Herding Cats:
A Primer for
Programmers Who Lead
Programmers

J. HANK RAINWATER

Apress™

Herding Cats: A Primer for Programmers Who Lead Programmers
Copyright © 2002 by J. Hank Rainwater

ISBN (pbk): 1-59059-017-1
Printed and bound in the United States of America 12345678910

Editorial Directors: Dan Appleman, Peter Blackburn, Gary Cornell, Jason Gilmore, Karen Watterson
Technical Reviewer: Dave Christensen
Managing Editor: Grace Wong
Project Manager and Development Editor: Tracy Brown Collins
Copy Editor: Nicole LeClerc
Production Editor: Kari Brooks
Compositor: Diana Van Winkle, Van Winkle Design
Illustrators: Melanie Wells; Cara Brunk, Blue Mud Productions
Indexer: Carol Burbo
Cover Designer: Tom Debolski
Marketing Manager: Stephanie Rodriguez

Distributed to the book trade in the United States by Springer-Verlag New York, Inc., 175 Fifth Avenue, New York, NY, 10010 and outside the United States by Springer-Verlag GmbH & Co. KG, Tiergartenstr. 17, 69112 Heidelberg, Germany.

In the United States, phone 1-800-SPRINGER, e-mail orders@springer-ny.com, or visit http://www.springer-ny.com.
Outside the United States, fax +49 6221 345229, e-mail orders@springer.de, or visit http://www.springer.de.

For information on translations, please contact Apress directly at 901 Grayson Street, Suite 204, Berkeley, CA 94710. Phone 510-549-5930, fax: 510-549-5939, e-mail info@apress.com, or visit http://www.apress.com.

The source code for this book is available to readers at http://www.apress.com in the Downloads section. You will need to answer questions pertaining to this book in order to successfully download the code.

To David, my beloved son, your memory inspires me each day. Wish you were here
to laugh with me in all the strange and wonderful hours and days ahead.

His spirit lives on
In the voice of the songbird
In the flash of the firefly

His essence is felt
In the gentle breeze that caresses
With a coolness and flowing grace
Recollecting to us once again
Exactly who he was—

A loving gentle soul embracing life
With the innocence of a child
The maturity of an adult
The wisdom of an old soul

Contents at a Glance

Foreword xiii
About the Author xvi
About the Technical Reviewer xvii
About the Artist xviii
Acknowledgments xix
Preface xx

Chapter 1: Adapting to Your Leadership Role 1

Chapter 2: Managing the Leader 21

Chapter 3: Leading the Herd 41

Chapter 4: Organizing for Success 61

Chapter 5: Managing Meetings 87

Chapter 6: Philosophy and Practice of Technical Leadership ... 103

Chapter 7: Leadership in Eclipse 129

Chapter 8: Leadership Redux 151

Chapter 9: Working with Your Boss 179

Chapter 10: Words without a Song 193

Afterword: Into the Fray 217

Appendix A: Caring for Your Pet:
            The Administrative Director Software 221

Appendix B: Poking Your Pet in the Eye:
            Code Review of the Administrative Director 227

Bibliography: Resources for Cat Herders 235

Index 243

Contents

Foreword .... *xiii*
About the Author .... *xvi*
About the Technical Reviewer .... *xvii*
About the Artist .... *xviii*
Acknowledgments .... *xix*
Preface .... *xx*

Chapter 1 Adapting to Your Leadership Role *1*

Do Real Leaders Wear Black? *2*
    How Important Is Being Cool? *3*
    Be More Than Cool: Beware *4*
Leading Weird, Eccentric, Strange, and
Regular Folks into Great Work *5*
    Recognizing Programmer Breeds *6*
    Working with the Breeds *12*
Glory, Honor, and Greenbacks *15*
    Motivating with Money *16*
The Thunking Layer *17*
How Are You Adapting? *19*
What Lies Ahead *20*

Chapter 2 Managing the Leader *21*

A Look in the Mirror *21*
Heaven, Hell, Purgatory, and
Your Place in the Software Universe *23*
    The Nature of Work Has Changed for You *24*
    You Must Re-evaluate Success, Passion, and Ambition *24*
Natural Selection and Time *25*
    Avoid Unnecessary, Ineffective Meetings *26*
    Don't Organize Too Little or Too Much *27*
    Don't Expect If You Don't Inspect *27*
    Plan Your Architecture before Choosing Your Technology *28*
    Balance Purity with Practicality *28*
    Delegate Tasks, Don't Do Them *29*
    Document What You Do or Plan to Do *29*

Measuring Your Productivity *30*
Watching Your Weaknesses *31*
And the Answer Is *34*
Putting It All Together *38*

Chapter 3   Leading the Herd *41*

Managing Administration *41*
Deflecting Distractions *44*
Dealing with Creeps *46*
Gathering Strays *51*
Danger, Will Robinson! *52*
Building and Maintaining Your Staff *53*
    Hiring Practices *53*
    Firing Practices *56*
    Promotions and Raises *56*
    Grooming Your Replacement *58*
Enough Already! *58*
More to Come *59*

Chapter 4   Organizing for Success *61*

Organize Information into Knowledge and Action *62*
    The Paper Chase *63*
    The Paperless Chase *65*
Customize Your Administration *70*
Organize to Control *71*
    Information Flow *72*
    Assignments *73*
    Architecture *73*
    Working Hours *74*
    Expectations *75*
    Attitudes *76*
Helping Your Company Organize *77*
    Product Management *78*
    Project Definition *79*
    Process Management *80*
    Testing *82*
    Facility Management *82*
At the End of the Day *84*
Next on the Agenda *85*

Chapter 5 Managing Meetings 87

The Weekly Staff Meeting 87
Leading a Design Meeting 90
The One-on-One Meeting 95
Meetings with Other Groups 97
Project Retrospective Meetings 98
Conference Calls 99
In Between Meetings 100
Meeting for Consensus and Action 101
Our Next Meeting 102

Chapter 6 Philosophy and Practice of Technical Leadership 103

Seize and Hold Your Technical Role 103
Construct or Plant? 105
The Primacy of Architecture 106
    Design Forces in Architectural Planning 108
    Analysis Viewpoints: Managing the Forces 109
A Fresh Look at Design 110
    Design Step 0 111
    Design Step 1, 2, 3, 2, 1, 4 113
The Code Police 118
    Enforce the Laws 118
    Common Violations 119
    Go to Jail, Go Directly to Jail, Do Not Pass Go 122
Philosophy in Action 123
    A Case Study of Philosophy in Action: Leonardo da Vinci 124
    A Dose of Reality 126
A Bird's-Eye View 126
Leading to Excellence 127

Chapter 7 Leadership in Eclipse 129

The Face of Darkness 129
Antipatterns in Management 130
The Shadow of Micromanagement 132
    Advice for the Micromanager 136
Dimming the Light: Unfocused Managers 137
The Blinding Light of Misapplied Genius 140
Dark Empire Builders 142

Flirting with Darkness 144
    You've Reached Your Limit 145
    You're over Your Head 145
    Criticism Pushes You to Rage 145
Surviving and Emerging from an Eclipse 146
Avoiding Eclipses 147
Moving On 149

Chapter 8 Leadership Redux 151

Foundations of Leadership 151
    Understanding 152
    Communicating 154
    Delegating 156
    Monitoring 158
    Participating 159
Building Upon the Foundation 161
    Mentoring 161
    Rewarding 162
    Correcting 164
    Envisioning 165
    Adapting 166
Will They Follow? 167
    Force 167
    Duty 168
    Admiration 168
    Reward 169
    Knowledge 170
Generational Dimensions to Leadership 170
Marrying Style to Substance As a Leader 172
    Andy Grove: Aggressive and Paranoid 173
    Bill Gates: Driven and Calculating 174
    You: _____ (Fill In the Blank) 174
Summing Up 175
    Practice Makes Leadership Real 176
    Build on the Cornerstones 176
A Look Ahead 177

Chapter 9 Working with Your Boss 179

Understanding the World of Your Boss 179
Honesty and Deadlines or Slips, Lies, and Videotape? 181
Helping Your Boss Plan for Success 183
Knowing Your Limits 185
Expecting the Unexpected 187
Overcoming Organizational Inertia 187
    Point Out Industry Trends 188
    Experiment with New Methods and Techniques 189
    Be Sensitive to Timing 189
    Recognize the Customer Is First 190
Summary of Guidelines 191
The End Is Near 192

Chapter 10 Words without a Song 193

The Distributed Workforce 194
    The Challenge 194
    A Solution 195
Multicultural Factors in Management 198
    Language and Culture 198
    Motivating and Controlling the Team 199
Evaluating Software Development Methodologies 201
    Software Engineering 202
    Microsoft Solutions Framework (MSF) 203
    Extreme Programming (XP) 205
    Agile Development 207
    Craftsmanship: The Heart of Any Successful Method 209
Revolutions in Technology 210
Economic Woes 212
Alone at the Top 213
    Devoting Time to Research 213
    Turning Administration into an Engineering Discipline 214
    Making Strategic Planning a Science 214
    Learning to Increase the Value of Your Relationships 215
Finale 216

Afterword: Into the Fray 217

The Rudder 217
The Sail 218
The Anchor 219

Appendix A   Caring for Your Pet: The Administrative Director Software ...221

Appendix B   Poking Your Pet in the Eye: Code Review of the Administrative Director 227

Context and Origin of the Software 227
The Rules of the Game 228
  Did I Follow Appropriate Standards? 228
  What About Cohesion and Coupling? 230
  Other Strengths and Weaknesses 232
Summary 233

Bibliography: Resources for Cat Herders 235

Software Development 235
  The Classics 235
  Cream of the Crop 236
  Noteworthy 237
  Helpful 240
General Management and Leadership 241
Software Language-Specific Works 241
Miscellaneous Works 242

Index 243

Foreword

Reading Hank's wonderful book on "herding cats" took me back a number of years (too many) to the time when I made the transition from programmer to manager of programmers. Like the readers of this book, I was a supremely confident programmer/analyst. Without dating myself too much, my specialty was the PLI language and IMS DB/DC database. Throw in a little Ramis, FOCUS, Easytrieve Plus, Datacom/IDEAL, CICS, and VSAM, and you had the foundation for a pretty well-rounded mainframe programmer. These technologies might seem like ancient history to today's code jockeys, but I assure you that at least some of them were cool—even "way cool"—in their day.

Like Hank, I began taking on informal responsibilities for managing and mentoring other people, usually younger staff that we were hiring. Then, I took on formal technical management responsibilities. In that job, I was a full-time programmer/analyst with formal people-management duties as well. It was then that I began to see the good and frustrating parts about being a people manager. I still remember being in a meeting with a group of my peers. Our manager was talking to us about the expectations he had for us and how we must improve our management skills. One of my peers raised her hand and stated what many first-time managers must feel. She said she could be a much better manager if she only had better people to manage.

It's hard to say why certain things will stick in your memory years later, but that quote does. I wonder how much smoother the transition to management would have been if we'd had a resource like Hank's book available to us then. We were all programmers who were being asked to take on people-management responsibilities for other programmers. We were discovering that old buddy relationships changed almost overnight. I was determined that my attitude wouldn't change, but I couldn't control the behavior of the people who worked for me. Of course, we were still friends, but on a different level. My relationship with members of my programming team changed forever.

Over the years, I feel fortunate to have had an opportunity to be a part of over 200 people-management relationships as a team leader, project manager, group manager, department manager, and director. I've also been fortunate to have had the opportunity to hone my people-management experience with training classes and seminars. Finally, I'm grateful, too, that I understood early the value of reading. After all, in general, the person you are today is based on a combination of what you've experienced and what you've read.

My background as a programmer moving into the management ranks gives me an appreciation for the valuable insight Hank provides in this book. The results of his effort will be valuable for anyone who is in a similar position. Hank hits the nail on the head in his opening chapter when he talks about "your ways are not my ways." After all, isn't that the crux of much of the frustration we feel as we move into the management role? If you really take that to heart, Hank will have helped you tremendously in your new role.

To paraphrase a former colleague, management would be much easier if only everyone was just like you. Fortunately, however, everyone is not just like you. People have different motivations and different skill levels, and you really never know what makes them tick. These differences don't mean that they're better or worse than you—they're just different. Being a manager means that you need to manage and lead these "cats." Understanding something about how the cats behave and interact goes a long way toward being able to lead them effectively.

I remember a discussion with my boss about a problem with a member of the staff that was caused by another programming manager. My boss said to me, "Tom, as long as I'm the manager here, I'll never promote another technical person into the management ranks." Perhaps a year later, when I reported to a new manager, we were discussing a technical manager who was having tremendous success managing and motivating his staff. This manager's comment to me was, "Tom, I think in the future all of our managers need to come from the technical ranks."

These comments confirm that no two people are cut from the same cloth. People have differing talents, abilities, desires, and biases. You need to understand your own strengths and weaknesses (discussed in Chapter 2) and utilize your skills as best you can to make sure your entire team is successful (see Chapter 3). Programmers who are managing programmers for the first time find themselves at a career crossroads. Some end up moving permanently into the management ranks. Others are better suited to providing long-term value in the programming role. The rest will enjoy the dichotomy of being a technician as well as a manager.

If this book had ended after these first three chapters, new cat herders would have gotten their money's worth. (The book would have been short, but still very valuable.) However, Hank proceeds to discuss other topics that new managers will find extremely helpful.

The first is that you now have formal administrative responsibilities. People-management skills are vital to the success of the company, but administrative skills are what keep the machinery of the organization humming smoothly. You're going to get many requests for information and you may have to do performance reviews. You're the focal point for your group in the management hierarchy. If you're disciplined and organized, you can keep up with the administrative aspects of your job. If not, you'll become a broken cog in the machine and require the constant prodding follow-up of your own manager. You can thank Hank for making you aware of this common administrative role and helping you understand that it's not just a burden placed specifically on you.

The chapter on managing meetings (Chapter 5) gets into a much underappreciated set of skills. Just knowing that you must manage meetings to begin with is a pearl of wisdom. Have you attended meetings that were unfocused and out of control? (Perhaps the better question would be, What percentage of meetings you've attended has been this way?) If you have, now you know why: No one proactively managed those meetings. If you can take the lead in making meetings more productive and focused, you have Hank to thank.

Another section of the book that I particularly enjoyed was the chapter on managing the relationship with your own manager (Chapter 9). This is a valuable concept to understand and one that many people realize too late. Yes, your manager manages you. However, you can be proactive in managing the relationship between the two of you. It's funny, but if you make it your job for your team to be successful and make it your job to make sure your boss is successful, you'll find that you are successful as well.

I can't go into all of the chapters in detail or convey all my comments on Hank's material—that would make my Foreword longer than the book itself. (One last note, though: Be sure to read the sections on multicultural and distributed teams. Very valuable stuff!) Suffice it to say that I think this book will help programmers who find themselves in the position of managing programmers. The analogy to herding cats is accurate. Many animals have a herd mentality and will be easily led as a group. I have two cats of my own and I know that they don't have that instinct. It can be hard to lead even one cat (or programmer) in the direction you want. Leading and managing four or five—or a dozen—takes your focus, and it takes a new set of skills. Let this book help you build awareness for the expectations of your new role and leverage Hank's experience to make the path to success a smoother and shorter one for you.

Tom Mochal
Author of *www.TenStep.com*
President, TenStep, Inc.

About the Author

Hank Rainwater currently leads programmers who build software for the insurance industry at Risk Sciences Group in Atlanta, Georgia. His career in science and engineering has spanned over three decades and has included writing Fortran programs on punch cards; teaching college mathematics; conducting research in radio astronomy, missile guidance systems, and remote sensing technologies; and managing the building of embedded digital control systems. As a software professional, Hank has served as a consultant, teacher, programmer, and manager of development teams in several industries.

His educational background includes an undergraduate degree in physics and graduate studies in mathematics and physics. Hank holds a master's degree in theology and spent several years in the ministry, where he served as a pastor and teacher in the United States and overseas.

Hank believes that leadership skills are crucial to managing programmers.

Prior to his career in software development he didn't understand the implications of this statement. After years of experience, he has learned to let

his hair down, so to speak, and loves the interactions between creative individuals who seek to turn code into marketable products. On a good

hair day, Hank looks like an ordinary man on the street.

About the Technical Reviewer

Dave Christensen is currently employed as a senior technical systems analyst with Potlatch Corporation's Minnesota Pulp and Paper Division, headquartered in Cloquet, Minnesota, where he created Web-based applications for competitive advantage. He's also president of Proxis Productions (http://www.proxis-productions.com), a consulting company that specializes in designing distributed Web applications for the enterprise. Proxis Productions was founded in 1995 to create CGI (computer generated imagery) for the commercial and video game industries, but the emergence of the visual Web gave Dave the opportunity to merge his visual and technical passions together in this new medium. Dave holds a degree in English literature/ pre-med with a minor in theatre from the College of St. Scholastica.

God has richly blessed Dave, and when he's not at work he enjoys the time he can spend with his greatest blessings, a beautiful wife and two amazing children who always surprise him. Together they enjoy being surrounded by God's creations and have way too many pets, including two dogs and a set of cats whose personalities can be found in various places within this book. Dave also collects rare fish and enjoys the process of restoration. He has a passion for seeing the hidden potential in the things around him. He's worked on cars, houses, and people.

About the Artist

Melanie Wells is a seasoned graphic design artist with a decade of experience in a variety of fields. Her work has included creating book illustrations, logos for corporations, Web pages, brochures, show and store displays, mailers, magazine ads, catalogs, package design, sportswear, product design, and more.

In addition to graphic design, Melanie has a passion for fine art. Whether she's creating a corporate identity or an oil painting on canvas, Melanie's first passion in life is art.

Acknowledgments

Special thanks to Dan Appleman at Apress for considering my first draft chapter and seeing the merit in a book not exclusively focused on a current programming language. Thanks, Dan. You've inspired me and many others over the years, and I hope to follow in your footsteps.

To Karen Watterson, your guidance during this project has been decisive in helping many ideas that were only seeds become fully formed. Your scope of knowledge, experience, and e-mails at all times of the day and night were a constant inspiration to me. Thanks, Karen.

This book was a new kind of development effort for me, and Tracy Brown Collins was a great project manager. Thanks for all the keen literary insights and helping the team make this book a reality.

Dave Christensen was the primary technical reviewer for this book and was a great help in keeping me from putting my foot in my mouth. I still have managed to do this a few times, but his observations and insights were responsible for many improvements. I "borrowed" some of his comments more than a few times. Thanks, Dave, for all the hard work.

I also am very grateful to Nicole LeClerc at Apress for correcting my grammar. We programmers are not always good at elaborate syntax, preferring the arcane and obscure style of code. She taught me things I missed in high school about voice, punctuation, and other things that have made this book more readable.

Jessica Landisman spent many hours annotating, correcting, suggesting, and commenting on several early drafts. As an expert seasoned programmer, she is the best, and I'm deeply grateful for her support.

A special thanks to Kathy Haynes, who pored over the manuscript in its various stages and made innumerable improvements each time she touched the pages. She's my expert authority on authentic Southern English, being from LA (Lower Alabama).

Melanie Wells, a brilliant artist who works in many mediums, created the graphics for this book. She has a great talent for seeing words and translating them into visual images. Thanks, Melanie, for making the cats so cool!

Finally, I express a deep sense of gratitude to my dad, Julius Rainwater, who created prototypes for many of the graphics that grace the pages of this book. As an engineer, entrepreneur, great father, and most excellent role model, words fail to express my debt to him and appreciation of his many talents. And Mama, without you nothing I've ever done would have been possible, including this book!

Preface

"There is no truth, only stories."
—An anonymous Southern writer

This book is intended to open your mind to what it takes to lead people like yourself. Take heart: It can be done, in spite of what you've heard. You just have to undergo a gestalt in your thinking. What does this word "gestalt" mean? Webster's defines it as "a form or configuration having properties that cannot be derived by the summation of its component parts." In the language of object-oriented programming, more familiar to you as a programmer than Webster's, it means your mental architecture is about to undergo a transformation: You'll inherit management skills, overload your typical parameters of thinking with new types and meanings and, in general, undergo something like polymorphism with respect to your character. You'll then have encapsulated a whole new art form in your programmer brain—that of leadership and management. I'll draw a distinction between management and leadership: Both are needed but leadership is the primary strength you'll need and learning to be a better manager will help you achieve this.

I'll take a light-hearted approach to a very serious subject. The so-called buck will now stop with you. This buck is worth a lot more than a dollar to those to whom you report. The timeliness and quality of your company's software is in your hands and I hope to give you something new to do with your digits rather than just punch out code day and night that all ends up as 1s and 0s.

Looking at the chapters ahead, you'll find the following:

> **Chapter 1: Adapting to Your Leadership Role.** Leadership requires new skills compared to writing code. This chapter describes how to adapt to your job by examining the varieties of programmer personality traits that affect your ability to manage and direct development activities. You'll accept the dreadful otherness of the biblical challenge, "Your ways are not my ways," and you'll boldly attempt to uncover the ways of the weird and creative programmers you manage. After all, you are one, so what's not to like?

> **Chapter 2: Managing the Leader.** You'll look deep into your soul (try not to be scared) and apply management techniques to yourself. *You cannot lead and manage others until you manage yourself.* As Winston Churchill said, "The further back you look, the further ahead you can see." Take this as an aphorism about introspection rather than history.

Chapter 3: Leading the Herd. Leadership requires a whole new set of skills on your part, not just programming smarts. You'll identify key areas you must give diligent attention to or else you'll find yourself being led in the wrong direction and your team scattering like frightened cats. I don't want you quoting Lord Byron and being among "the few whose spirits float above the wreck of happiness."

Chapter 4: Organizing for Success. A break from all the warm fuzzies of dealing with people. Improving your personal organizational skills will help you do a better job of managing your administrative life. I'll also challenge you to examine the organizational structure of your company and look for ways to make your development efforts more effective. This will help you have time to be a leader, the main job you should be about.

Chapter 5: Managing Meetings. You've been used to conferring with yourself as you program—now you must include others. No more staff meetings as you shave in the morning, looking in the mirror at that great-looking guy. Now you'll be gazing into the face of others like yourself (maybe not as good-looking, though) and, amazingly, people who don't actually code for a living. Patience will be required in your new role as a leader of meetings. Don't despair, and remember what Leonardo da Vinci said: "Impatience is the mother of stupidity."

Chapter 6: Philosophy and Practice of Technical Leadership. I'll survey technical principles in this chapter and focus on the philosophy behind the details. Making technical choices is harder when you have to do it for your whole department, rather than just your individual coding assignment. You may already be an expert at using technology, but here you'll drill down on the consequences of your corporate technical decisions. Architecture, design, and code reviews will be highlighted.

Chapter 7: Leadership in Eclipse. The dark side of leadership may plague you (or your boss) from time to time. Some styles of management are not healthy to exercising constructive leadership and you want to avoid them. Seeing how your leadership can be eclipsed by the shadows of bad management will be illuminated and remedies proposed.

Chapter 8: Leadership Redux. Software is built on good architecture, whereas leadership is grown from your character. This chapter pulls together all the threads of leadership into one tapestry. To paraphrase Emerson, "Redundancy is the hobgoblin of authors, adored by publishers and readers and booksellers." More important, laying out the foundations of successful leadership and showing how to build upon it is crucial for your growth in your job.

Chapter 9: Working with Your Boss. Notice this chapter's title isn't "Managing Your Boss," because this isn't really possible. You must manage, however, your relationships with those to whom you report with as much care as you do with those who report to you. Subordination is not a bad 13-letter word. Helping you become a team of two with your boss is outlined and elaborated upon here.

Chapter 10: Words without a Song. This chapter presents a wide range of topics that often fall outside your daily activities as a leader of programmers but are essential to herding cats. Managing a geographically dispersed team, evaluating trends in software development methodologies, and other important themes are explored. The goal of this chapter is to help you turn chaos into order without going mad.

Afterword: Into the Fray. I'll leave you with some parting words of wisdom, or what passes for it in this crazy wonderful world of software development.

Appendix A: Caring for Your Pet: The Administrative Director Software. This appendix contains the details of the software described in Chapter 4. I believe in sharing source code so you can build upon the good ideas of others. You can download the source code as long as you buy this book and know the secret word. You can then determine if my ideas were any good as they became code.

Appendix B: Poking Your Pet in the Eye: Code Review of the Administrative Director. Applying the principles of code review outlined in Chapter 6 to the software described in Chapter 4 and Appendix A is the topic here. I'll attempt to be as objective as possible since I'm reviewing my own code and point out its weaknesses and strengths. The main purpose is to give a little real-world experience at being a code cop.

Bibliography: Resources for Cat Herders. I've annotated all the references quoted in this book plus a few not explicitly quoted that are worthy of your perusal. Many others have gone ahead of us in our leadership journey, and I share with you some good companions you should get to know.

Index. You know what this is. Here you can look up things that sound interesting without having to read the whole book. This is the same approach you would take to learn programming by reading the language reference guide. You may know the syntax, but without the context Bad Things will happen.

Scattered throughout the book are small sidebars called "Cat Fights." These are true stories from the world of programmer management compiled to edify and horrify. They illustrate many of the principles presented in this book. Names, places, programming languages, and application types have been changed to protect the innocent and disguise the guilty. These stories are quick to read and provide examples of what not to do. It seems we learn best from our own mistakes, and these stories are told so you can learn from the mistakes of others. Recall what Albert Camus said: "It is puerile to think that pessimistic thoughts must be despairing ones." The negative can turn out to be positive with the right physics—namely, leveraging the experiences of others to nudge your own in a successful direction.

Another feature that will appear on a number of pages is a small graphic of a cat's paw highlighting key principles from the text. I call these "Paw Prints," to stay in keeping with the theme of herding cats. This feature may save you money because you won't have to use a yellow highlighter to pick out the things that are important to you. No, use your highlighter as much as you want. What I think is important is that you give thought to how you're doing your job, and anything I might say that would help you is my fondest wish and purpose in writing this book.

Who Should Read This Book and Why

Programmers who've been promoted to project managers, team leaders or, if you prefer lofty titles, directors of software development, will benefit from this book. If you lead a relatively small team of programmers (say, four to seven people), work in a small- to medium-sized company, and are engaged on a number of development efforts simultaneously, you're reading the right stuff. If you're going to build, say, the next great worldwide airline reservation system with 100 programmers over the next 12 months, this book might not be adequate for you. Perhaps a dual master's degree in project management and psychology would be more helpful. Good luck.

If you're managing programmers, but just managing, and you feel more like you're doing triage on projects and people rather than being a leader, you need help. This book is it.

Maybe you've been a manager for many years and need to review your skills as a leader. This book is it.

Perhaps you finally got that promotion you were hoping for, or dreading. All the clever code and outstanding software you created on time over the years has paid off. Management saw you as an outstanding candidate for managing programmers. Perhaps you were slightly less weird than your fellow programmers. You may have even been wearing shirts with collars and this tipped your hand. Maybe the other guy quit. Whatever the case, welcome to the new world of leading programmers. This book can be your guide.

Whatever your age, gender, or position, this is a book that will help you become a better leader for your programmers and is brief enough to mentally digest. While you sip your cappuccino here in the bookstore, mull over your decision to buy this book after you ask yourself the following question: "Can I be a better leader than I already am?" You should answer "Yes," and I believe this book can help you.

Style and Perspective

Management literature is replete with suggestions, recommendations, and scientifically determined techniques for getting work done through others. After all, that's what management is about: motivating and controlling, in the best sense of these words, work you delegate to others in order to accomplish a shared corporate goal. This book is not a tome on the science of management but rather an expression of the view that creating great software is an art learned from experience, the best teacher. What you'll find here is a synthesis of ideas learned from this constant and faithful teacher. The ideas of others who've contributed academic thought to my experience will emerge in this writing—of this, I have no doubt. Since you're probably spending time reading this when you should be on the phone or in the next cube monitoring the progress of your programmers, I've attempted to keep the writing here short and sweet and, for entertainment value, humor is used from time to time to lighten the mood.[1]

While I often use the masculine form of pronouns in this book, the author's note at the beginning of Chapter 9 should clarify my position on this sometimes delicate issue. This book isn't gender specific—but I expect any reader to benefit from the subject matter.

This primer will focus on two primary areas of programmer management: people and process. In this short list, people are by far the most important. Get great people and you can build great software in spite of poor business processes. Improve the process and with good people, you can code the moon.

---

1. Most of the humor is in the footnotes so you won't be distracted from the main flow of the text. It's also a bit on the nerdy side; for example, what does "backward-compatibility" mean? It means the new operating system will also crash your existing software.

CHAPTER 1

Adapting to Your Leadership Role

In the beginning of any new job, we all have great hopes and, to some extent, a reasonable amount of fear that we might fail. As a successful programmer, you have, no doubt, had your share of new beginnings on projects and at places of employment. Now that you've been given the reigns to lead a group of programmers, a very new and perhaps daunting task is before you. You must evolve from programmer to leader as quickly as possible to thrive in your new software development role. This will entail adapting to a new social context and adopting new ways of interacting with your work world and the people in it.

Adaptation, a driving force of biological evolution, has been successful in helping our species climb out of the ooze and up the ladder of life to sentience. It took millions of years, but here we are, using language and dealing with abstract concepts such as computer programming. How did we get to this point? You'll have to ask your local biologist that question, but in the pages of this book, you'll rely heavily on your ability to adapt in order to face the challenges of leading programmers.

In this first chapter, you're going to become somewhat of an anthropologist. You'll look at the very human enterprise of writing code—specifically, you'll examine the types of individuals who engage in this wonderful activity. In learning more about the people you manage, you gain insights into how to successfully lead them. Many different ideas about how to lead programmers have currency today. Each generation of leaders starts from their own unique perspective and builds upon what they know and what they find works as a management and leadership style. I'm from the generation that grew up with slide rules and punch cards, and this will, no doubt, color my presentation. However, in years of working with programmers much younger than myself, I've learned that my generation doesn't own the only methods that work. I've had to adapt numerous times to the changing needs of business, revolutions in technology, and growth and stubbornness in my own character as I faced the challenges of leadership. I'll share these experiences with you, and I believe we'll have a great journey together.

Do Real Leaders Wear Black?

Some do, and some even sport ponytails, depending on their hair situation, to fit in better with some of the younger geeks or (depending on your generational preferences) nerds. You may prefer neither of these terms and see yourself as a modern leader of business, guiding men and women like yourself who find programming a great intellectual thrill. Thus, the affectations I've alluded to, including the one referred to in the title of this section, shouldn't be taken too seriously. Do take seriously, however, your ability to personally relate to and identify with your programmers. Now that you're the leader, you can't fit in like you once did as part of the group, and you shouldn't really try too hard because you're the boss and you'll need to use this advantage from time to time in the course of conducting the business of constructing software. Someone once said, "Give me a lever large enough and I can move the earth." Being the boss can be such a lever.

You may not be convinced that image isn't important. It took me a long time to realize that what I looked like on the outside wasn't necessarily a reflection of my character. I still enjoy the trappings of "nerdom," but I also know that leading my team requires much more than just style. True, a certain image can go a long way toward reassuring your folks that you're one of them. But is it a crucial leadership skill? You may remember from the movie *The Net* how Angela (Sandra Bullock) was accepted by her online pals. They all said she was one of them and thus accepted her into their weird little circle. Of course, in the end it turned out that this wasn't really such a great thing. Learn from this: Image is truly only skin deep. What counts is character. That's why all the management techniques you may have learned and try to practice fail so often: They are techniques you have grafted onto your brain rather than nourished and grown from your heart.

How Important Is Being Cool?

So, continuing in this serious tone, should you wear black and embrace the affectations you believe contribute to coolness as a leader of programmers? Take the "Assess Your Level of Cool" test in the sidebar and see how you do. Note that some prefer the term "Ninjitsu"[1] rather than "cool," but I'm from the old school.

---

1. You know what a Ninja is—this word refers to the quality of being one, as in black-belt programming.

Remember, this is a self-help book, so you have to do some work. Pop quizzes aren't just given by stuffy old college professors—they show up in your daily work life all the time.

....

Assess Your Level of Cool

Select one or more answers to the following questions.

1. A "hacker" is a person who

    a. Makes furniture with an axe

    b. Programs enthusiastically as opposed to just theorizing about it

    c. Enjoys the intellectual challenge of creatively overcoming or circumventing limitations

    d. Maliciously tries to discover sensitive information

    e. Was a character played by Angelina Jolie before she was a tomb raider

2. A "cracker" is

    a. One who breaks security on a system

    b. A Southern white boy like your author

    c. Thinner than a cookie (see question 6)

    d. Considered to be a larval-stage hacker

3. "Phreaking" is

    a. The art and science of cracking the phone network

    b. An old nerd trying to be cool

4. "Ping" is

    a. Packet Internet groper

    b. The sound of a sonar pulse

    c. The other half of pong

    d. A quantum packet of happiness

5. "Worm" refers to

    a. A write-once read-many optical disk drive

    b. A virus program designed to corrupt data in memory or on disk

    c. A bilaterally symmetrical invertebrate

6. A "cookie" is

    a. A token of agreement between cooperating programs

    b. Something Amos made famous

    c. Something used to store and sometimes learn about the browsing habits of users

....

How do you think you did on the test? I once gave this assessment to a group of nonprogrammer types during a lecture on computer security to illustrate the kinds of people who get involved in hacking as well as protecting computers from threats. They didn't do very well on the test, but I bet you did way above average. All the answers are correct for each question.[2] Well, maybe choice b in question 3 is a bit of fiction, but this test does illustrate how programmers have been traditionally characterized as belonging to a particular subculture. Sometimes it's called, in the nonpejorative sense, the "hacker" culture (see the nice answers for question 1). Today these hacker stereotypes are disappearing. A programmer today more than likely holds an undergraduate degree in computer science and an MBA to boot. Nevertheless, each corporation has a culture, and your team has one as unique as the people who comprise the group. However the culture is defined, it is within this context that you lead and manage your people. Understanding the warp-and-woof (ways of interacting and thinking) of your programmers' culture can help you relate better to them and aid your leadership efforts. So wear a cool black T-shirt with an esoteric message emblazoned on the front if you desire, but there are more effective ways to relate to your people than just adopting or reinforcing a stereotypical image. This is the key theme of this chapter.

 Hacker stereotypes are disappearing. A programmer today more than likely holds an undergraduate degree in computer science and an MBA to boot.

Be More Than Cool: Beware

Of course, if you're a dyed-in-the-wool hacker yourself, relating to programmers may be no problem. However, beware: Good programmers, while often promoted into management, don't often make the best managers or leaders of programmers. You have a great desire to work on the coolest projects when you should delegate. You often spend many hours on code review, when an hour would do, trying to get every little comment and indentation just right. There are times when you give up trying to help others understand what you want and you just do it yourself. Don't misunderstand me here, you must be concerned about the details of the code for which you are responsible, but the programmer-cum-manager is often guilty of not seeing the forest for the trees.

---

2. You can look up most of these terms in *The New Hacker's Dictionary*, Third Edition, by Eric S. Raymond (The MIT Press, 1998).

> *You must be concerned about the details of the code for which you are responsible but the programmer-cum-manager is often guilty of not seeing the forest for the trees.*

At the other extreme, you may manage during the day and write code at night, depending on whether or not you have a life. Perhaps coding is your life and managing is your day job—this can work unless you lose your passion for the work. Maintaining your passion is essential in my understanding of what it takes to lead programmers. You will work through a number of management skills in this chapter and the chapters ahead, and these skills will help you balance your work life and keep your passion strong for your job. One key management skill that allows you to have time to lead is delegation. It is a cornerstone of leadership, and I focus heavily on it in Chapter 8. For now, realize that delegation involves trusting your staff. Trust takes time to build and is essential to successful leadership. Trust also is a reciprocal human activity. In this chapter, you'll learn to trust your instincts about people as you refine those instincts with a bit of anthropological insight into the mind and hearts of programmers.

Leading Weird, Eccentric, Strange, and Regular Folks into Great Work

Now, I don't want to take all the fun out of managing programmers, even though it has often been described as an exercise in "herding cats"—a reference, no doubt, to the independent nature of the creative individuals who choose to write code. The fun part is that these sometimes troublesome, always needed, and usually fascinating employees can be a blast to work with. Getting to know them better will improve your management style.

If you are a true lover of programming, you understand what it means to be close to your code—it may seem like second nature to you. As Ellen Ullman writes in *Close to the Machine*:

> *A project leader I know once said that managing programmers is like trying to herd cats . . . I mean you don't want obedient dogs. You want all that weird strangeness that makes a good programmer. On the other hand, you do have to get them somehow moving in the same direction.*[3]

---

3. Ellen Ullman, *Close to the Machine* (San Francisco: City Lights Books, 1997), p. 20.

This "same direction" is the goal of programmer management, but since each programmer is different, you have to lead in a unique way for each of your people. You can't lead programmers if you don't understand them. In the following section, I outline various programmer "types" and the traits that define them. You may recognize some of your employees in this list of types, which I'll call "breeds," as this is a book about cats.

Recognizing Programmer Breeds

What's a typical programmer like? Can you stereotype programmers just for the purpose of understanding them? Maybe. Like so many personality assessment tests from the field of psychology, it is helpful to look at programmer traits in isolation and recognize that many of these characteristics can coexist in the same person even if they seem contradictory. I've grouped the breeds into three categories: major, minor, and mongrel. *Major* refers to the most common types you'll find in the workforce. The *minor* breeds are sometimes seen, but not as frequently as the major ones. *Mongrels*, as you might expect, are not very desirable, but they do exist in the workplace, and as a result you need to recognize them. Mongrels can work out fine, as long as you help them build up their skills to overcome the weaknesses they inherently bring to the coding process.

As mentioned previously, any individual can be an amalgam of the characteristics identified with a breed—this makes working with that person a challenge but well worth the effort. Programmers are a wonderfully complex people. Relish the differences and unique styles of each breed. You'll probably recognize many of these traits the next time you look in the mirror.

The Major Breeds

The following are the major breeds and their characteristics.

The Architect.[4] This breed is highly prized by most managers and can be a valuable asset to your team. Architects are mostly concerned with the overall structure of the code. They dream in objects and printable whiteboards are their best friends. They live to solve business problems by abstraction and system analysis and then create concrete solutions in code. This is a necessary component of programming, but it isn't sufficient for the task. An architect may often have great ideas, but his or her

---

4. I'm using the term "architect" here in the sense of a programmer, not a full-fledged software architect. See Chapter 6 for a discussion about the importance of architecture in the grand scheme of development.

code may be so skeletal or obtuse that no one can pick it up and extend it. The rare architect can create a good system in his head, or preferably in Visio, and then flesh out the code and almost become a one-person show. The downside of this is that sometimes the architect's code may become a one-owner pet: It can't do tricks for anyone else.[5] Some architects are only interested in getting the code started and then handing it over to someone at a "lower" level for completion. You'll sometimes find strange constructs in an architect's code, such as message boxes in error traps when the code is supposed to run as a DLL on a server.

The Constructionist. This programmer just loves the process and result of writing code. Constructionists don't always have a master plan, but they are often fast and their code is usually fairly free of bugs even in the alpha stage. Constructionists' code originates from intuition and thus they appear to code by the seat of their pants. A constructionist also may have really great intuition and the master plan is in his or her head, so the code flows naturally from this source. Ask a constructionist for documentation and he or she will say the code is self-documenting. Tell a constructionist he or she must write documentation and you'll probably get some pretty good stuff. Of course, the code should be self-documenting, but in his or her heart, this programmer loves the act of creation and puts this first in his or her activities. The constructionist does so many daily builds that even Microsoft would be amazed. This can lead to solid code, but sometimes, as the scope creeps (and it always does), the solidity of the code can fracture and the constructionist will find him- or herself hacking away at solutions to preserve a personal sense of completeness and having done the job well. Team a constructionist up with an architect and you'll have a solid team. Find a constructionist in the same body as an architect and you'll solve most of your people problems.

The Artist. Writing code *is* as much an art as a science—that's why universities often put both departments in the same college and call it the College of Arts and Sciences. Take away the artistic side of programming and you'll lose many who find a great deal of job satisfaction in the craft of coding. The artist is in love with the act of creation: taking business requirements, mapping them to programming constructs, and elegantly making user interface objects present themselves with grace. Some artists, when they work on components that have no visible interface, will create beautiful symmetries of logic. The downside of being an artist is that it often leads to extended coding time as the programmer tries to see

---

5. This concept is important because one authority estimates that at least 70 percent of software cost is related to maintenance. See William H. Brown et al, *AntiPatterns: Refactoring Software, Architectures, and Projects in Crisis* (New York: John Wiley & Sons, 1998), p. 121.

how many equal signs he or she can put in one line of code and still get the correct Boolean result. The upside is that code that doesn't reflect artistry is often lacking any real design and craftsmanship on the part of the programmer. Take out these artful qualities and you have a time bomb waiting to go off under the fingers of your users. The artist shares qualities with the constructionist and architect but has a flare for style.

The Engineer. You have to love these boys and girls. They will buy every third-party tool available, write dozens of COM objects, and hook them all together such that they actually work in version 1. It is only when version 1.1 needs to be built that their love of complexity rears its ugly head. Programming is often described as software engineering, and many aspects of our profession can be constrained and guided by this approach. Just don't let the engineer run the whole show for you. Engineered software isn't a bad thing because in the best sense of the term, engineering is the application of scientific principles to software problems. You need programmers who aren't afraid of complexity, but you don't want those who are just in love with creating it needlessly. I don't mean to give a bad rap to engineers—I was one for many years on the hardware side of computers. Nevertheless, it is this hardware dimension that sometimes runs counter to the aspects of software that make it soft (i.e., flexible and easy to reuse). Hardware usually serves one distinct engineered purpose, and you don't always want your software to be like this.

The Scientist. These are men and women after the hearts of Babbage and Turing. They would never write a GoTo in their life. Everything would be according to the fundamentals of computer science, whenever the day that programming is more science than art comes. And this is often the problem: They are overly concerned with purity, while you are concerned with tomorrow's code-complete date and producing good enough software. Scientists are useful and their ideas are often essential in solving particularly tough coding problems. Just watch out that purity doesn't overshadow practicality. Engineers and scientists have some similarities in that they both value the complex—sometimes you might think they worship at the shrine of whatever god represents complexity. (They often do bring their offerings to the temple!) Value the insights of the scientist and use their creations when appropriate, but beware of the legacy of complexity that will be perpetuated if they have free reign in the code.

The Speed Demon. As the name implies, these men and women are fast. No comments, no indentations, and bad variable naming conventions, but they do produce and it often works pretty well until the first untrapped error occurs. Sometimes these coders are just young in the profession and want to impress you because they think speed is the primary behavior you expect as a manager. Haven't we often given that impression? Perhaps we managers are to blame for speed demons. Our bosses hand down the milestones they gathered from some meeting of the great minds and our job is to make it so. Haven't we often heard how foolish it is to establish a coding deadline before the requirements are gathered? *Get over it.* The real world is like this, and users and the marketplace often demand that we promise before we plan. That's why you are reading this book—you want some help in the fast, cruel, and often unforgiving world of software development.

The Minor Breeds

The following are the minor breeds and their characteristics.

The Magician.[6] You don't know how this programmer does it, but he or she always seems to solve the apparently intractable problems with unique solutions that no one thought of before. The magician also does it on time and sometimes it is understandable and maintainable software. A little magic can go a long way in our craft; too much and you may find yourself a sorcerer's apprentice rather than a clearheaded manager of hardworking people. In other words, if you depend too much on the magician, he or she will eventually let you down: No one can perform magic every time.

The Minimalist. This programmer produces sparse code, though it is often very powerful. Every procedure fits on a single screen in the code editor. Objects are nice and tidy and have a single-minded purpose. Sounds good, doesn't it? It can be, as long as the minimalist isn't just trying to get through the job so he or she can move on to the next, more exciting project. Sometimes—and this is a trait sometimes shared by architects—minimalists are easily bored once the problem is solved and they don't want to get down and dirty with the code as problems show up in alpha testing. Some minimalists are rather picky about the applications they want to work on. They are often very bad at code maintenance.

The Analogist. Okay, I may have made up this word and no, it isn't the nurse that puts you to sleep before a surgery—this is the programmer who really isn't very good at abstraction but is excellent at analogy. Analogists drive you mad during the design meeting as you constantly tire of their analogies, but often they do grasp the problem at hand and

---

6.   Some may prefer the term "guru" or "wizard." I like "magic."

can often produce practical, maintainable code. Sometimes they have favorite analogies that they try to apply to every software issue. They like to think of components as moving parts and when things are working well they will say their code is "firing on all cylinders." Their analogies are always tied to some tangible object rather than an abstract one. You get the idea. Mix them with an architect and, if they don't kill each other first, you'll have some righteous software. The only danger with an analogist is that he or she may not do sufficient abstraction to create objects that have a clean interface for hooking up to other layers in the software. Being able to create a sufficiently abstract object interface is one of the great strengths of object-oriented (OO) programming, and sometimes the person who must always think in concrete ways will be unable to get the job done adequately.

The Toy Maker. This programmer overemphasizes the joys of technology. You have a person who loves new toys but you get the same old woes. In all honesty, all of us in this great craft love the toy aspect of technology. I remember my first computer: It was analog, you turned dials that closed switches in a predetermined hardware algorithm. It was sort of a slide rule on steroids and I loved it. I still love the joy that comes from working with neat technological tools. With toy makers, temper their love of toys with the purpose of their employment: to produce business solutions. Just because they managed to fit 30 user interface controls on a screen that is supposed to work at 800×600 doesn't mean they have met users' needs.[7] Toy makers, while showing a good grasp of the technology, fail to consider the end purpose of the software. They often think that their job is to have fun with the tools, rather than consider the aspects of programming that make maintenance possible without massive efforts.

The Mongrels

The following are the mongrels and their characteristics.

The Slob. There isn't much good to say here. Some folks are just sloppy and it shows in their code. They ignore small things such as properly spelled variables in correct Hungarian notation. Perhaps personal problems prevent them from doing good work. Perhaps they need some guidance in how to write effective code. They start out with one style and after one or two procedures they have adopted another. Following their code is painful and sometimes you have to rewrite it late at night just to be sure

---

7.   Don't you hate users? What fun we could have if we only wrote software for programmers.

you meet the deadline. You, their manager, failed—they didn't, they are just slobs who probably should be transferred to beta testing. No, strike that, this would only move the problem down the path a bit and it could come back to bite you. Some slobs can be rehabilitated if they really love writing code and should be given more personal attention and mentoring. Those that can't may just need a metaphorical kick in the seat of the pants or an introduction to a job placement counselor.

The Intimidated. This programmer doesn't know where to start. He or she is constantly looking at (or waiting for) the specification, trying to find a point to begin. Not to worry, being timid can be a good thing when it leads to careful code, even if it is the result of the poor programmer not wanting to create runtime errors. Your job is to give the intimidated some prototype code that illustrates where to begin and a style to emulate. Often, those with only a few years in the profession exhibit some timidity and by nurturing them you can change their nature. You may also find timidity in an experienced programmer who hasn't had such a great track record. Maybe his last performance review was bad and he wants to do better but is afraid of screwing up. Lack of confidence often shows up as timidity, so bear with him and enable him achieve a little success as you hold his hand from time to time. I cover mentoring, which is the best way to nurture a timid programmer, in Chapter 8. You'll discover that being a mentor is one of your primary roles as a leader and it will pay you back handsomely for the efforts you put into it.

The Amateur. Amateurs are programmer wannabes. They come into the ranks of hackers as power users of some macro-writing tool. They left their cozy role in support or testing because they think programmers are way cool. Of course, we *are* cool but this is just a by-product of what we do. These folks need education and you must carefully assess their progress up the learning curve before you let them handle mission-critical application creation. These wannabes often become disillusioned with the job once they learn how hard programming can be and how much attention to detail is required. They often fail to see that object-oriented methods are superior to the procedural paradigm because they just haven't had the right epiphany. In defense of amateurs, remember the following saying: "Amateurs built the ark, professionals built the Titanic." Sometimes the fresh viewpoint of an amateur can be helpful to us old, sour techno-grouches.

The Ignoramus. This programmer is also known as Mr./Ms. Stupid, or worse, he or she is dumb and doesn't know it. Watch out for these people. You may have inherited them—please don't hire them. Now, I'm not being prejudiced toward the mentally challenged, but they just don't have a useful role in a profession that requires constant learning and self-discipline. Ignorance can be tolerated as long as it isn't willful. Maybe move this person to the testing department, because sometimes users who are stupid find the bugs.[8] Another word about stupidity: We all suffer from the constant problem that occurs between the keyboard and the chair. If writing code didn't require some smarts, everyone would do it, right? Just be sure you don't mistake ignorance for stupidity. Ignorance can be cured, stupidity should be shunned. If you came on board a department that wasn't assembled by a professional programmer, you may find some of these breeds in your midst. Some nontechnical business leaders may have put the group together from folks who had sold themselves as programmers but don't have the gift.

The Salad Chef. A love of cooking up software reigns here. This breed consists of a bit of the engineer, the slob, and a not-so-gifted artist combined, but the ingredients are out of proportion. The result is a smorgasbord of coding styles and add-on components, and a general disorderliness of code. It might look appealing, but one bite and you know you're going to die. Send this programmer to a cooking class and be sure you don't have a full-blown slob lurking underneath what appears on the surface to be talent. This mongrel breed might appear seldom as a pure form, but I mention it because the trait shows up in a number of programmers' coding styles. If they can't conform to your corporate standards, you'll have a full-time job on your hands just trying to figure out what they have done and how to maintain their code. Your role as a code reviewer (see Chapter 6) will be crucial to rehabilitating the salad chef.

Working with the Breeds

Programmers are people first, so all the traits in the previous section may exist to a greater or lesser degree in the same person. Some of these traits are in opposition to each other, but don't worry about this. Every human walking the planet tonight is a bit of a contradiction, and you and your programmers are no different. What is important for you to do as the manager of these wonders of nature is respond with understanding, appropriate motivation and, above all, wisdom that's best gained by experience on the job learning to know your folks. Try to identify your programmers by the facets of their characters that shine the brightest under the sunshine of new endeavors and the lightening flashes of those projects near their deadlines.

---

8.   I prefer the term "program anomaly" or "undocumented feature offering (UFO)" over "bug."

> *Try to identify your programmers by the facets of their characters that shine the brightest under the sunshine of new endeavors and the lightening flashes of those projects near their deadlines.*

What breeds would make up a good team of programmers, assuming you could create your department from scratch? My first choice would be to have a good balance between architects and constructionists. These two breeds bring the best of needed skills to software creation: One has a high-level view, and the other is good at the details. An artist might be your second choice to mix in from time to time. Alas, you probably will not be able to assemble your group from the ideal candidates. You'll need to work with what you have, and thus your ability to deal with the blended nature of the traits I've stereotyped must be shaped by your insight, patience, and mentoring—leadership requires all three working in concert.

Another personality type you should be on the lookout for is the cowboy programmer. This type doesn't fit well into the other breeds listed previously because it is best described as an overall attitude. This attitude describes the programmer who may be really good at what he or she does but practically impossible to manage. Cowboys have the idea that they can pick and choose the programming work they want to do, and they can do it on their terms, according to their schedule, and by whatever means they see fit to employ. You could call this type a lone wolf (or a stray cat, in keeping with the context of this book). These cowboys can work miracles or wreak havoc, depending on your needs and ability to tolerate personal eccentricity. Be careful with cowboys—they will never be part of your team. Use them only as a last resort or if the project is truly a stovepipe or silo job that you don't expect your team to maintain.

Why do we find all these interesting personality characteristics in programmers? I believe it is because the nature of the software developer's work attracts a certain breed of human. In the classic book, *The Mythical Man-Month*, Frederick Brooks[9] describes our craft as one that provides five kinds of joys:

1. The joy of making things

2. The joy of making things that are useful to other people

3. The fascination of fashioning puzzle-like objects of interlocking moving parts

---

9. Frederick P. Brooks, *The Mythical Man-Month: Essays on Software Engineering, Anniversary Edition* (New York: Addison-Wesley, 1995), p. 230. This is a timeless classic—very few books in our field are reissued after 25 years, and this one is truly worthy.

4. The joy of always learning, of a nonrepeating task

5. The delight of working in a medium so tractable—pure thought-stuff— which nevertheless exists, moves, and works in a way that word-objects do not

These joys attract the kind of people you manage, and understanding what motivates them (and you) can be a tremendous aid to your leadership role.

Cat Fight! A Hissing and Scratching Contest

John and Kevin were constantly at odds during the design meeting. We had begun to discuss how the user would log into the system, and they were arguing about low-level details of construction techniques. The meeting was not progressing and there were many more features to be designed, or at least everyone thought so in spite of the lack of a clear agenda for the meeting. John and Kevin always fought because John, who was a consultant, and Kevin, who was a long-time employee and a very creative programmer, had very different motives and plans for the meeting. They were more interested in proving who was the smartest than designing a system, even though John had been designated as the development leader, a job Kevin desperately wanted. It didn't help that the boss wasn't in the meeting; there was no one to act as a negotiator.

A day went by, and the other programmers grew more silent as John and Kevin fought over each piece of the design. By the end of the second day, very few whiteboard printouts had been produced and what had been done came at the cost of long hours of tedious battling between the two scrapping cats, John and Kevin. The rest of the team became so discouraged that they began to doubt whether the system would ever be built. To compound matters, the team had been tasked to get this new system created as soon as possible because the legacy system was hurting the company in the marketplace.

This short story illustrates some of the difficulties with consultants and employees working on the same team, especially when the boss isn't in the room. You might question the choice of a consultant as the development leader, too. You also can see that a design meeting without a careful plan, an agenda, and a method for resolving differences can waste time and place the whole idea of "design before coding" in jeopardy. The dynamics of interpersonal relationships on the development team also illustrate the need to know your people before you create team leadership roles.

The end result of this particular story was that the project was canceled and a competing team in another division designed and built the software. The absent manager also had some dreary and difficult days explaining to his boss why they didn't step up to the plate and hit a home run after many promises and reassurances were given prior to project commencement.

Glory, Honor, and Greenbacks

Everyone with a job wants to be appreciated and to feel his or her contributions are meaningful. Even incompetent workers want to feel appreciated, in spite of the fact that they make negative contributions to the company. Sure, we all say coding is its own reward, but take away our paycheck and see how long we pound the keys. Pay us well and we will still crave recognition among our peers and an occasional pat on the back from the boss. Real cats may preen alone in a corner thinking no one is watching, but programmer cats really do like to preen in public. The practice of creating Easter eggs, though somewhat out of style at present, was always a sure sign that programmers wanted and needed an audience. You, their leader, are sitting in the first row and they are looking for your applause. Of course, some don't deserve applause but are truly in need of a serious word of prayer.[10]

There is a time to praise and a time to pause and consider if you're getting your money's worth out of your people. This is your challenge as a leader and manager. If you praise them, make sure it is in public. If you criticize, do it in private. These guidelines are not just given because they conform to rules of polite society—they are necessary because of the affect your actions toward one team member have on the whole group. Public humiliation never makes a group function as a productive unit. Public praise, when done genuinely and because the recipient deserves it, can work wonders. Don't be flippant when you praise, shouting out "You guys did a great job!" as your team walks out of a meeting. Take the time to make it stick. Give thought to the reason for the praise and let your team know your thinking.

> *There is a time to praise and a time to pause and consider if you're getting your money's worth out of your people.*

Another word about praise. You may feel left out yourself, depending on how your boss treats you, when it comes time for compliments. As the leader, you are striving to make the group successful. When the group is successful, you praise it. Who praises you? Sometimes, the answer is "no one," and you may wish for a pat on the back from time to time yourself. This position, where your efforts and successes are the reason for the good reputation of the team, can be awkward if you seek fame for yourself. Leaders must learn to measure their confidence by how well those they lead perform.

---

10. This is a Southern expression for a trip to the woodshed, usually involving a spanking.

If you've risen among the ranks to become the leader, your job may be doubly difficult since you may be in charge of deciding the professional fate of your friends. Don't let friendship get in the way of business, but rather use it to motivate for the benefit of all. No one will feel you're manipulating friendship if in the end everyone enjoys the pleasure of success.

Motivating with Money

Well, I mentioned money previously, didn't I? Dang. I might as well get this over with since, as the Good Book says, ". . . money is the answer to everything."[11] A recent salary survey concerning programmers shows hourly rates range from $30 to over $150 per hour, with most of us in the middle of this wide spectrum. What determines if your folks are worth their rate? Performance, experience, effectiveness, timeliness, the current local market rate, and economic conditions are all factors, as well as your company's tradition of pay for high-tech workers. Your challenge when hiring new people or giving raises is to be fair and prudent at the same time.

Fair and prudent. Hmm, this is a difficult task because you may want to dole out the money as if it grew on trees thinking this helps job performance. Think again—a luxury today is a necessity tomorrow. Money is like power: It can corrupt, and don't make me quote another famous line from the newer portion of the Bible.[12] Getting back on track, how do you achieve a balance in monetary compensation matters? If you consider the task as one of balance, envision the scales of justice: On one side, you have a tray for fairness, on the other side, you have a tray for prudence. Fairness accepts weights that are equivalent to the programmer's experience and performance. Prudence accepts typical business smarts, such as watching the bottom line and the average salary of the programming staff. Keep these in mind as you make decisions about money—it's a good theory.

Theory? What about application? This is why money can be such a tough area to administer properly in your job. You have principles in mind you believe should guide your efforts to reward your staff, but at the same time, the economics of the current business climate and corporate policies you must live by may frustrate your planning. Salary can be supplemented with bonuses based on merit and/or corporate profits in some organizations. These incentives can work as long as the staff member's contributions can truly carry enough weight to affect the formula used to determine the bonus. You can try quarterly bonuses if you want, but I've

---

11. Actually, it accuses the fool of saying this. See Ecclesiastes 9:14–19 in a modern version for the context. Try not to get too depressed when you read this.

12. See the New Testament, 1 Timothy 6:10, where love, money, and evil are related together in a nice, logical syllogism.

found them problematic because once you start giving them, they begin to be expected. You should consult with your boss to work out a plan that fits within your organization. If you are the ultimate decision maker, do what you think is appropriate and keep in mind the issues of fairness and prudence.

The Thunking[13] Layer

Are you feeling all warm and fuzzy now? Probably not. You're most likely waiting for the bulleted list of things to avoid and things to embrace. There will be plenty of lists to look at in the chapters ahead, but at the moment I want to emphasize the role of thinking in your new role, rather than give you a long list of dos and don'ts. Thinking is perhaps the hardest thing we have to do as mangers and leaders, but it is crucial—absolutely crucial—to our success. As Jim McCarthy writes in *Dynamics of Software Development*:

> *The real task of software development management is to marshal as much intellect as possible and invest it in the activities that support the creation of the product.*[14]

Think while you're in the shower. Think while you ride your bike, take a walk, or go in-line skating. Think while you're listening to the dilemmas posed by design decisions. Think instead of watching TV or surfing the Web—they both may have 500 channels, but nothing is on, even if they relieve you of thinking. Think yourself full, work until you're empty, and then do it all over again. The result will surprise you.

Okay, let's do a little thinking about how to handle some typical situations.

Say you have a cat who is primarily a minimalist, but a very sharp one. You need him to enhance a product that he didn't write but that is critical for the current business goals. How do you motivate him when he takes one look at the other guy's code and says, "This is too complicated. It needs to be rewritten." He says this, of course, staring at code that took 2 years to write and is making the company money. The "other guy" is no longer around to explain the code, either. You have two choices: Give in, make him happy, and ruin any chance of meeting the deadline, or help him see how he can learn the existing architecture and make a significant contribution. Appeal to his sense of wanting a tidy architecture by asking him to document the existing code with the view that in the future, as time

---

13. You know what "thunking" is if you've been under the covers with compilers. You'll soon figure out my play on words.

14. Jim McCarthy, *Dynamics of Software Development* (Redmond, WA: Microsoft Press, 1995), p. 5.

permits, he can rewrite some of the objects to make them easier to follow. If he is a sharp programmer he ought to be able to figure out what another one has accomplished. Never hesitate to let competition serve a useful goal. For the minimalist, anything he didn't write is junk, but the truth may be that he is afraid he can't understand the code and doesn't want to admit it. Look for the hidden motivations that all of us share as humans and realize that programmers often hide behind intellectual excuses rather than admit their brains are not up to the task at hand.

How do you deal with an architect who thinks her object designs are far superior to anything that has been invented before and yet you think you see some weaknesses? Don't tell her that her design is flawed from the get-go or she will be on you like white on rice.[15] Ask her to explain how all the moving parts will work and to build some prototypes or test programs to illustrate the functions. If her prototypes don't show any problems, maybe you were wrong to see design flaws. Ask her to "componentize" her architecture if it seems like one massive and monolithic edifice. If the components can work together, maybe she has some good ideas. If the objects are too coupled and intertwined, she is too in love with complexity, which can lead to expensive software maintenance costs. A really great architect can create a framework that anyone who applies him- or herself can follow and extend. It also doesn't break when the next set of enhancements need to be added to the code. The key to working with an architect is to try to see the code through her eyes, not yours, even if she is blind in one and can't see out of the other.

> *Listen first and seek to understand before you use your authority as the manager to railroad a solution.*

What is the common technique I'm suggesting for dealing with these people-induced situations? It is to listen first and seek to understand before you use your authority as the manager to railroad a solution. Programmers are no different from the rest of the human race when it comes to confrontations: They want to have a fair hearing of their point of view. As Stephen Covey writes in *The 7 Habits of Highly Effective People*, "Seek first to understand . . . then to be understood." Building consensus in technical decisions is an art whose canvas is openness to the ideas of others. It takes patience to construct such a canvas, even though you often feel you don't have time to build software and have everyone agree about

---

15. The phrase "like white on rice" is Southern for "in your face."

the methods. This may be your *feeling* in many cases, but consensus should still be your goal.[16] I have more to say about building consensus in Chapter 5, which deals with leading and managing a design meeting. You may be surprised to learn that consensus is not built through compromise.

Another example will illustrate the concept of understanding before judging. Some languages, such as Visual Basic (VB), don't allow true object constructors. I've seen an artist use the VB class initialize event to do a reasonable amount of work for getting the object set to be used by the consuming (parent) class.[17] In VB, if an object can't be instantiated, the error is difficult to trap—you will simply get a failure to create the object. When I asked him why he chose to use this event to handle error-prone activity, he replied that it was elegant, clean, and didn't require any action on the part of the calling object to be ready to use the interface. My opinion, of course, is that safe error handling should precede any attempt at beauty. I didn't tell him this first. I listened to his reasons, described how things could go wrong with his object, and then demonstrated an example in code. He learned something from the code example lesson that he would not have learned as well if I had just said, "Change it, this is not right." Again, when you give someone an opportunity to explain his or her point of view, that person will open up to your perspective.

How Are You Adapting?

You've taken in a lot of ideas in this chapter. You may feel overwhelmed by the scope of adaptation required to become an effective leader. Not to worry. We humans are still 99 percent genetically identical to monkeys, and the 1 percent that makes us different didn't appear overnight. The chapters ahead will help you adapt, overcome, and succeed as you look at other aspects of leadership and management.

Let's review what's been covered so far to help cement the key principles in your heart and mind.

You must adapt. Learning new management skills so you can lead requires adapting yourself to a new social context at work. You're the boss and this changes your relationship to those on your team.

---

16. Many would say that if everyone agrees then when things go bad, everyone is to blame. This may be true, but as managers we should be more concerned with fixing problems than affixing blame. Success has many parents—be one.

17. The initialize event in VB accepts no parameters and does not return any.

Character development is more important than image refinement.
Leadership comes from within and is not manifested by an image. You're
still a programmer, but your role as a leader of programmers requires you
to work on deep issues involving insight into others' behavior as well as
your own.

Know your staff. Become an anthropologist of programmer culture and
people. Learn why your staff writes code the way they do and how you
can work with the best qualities and rehabilitate the areas that do not
lead to productivity. Herding cats means getting them to move in the
same direction: This is what a leader strives to do.

Reward your staff appropriately. Act on the need to praise with words
and compensate with money. Consider all the factors that constrain you
financially, but be fair and prudent. Lavish praise in public when appropriate and reprove in private.

Think. Learn to apply what you know about people to build consensus.
Listen to and understand other points of view before you make judgments. Cultivate your life of the mind: Make learning second nature in
your new role as leader. Off-the-shelf plans to solve people problems are
no substitute for you crafting plans and methods to deal with the problems and opportunities unique to your organization.

What Lies Ahead

In the next chapter, you'll turn an introspective eye on you, the manager, just as
you did on your staff in this chapter. I'll ask some hard questions about how you
approach your job as a leader of the critically important endeavor of building software in today's business climate. You must manage your staff to be a good leader,
but managing yourself comes first.

Managing the Leader

Creating great software on time is your goal and managing the process is your job so what do you do in your free time? Probably code. If you have ascended to management from the ranks of programmers, you had better continue programming or your passion for the craft will wane and your skills will fade. Another reason you probably seek or make time to code is the joy it brings you. If you are new to leading a software team, you are still adapting to this role and writing code feels comfortable because it is a familiar task you feel productive doing. I believe continuing to code is a necessary activity that, if managed well with the rest of your life, will keep you in touch with your roots. Roots are important for nourishing your passion, and as a leader you need to sink some new roots into the soil of your work life.

These new roots will spring from introspection, so while you are at this nighttime code feast, take a look at yourself. You spent the last chapter looking at interactions with your staff; now it's time to look at the one who leads: you. This chapter examines topics related to managing yourself. They are all designed to help you explore questions such as "What kind of leader am I?" and "Do I aim to please my boss or my staff, or both at the same time?" The answers are crucial to your growth and success as a leader.

A Look in the Mirror

Examining yourself objectively can be a difficult thing to accomplish since subjectivity is inherent in the process. To aid your introspection, look at the following list of questions and ponder them as you read this chapter. At the end, I offer answers that I believe are essential to strengthening your grip on your management activities and will help you serve as a better leader. You can't have a powerful tennis swing without a strong grip on the racket. Management is the racket, and the following questions demand your answers.

Do you

- Believe deadlines are sales-driven tools that don't really matter?

- Let the programmers make the ultimate architectural decisions because you are too tired and stressed to care anymore?

- Hope your experienced programmers will do the job right because you just don't have time to baby-sit?

- Consider that it will eventually all work out as the deadline approaches?[1]

- Think users will never try certain functions or combinations of functions that might crash the code because they are just not smart enough?

- Prefer to lead by consensus even when it takes an enormous amount of time and patience?

- Consider e-mail an effective communication tool for design?

- Hate talking on the phone for hours at a time to be sure everyone is on track?

- Think that committees can never produce adequate business requirements?

- Believe you are the smartest programmer in the company?

- Feel jealously and fear when looking at really good code that you didn't write?

- Do whatever it takes to meet a deadline?[2]

The answers you give to the preceding questions might differ from day to day as a function of your circumstances.[3] Nevertheless, there are some answers that are correct regardless of your current management context. The sections that follow will help prepare you for what I believe to be timeless answers. Some of these answers may be tough to acknowledge, but I believe that if you know yourself you can accept and act on these truths.

---

1. This is the same as preferring the blue pill to the red, as in *The Matrix*, an addictive movie for many programmers.

2. In the South, we would say, "I'll hair-lip hell to get it done." This means you won't let anything prevent you from accomplishing your goals. The origin of this term is derived from the image of hell as a terrible yawing mouth about to swallow you up, somewhat like an impossible code deadline. You stand your ground and slash at the mouth of hell with a sword, thus rendering the "lips" of hell hairlipped and overcoming its power to destroy you.

3. Remember what Obi-Wan said to Luke about the nature of truth and one's point of view when discussing Luke's father? (This was after Yoda died.)

Heaven, Hell, Purgatory, and Your Place in the Software Universe

The most significant improvement you can make to managing software development is to improve the manager.

The most significant improvement you can make to managing software development is to improve the manager.

William Blake wrote, "He who desires, but acts not, breeds pestilence."[4] If you don't correct your management weaknesses, you'll spread pestilence among your programmers. Continuing with some poetry (a close cousin to programming), note what Yeats wrote (from "The Two Trees"):

> *. . . gaze in thine own heart,*
>
> *The holy tree is growing there;*
>
> *From joy the holy branches start,*
>
> *And all the trembling flowers they bear . . .*[5]

You have to nourish the "tree." As Virgil led Odysseus through purgatory,[6] I'm here to guide you through your new place in the software universe.

Knowing your place in the scheme of things will help you become a better leader. Let's explore the regions of this new and wonderful universe.

---

4. This little goody and many other tidbits equally enlightening and depressing can be found in Blake's poems "The Marriage of Heaven and Hell." The one here is from a section entitled "Proverbs of Hell." See William Blake, *The Complete Poetry and Prose of William Blake*, ed. David V. Erdman (Berkeley, CA: University of California Press, 1982).

5. William Butler Yeats, *Selected Poems and Three Plays of William Butler Yeats*, ed. M.L. Rosenthal (New York: Collier Books, 1986).

6. You can refresh your classical learning by reading a modern translation of Dante's *Purgatorio*. Being a software development manager might seem like you're in the land between heaven and hell, but you're really not—it's just life as we know it.

The Nature of Work Has Changed for You

Well, for sure you are not in heaven. You probably figured this out the first month you had to plan the programming assignments for your staff. You might think *your* boss lives in heaven, but I can assure you he or she does not. You see your boss creating timeline charts and conducting planning meetings for the distant future at the enterprise level and never apparently doing any measurable work. This perception on your part is mistaken and indicative of how you need to change your way of measuring work. I will have more to say about this in a little while and especially in Chapter 9, where I focus exclusively on your working relationship with your boss.

Since you are from the ranks of the coders, you also have figured out that you're not in this place anymore either. Sometimes you referred to it as "programmer hell" because you were given assignments with unrealistic deadlines and had no one to consult with but yourself. As a programmer, you got used to the heat, enjoyed the camaraderie with your fellow coders, and just accepted it as your place in life.

You now have a new place as a leader of programmers. You are somewhere in between heaven and hell and thus enjoy the "benefits" of both places. In mythology, this in-between place is called *purgatory,* and it is a place to work things out, hopefully on your way to heaven. Purgatory has its share of suffering, but it isn't as bad as hell. You may not feel that you are suffering less in this new place you live called purgatory, but once you get use to it, it isn't really so bad. Actually, I can't think of a better place to be: You still get to write code, but you also have an opportunity to help others do an even better job of creating software.

You Must Re-evaluate Success, Passion, and Ambition

The geometrical aspects of heaven, purgatory, and hell have application to your place in the management hierarchy of your company. Realize that each step up the management ladder means you have a greater distance to fall. If you're on the right ladder (i.e., it is leaning against the right wall), take heart: At least you know where you are going. And, by the way, where are you going as a programmer-manager? Hopefully in the direction of success, both personal and corporate. Though success is measured in many ways, the one I find most helpful and operational is being able to enjoy your labor and not lose your passion for it. Passion may seem overrated, but it can put fire in your belly and help you overcome the unpredictable software development world around you. Passion is a fuel that can drive your leadership "engine." Tell your programmers to passionately pursue perfection. If they are seeking elegance and perfection, two goals that can extend coding time, remind them that elegance is obtainable perfection. Passion will motivate them to achieve these goals. Work to preserve your passion—it is the only way you can grow, adapt, overcome, and succeed. It is part of nourishing the tree from which the flowers of success bloom.

> *Work to preserve your passion—it is the only way you can grow, adapt, overcome, and succeed. It is part of nourishing the tree from which the flowers of success bloom.*

Learn to embrace your place and don't strive for more. Ambition can be a very destructive force when it takes your eyes off the moment and the tasks at hand. Be ambitious to thrive in your new role as leader and part-time coder. If any future promotion comes your way, be sure it is one you didn't actively seek—this is the best kind of ambition. You can make this kind of ambition work if you have the heart of a programmer and learn to develop the mind of a leader.

> *You can make this work if you have the heart of a programmer and learn to develop the mind of a leader.*

Natural Selection and Time

We know from the evidence of the natural world that time is the one ingredient necessary for the process of natural selection to weed out weakness and produce survivability. In the software world, you don't have the luxury of geological ages for time to do its work. It might seem to the consumers of software products that it takes ages to produce the next, less-buggy version, but they just don't understand the process. You do understand the process and must consider the role of time in your daily work activities. In the revolutionary book on software management, *Peopleware*, the greatest management sin is described as wasting people's time.[7] Are you wasting your own time in your management activities?

---

7. Tom DeMarco and Timothy Lister, *Peopleware: Productive Projects and Teams, Second Edition* (New York: Dorset House Publishing, 1999).

Time is either an ally or an enemy. Consider what Francis Bacon, the father of modern science, said:

> *He that will not apply new remedies must expect new evils; for time is the greatest innovator.*[8]

Give natural selection a little help: Consider administrative issues that can become time wasters, and innovate and act to control them before they control you. I describe a number of these time wasters in the sections that follow. I do not address here the details of the management techniques associated with these likely time wasters, but they do serve as seeds for topics that will be discussed more fully in later chapters. For now, I want you to realize that you are currently employing *some* techniques, whether you are conscious of them or not. It is the time spent in these activities that should concern you.

Avoid Unnecessary, Ineffective Meetings

As a manager and leader you will participate in and conduct more meetings than when you were a coder. Chapter 5 is devoted entirely to this subject. For now, consider which meetings are truly necessary and strive to make them effective.

One necessary meeting is a weekly get-together with your staff. Beware of spending too much time talking and not enough time deciding and acting. Don't have a meeting just so everyone can be guided to "rubber-stamp" your decisions. Encourage debate but seek decisions. They don't build monuments to committees even if they are necessary to drill down to the dirty design details. And remember, the devil is in the details, and the purpose of any meeting is to exorcise these devils. You control the meeting and thus the time. Set limits to the duration of all meetings: A 45-minute staff meeting is usually more than sufficient. An 8-hour design meeting may be required many times but have a detailed agenda and follow it if you are going to endure such a mammoth brain bashing.

> *Don't have a meeting just so everyone can be guided to "rubber-stamp" your decisions. Encourage debate but seek decisions.*

---

8. See Bacon's essays *Of Innovations* (1625). Another nice line from *Star Trek VII*: "Time is the fire in which we burn." This probably comes from some great classical writer, but I'll be danged if I can find out who wrote it, so we're stuck with Bacon.

Don't Organize Too Little or Too Much

Don't buy into the theory that a clean desk is the sign of a sick mind. It may have looked like Einstein's desk was cluttered in the pictures, but I guarantee you his brain wasn't. You need enough organization to be sure you don't forget a deadline, but not so much that you spend all your time just keeping track of things to do. Reaching a balance is tough but necessary. Organizing for success is a topic covered in depth in Chapter 4. Don't mistake getting the job organized with getting it done. Organizing is the beginning of the plan: Work the plan. Remember what Spock said: "Logic is the beginning of wisdom."[9] In the same way, planning is the beginning of executing.

Don't Expect If You Don't Inspect

You make assignments, get back to your duties, and hope that everyone is on task. Little do you know that Joe went back to surfing the Web rather than making those API calls work correctly after you explained his assignment more carefully. If your delegations don't have intermediate milestones as an integral part of the task, you have failed to understand the mind of a programmer, even though you are one. Human nature is to see a deadline 1 month out and expect there is plenty of time to get the job done. Time is wasted when progress isn't measured. Completing a new product feature isn't a Boolean task, it is an incremental and iterative process that offers many opportunities for inspection. Let's say you tell the testing department that the code-complete date is January X. This had better not be your working code-complete date! You won't make X if you don't first achieve X − Y repeatedly where Y is adjusted every week to include some portion of the product's functions. (Can you say "daily build"?) You have probably heard that the price of freedom is constant vigilance—the price of on-time software is constant diligence.

 You have probably heard that the price of freedom is constant vigilance —the price of on-time software is constant diligence.

---

9. From *Star Trek VI*—you know, when Spock had the drink with Valaris after their talk about man's expulsion from paradise. Hmm, maybe paradise is being just a programmer compared to being a manager—you decide.

Plan Your Architecture before Choosing Your Technology

The magic bullet or golden hammer (whatever you want to call it) technology doesn't solve business problems, people do. Sure, you employ technology to implement a solution, but you are wasting time if you think buying the latest add-on to your development environment is going to increase productivity. The next version of your programming language may not solve all your problems either. Many promises are made by competing vendors of software development tools. Our industry is divided along two lines: Microsoft and everybody else. Now, I realize that this bifurcation is a bit simplified, but it will serve to illustrate my point. And that point is this: Microsoft has produced solutions that you would like to think are not proprietary just because they are a large, influential corporation. No matter how large or how much power they have to sway the industry, their technology is conceived based upon a predetermined architectural plan. The Java world, typified by Sun, is little different, though it is somewhat more fragmented than Microsoft and they, too, build their products around a particular architectural scheme. You may use Enterprise JavaBeans or .NET to your heart's content as long as you accept the associated architectural constraints. I encourage you to determine your architectural needs and plan a system before you choose a technology of implementation. You'll just have to do it all over again if the new whiz-bang tool doesn't pan out. You've heard it said many times: If you don't have time to do the job right, when will you have time to do it over again?

Balance Purity with Practicality

Balancing purity with practicality is tough for the lover of software construction tools. The concept of "good enough" software, probably pioneered by Microsoft, has merit. You can spend an inordinate amount of time making a program pure rather than practical. What you want to achieve is software maintainability, and practicality is often a better measure of this goal than purity. Sure, purity can help, but at what cost? I'm not talking about creating sloppy or hasty code, I'm thinking clarity and software that can be picked up and extended by others and not just the creator. The problem with purity is that it is like beauty: It is perceived by the eye of the beholder. Your eyes need to have practical lenses glued on permanently.

Delegate Tasks, Don't Do Them

The classic management trap for the programmer-cum-manager involves delegation. You know how to accomplish a particular solution in code, and it takes time to educate your staff members who don't necessarily see the solution. An old Chinese proverb applies here: "Give a man a fish and he can eat for a day. Teach a man to fish and he can eat for a lifetime." If everyone was as sharp as you, wouldn't your job be easier? Perhaps. Invest time in teaching now, and you'll save time down the road as your people become more capable of solving problems without your direct help. Then delegation will become an effective tool rather than you feeling you're shouting into the wind as you dole out coding assignments.

Document What You Do or Plan to Do

A tough task for those who like to code or manage by the seat of their pants is documentation. Go ahead and produce the screen prototype if you need to, but do it only for the sake of doing screen captures that will flesh out a design document to hand off to the appropriate programmer. Don't give the prototype directly to the programmer you ask to complete the project. It might seem this will save time, but it might just lead the programmer down the wrong path and result in a false start. Don't think that the business requirements are a sufficient basis for writing code. They should only be the starting point for a design document that outlines the architecture, and then you can talk about the code objects that implement the solution. You'll always be tempted when the time pressure is on (and when is it not?) to take a shortcut, but only if you are extremely lucky will you have extendable software without a clear design.

You may feel you are surrounding yourself with paper diagrams from time to time, but this is better than code stored away in a repository without any written clue as to how it works or what problem it was intended to solve. Writing documentation is very different than creating software, but it is a necessary first step to turning ideas into products. The next step will likely be a prototype, but view this as an extension of the documentation, not as the start of the project. Prototypes prove the documented concept, whereas the product is the implementation of the proven design.

Prototypes prove the documented concept, whereas the product is the implementation of the proven design.

Measuring Your Productivity

As I mentioned earlier in the chapter, administrative activity doesn't *feel* as productive as writing code when you first switch gears from full-time programmer to full-time manager and part-time coder. This fact introduces the point of this section: Learn to distinguish between nervous energy and true creativity. Say what? Okay, here's what I'm talking about. If you are used to spending hours and hours in a head-down code mode, you understand nervous energy. It is the state of your mind after the third can of Jolt[10] and you still have a bunch of code to write, but you can almost taste the final result. True creativity is seeing the end and all the steps necessary to get there but knowing that quality will result from a more measured pace. I know this was a mouthful, but you really need to chew on this concept.

As a programmer, you were used to measuring your productivity by the number of successful functional points you created in any given day. This measure will fail you as a manager. You'll be disappointed and feel unsatisfied with the way you're spending your time until you adopt a new mindset. As a manager and leader, you need to measure your productivity by how much your staff accomplishes as a team under your leadership. You can't always measure this each day, and that can be a problem if you're in need of constant internal affirmations that you're doing a good job. A solution to this daily need? Drop by your programmers' cubes every day or pick up the phone and see how they are doing. As they learn to expect your daily interaction, two things will happen: They will never know when you are coming and thus always try to be about their job, and you will have to determine their daily progress and adjust your timelines and future efforts accordingly. Both reactions can both be known by each party, but it's nice to pretend that neither actually knows this is going on.

 As a manager and leader, you need to measure your productivity by how much your staff accomplishes as a team under your leadership.

---

10. Substitute your own caffeine-loaded liquid here. I prefer programmer-strength coffee, which is opaque and able to almost stand on the desk without a cup.

In his highly insightful book, *The End of Patience*, David Shenk writes:

With hypertext, endings are irrelevant—because no one ever gets to one. Reading gives way to surfing, a meandering, peripatetic journey through a maze of threads. The surfer creates his own narrative, opting for the most seductive link immediately available. As a research technique, this is superb. As a mode of thought, however, it has serious deficiencies.[11]

As an analogy, this quote suggests the following: Don't measure your productivity by how quickly you can jump from one project or person to another. Keep large-scale goals in view and measure the small steps necessary to reach a happy ending. Don't make up your own story about how the development is going—let the facts dictate the reality, not your hopeful imagination. Operative words from the previous quote are "seductive" and "thought." Don't be seduced by the immediate joy of writing code; instead, give thought to the task of facilitating others to experience this joy guided by your leadership.

I mentioned earlier that deep thinking is required to manage programmers and the task of software development. Add to this list patience, a quality not often found in the programmer's soul but in dire need of being grafted into that of the programmer/leader. Direct some of this patience toward yourself and realize that patience is a friend of both a programmer and a leader of programmers. Structure—the mental discipline you bring to your job—is patience's facilitator.

If you are new to the job of managing, don't expect to feel comfortable for the first 6 months. Let this discomfort remind you that you still have a lot to learn and that learning new ways of being *and feeling* productive takes time and will pay off in the future.

Watching Your Weaknesses

You are a great programmer, right? I'm sure you are but you aren't perfect yet. Beware of how your weaknesses as a programmer will make you overlook things in those on your staff with similar characteristics. If you don't like to document and design before you code, then you will probably let others get away with this, too.

Rarely is this a good thing. If you are a minimalist when it comes to error trapping (never a good quality), you might not catch this in your next code review of Sally's project, where she thinks the procedures are so straightforward that error trapping would be a waste of space.

---

11. David Shenk, *The End of Patience: Cautionary Notes on the Information Revolution* (Bloomington, IN: Indiana University Press, 1999).

If you don't like to document and design before you code, you will probably let others get away with this, too.

I could continue to make a list of programmer weaknesses but I will leave this to you. What you can't leave to another day, however, is the fact that you must constantly be watchful of your own faults as a coder so that you don't excuse in others what you might excuse in yourself. This might seem like a contradiction, and it is, so working to remedy your shortcomings as a programmer will go a long way toward not infecting your staff with the same problems.

To help you overcome your weaknesses, realize that many others have traveled the same path as you. Some have left breadcrumbs behind for you to follow. These breadcrumbs are commonly known as books and sometimes URLs. In other words, I recommend a diligent reading program to combat your lack of knowledge and/or experience. You need to read with a number of different agendas. Here are some suggestions:

1. **Read to keep up**. This involves reading trade magazines, books on your primary language, and journals concerning techniques you need to employ to do your job. You must do this almost every day just keep from falling behind in necessary work skills.

2. **Read to stay aware**. This concerns the breadth of your knowledge, and some of the same sources you use for keeping up apply here. The agenda in this area is more focused on those things that you might not use right now but may in the near future. Internet newsgroups, forums, and other such wonders of the information age can be a great help. Be aware, however, that the information age isn't the knowledge age.

3. **Read to grow deeper**. You will find this task difficult to manage, but you must make time to gain a more thorough knowledge about the technology and techniques that impact your daily job. Here you might peruse the bookshelves of your local library or bookstore or the Internet until you find a publisher that puts out works that really help you. Depending on your particular programming community, the publisher will vary and only you can determine who puts out the good stuff. Avoid the "cookbook" approach to growing deeper. You need more than just a list of tips, you need to bite off more than you think you can chew until your capacity for learning increases.

4. **Read to grow wiser**. Our field isn't the only one with smart people. Other scientific and literary disciplines can offer you real insight into lateral thinking. Often in our profession, we engage in vertical thinking only. *Vertical thinking* means progressing from one logical conclusion to the next and ruling out that which doesn't fit into our preconceived notions of what is appropriate for a solution. Lateral thinking is what brings about original ideas and is often the mark of genius.

A special word of caution for the lover of technology: Businesspeople are smart, too. By "businesspeople" I'm referring to those who have participated in the building of great corporations and government agencies over the years. I have to admit that it took me a long time to learn to appreciate the skills required to run a business. I was guilty of being an intellectual snob, thinking that unless you understood all the details of technology, you were not truly among the best and brightest. This is a weakness. You can learn from leaders in many fields, not just those associated with technology. Broaden your intellectual pursuits to include human endeavors that have little to do with the application of technology directly, but rather the application of business acumen. As a leader, your primary job is to focus people to solve business problems, and technology is just one of many possible solutions. You need to become familiar with other paths to problem solving, so read outside of the technology field.

Here is an example of what I mean about business smarts. Jack Welch, the longtime head of GE, writes:

> *I believe that business is a lot like a world-class restaurant. When you peek behind the kitchen doors, the food never looks as good as when it comes to your table on fine china perfectly garnished. Business is messy and chaotic. In our kitchen, I hope you'll find something that might be helpful to you in reaching your own dreams.*[12]

Sounds a bit like the software business, doesn't it folks? Welch has much to say in this book germane to leading programmers as he writes about leading one of the largest and most profitable companies of the past 20 years. Learn from those who have made the leadership journey ahead of you. Follow their trail.

The Bibliography at the end of this book is annotated to help guide your journey. Turn there for some good books to own and read. Books aren't just for lining your walls to impress your friends, office mates, and coworkers. The good ones are the testimony of a life, often in the process of being lived. Learn to know the authors who seem to speak directly to you and listen to what they have to say.

---

12. Jack Welch, *Straight from the Gut* (New York: Warner Business Books, 2001), p. xv.

And the Answer Is . . .

The questions that began this chapter were designed to offer a springboard for introspection. Now that you have jumped into your psyche with both feet, let's look at the range of answers for these questions and the motives behind the questions.

Do you

- **Believe deadlines are sales-driven tools that don't really matter?** They do matter. Software may be given away by your company to sell its services, but marketing is about feature sets, and even if customers don't use all your product's features, those features need to exist on the sales brochure. Some high-dollar clients may require one particular feature that no one else wants, but having it in the software can make a huge difference to your bottom line. Marketing can be a dangerous force in software development, but it is also a necessary one. You don't want your development cycle totally driven by the sales department, but it will be one of the driving forces in creating your code-complete dates. Get to know the sales force and become their friend. Earn their trust by delivering on time and learn from them what your competition is up to in the market. (See the Cat Fight sidebar at the end of this series of questions for a story directly related to this question and answer.)

- **Let the programmers make the ultimate architectural decisions because you are too tired and stressed to care anymore?** You will be tempted to delegate some tough decisions, especially in the early days of your management career. This can work if you have good people, but be sure the reason is that the best ideas aren't always coming from your head rather than you're weary of making decisions. A failure to be decisive is an active decision. Passivity doesn't really exist, and if it did, you would soon find someone else in charge of your work life.

- **Hope your experienced programmers will do the job right because you just don't have time to babysit?** This is closely related to the previous question and again, if you have good people, they may not need your full-time attention. Just don't forget what I mentioned previously about having expectations without performing inspections.

- **Consider that it will eventually all work out as the deadline approaches?** Call it wishful thinking or, more in line with the behavior of a child, magical thinking. Whatever you call it, it is dangerous and is usually a result of bad stress working on you. Many people view stress as a common fact of life that doesn't always lead to harmful effects. Stress can be a very powerful force that can motivate and direct your efforts if you learn to be energized by it rather than conquered. If you can't be energized by your job, maybe you have the wrong one. Don't fear failure, it will come; don't fear missing a deadline, it will happen. Learn from your mistakes because if you can't learn to handle failure gracefully, you'll never learn to handle success.

- **Think users will never try certain functions or combinations of functions that might crash the code because they are just not smart enough?** More wishful thinking here. This is why programmers make bad beta testers: We know unconsciously that certain functions will fail and so we never try them. The bugs will eventually show up, so don't let haste govern your quality assurance efforts. As the development leader, you may have to do a good bit of testing in the alpha stage yourself just to catch sloppy programming.

- **Prefer to lead by consensus even when it takes an enormous amount of time and patience?** I touched on this question at the end of the previous chapter and now that I have covered the role of time and the need for patience, I believe the answer is intuitively obvious. In case your intuition is a bit rusty, consensus should always be your goal and you must marshal all the diplomacy, patience, and deep technical thinking you can to achieve it. See Chapters 5 and 6 for more on this subject.

- **Consider e-mail an effective communication tool for design?** Of course it isn't, but sometimes it's all you have to work with if your staff is geographically challenged. Sharing edits on a document is better than chasing a long thread of e-mail, but because e-mail is so convenient, people tend to use it first. Just be sure that e-mails don't pile up without compiling them into one document that expresses all the ideas pertinent to the design.

- **Hate talking on the phone for hours at a time to be sure everyone is on track?** Get over it. This will become a necessary evil unless everyone you work with is in shouting distance. In some cases, the phone is your only way of conducting daily inspections. Instant messaging software can sometimes take the place of the phone, but it too often is a time waster.

- **Think that committees can never produce adequate business requirements?** Sometimes committees fail, but they are usually necessary in a large and diverse organization. You will probably be a member or leader of more committees now that you are in charge, so you had better learn to use them. Under the best conditions, committees can be a powerful way of pooling intellectual resources, so don't underestimate their importance. After all, no one person usually has all the business knowledge and without knowing the requirements, you'll have software built by programmers just having fun.

- **Believe you are the smartest programmer in the company?** You probably answered this in the affirmative. This question's motive is to help you adjust your ego. Always seek to surround yourself with people who are even smarter than you are if possible. Never be deluded into thinking you're the only one who has all the answers. Most original thought is just fancy brain chemistry and someone else may have better molecules than you do.

- **Feel jealously and fear when looking at really good code that you didn't write?** This is a trick question. If you take pride in what you do, it is only human to feel a bit of jealously when you see something done better by someone else. Underneath this jealously is usually the fear that you've been outsmarted or, even worse, someone has accomplished something and you can't even begin to understand how he or she did it. This is sort of the internal emotional state of the "not invented here" syndrome that often plagues development departments. Recognize these emotions for what they are and move on. Your job is to get the project completed with quality and in a timely manner, so use whatever works to help you accomplish this.

- **Do whatever it takes to make a deadline?** Back to the first question. Deadlines missed can hurt a company financially and ruin your career. Does any more need to be said? Yes. A constant theme in good management of software development is diligence, vigilance, and careful attention to detail. The determination of a deadline falls within the scope of these management components. You may remember from *Star Trek* how Scotty earned his reputation as a "miracle worker,"[13] and you might need to employ with prudence a similar technique. Don't just multiply your initial estimate of time to completion by a random number, but do give your people some fudge time and have an internal code-complete date sometime prior to the one you give out to the testing department. The more you practice estimating deadlines, the better you'll become at this art form.

These questions were not a test—they were an exercise in thinking about your attitudes as a leader in order to expose weaknesses that can hinder your success. In the previous chapter, I described how you need to adapt to your role as leader. The greatest adaptation will occur in the realm of your attitudes.

---

13. You figure out which *Star Trek* movie this comes from, when Kirk asked Scotty if he always multiplied his repair estimates by a factor of 4.

Cat Fight! A True Death March

The deadline had passed without code completion a few days prior to a lovely spring day in May. The birds were singing and the air had a fresh clarity that reminded Roger of all the bright promise of the season in spite of the recent glitch with the embedded processor software.

As he pulled into his vice president's slot in the parking lot of the recently built, fancy corporate headquarters building, Roger noticed that Jeff's car wasn't in the parking lot. Well, another talk about timeliness was in order this morning! These talks had happened often in the past few months between Roger and Jeff. They were both aware of the seriousness of meeting the deadline for the new software. It seemed that Jeff would always say he was sorry and would try harder this week to get the system up and running. The vice president of sales already had signed contracts for the installation of the new control system Roger and Jeff had yet to complete in a large nationwide business with many facilities. The president had made it clear that this new deadline must be achieved since several had already passed with no joy.

Roger mused about what he could say to Jeff that would be new and somehow motivate him to get the job completed. He knew Jeff had been staying late and on weekends—he had called just to be sure. If only the code didn't have to be written in C, maybe Roger could have helped. Oh well, thought Roger, he had done his best.

About 30 minutes into Roger's day the president poked his head into Roger's spacious office and said, "Come down to my office for a few minutes. I want to have a little chat." Roger cringed and thought, A little "chat"—typical CEO talk for a tongue-lashing. As Roger seated himself in front of the president's desk, the secretary closed the door to the office. The president looked Roger in the eyes and said, "Do you know what this is about?" Roger didn't have a clue. He was speechless but mumbled out a few words about how sorry he was that they had missed the deadline again. The president was nonplussed and simply said, "Pack your things. You're fired. I told you a month ago we must meet this latest deadline. Pick up your severance check from my secretary. I want you out of the building by noon. Good-bye."

What can you learn from this story? A lot—the clues are all over the place. First, this story deals with an apparently successful and wealthy company with a very aggressive VP of sales. He already had signed contracts for a system that wasn't even finished. The other unfortunate VP was obviously in charge of software development but didn't actually have the technical skills to understand the programming problems faced by Jeff. In addition to this lack of knowledge, instead of spending extra hours with Jeff at nights and on weekends to see that the job really got done, he used the phone to "check up" on Jeff.

Many mistakes were made by this fired VP. First, there was a lack of recognition about the importance of deadlines. This flowed out of a disregard for business commitments. "I did my best" are famous last words with a mixture of magical thinking thrown in for good measure. Second, the VP was out of his depth. He didn't know C but was managing a programmer who obviously did (just not very well, apparently). Third, the VP failed to identify the actual problem with the software or programmer—he never uncovered or addressed the root causes of the pending disaster. The autopsy is complete: He was fired, so it was a true death march in the sense of the death of a job.

Putting It All Together

I have held up a mirror for you in this chapter, a metaphor for self-examination and introspection. It may have been painful, but without pain you can't grow as you must in order to lead men and women in the struggle to build software under deadlines. Is there one secret to managing yourself? I haven't found just one, but I do know that my determination to do my best has taken on new meaning as I have managed programmers. There are times when saying "I've done my best" becomes famous last words—it is what we say when we fail. Don't think of it in these terms. Giving your best means expending the maximum effort to succeed; efforts can be measured daily, success sometimes only at the end. So, if there is a secret it is this: Inspect your own leadership daily and get better the next day. Your daily inspection checklist is as follows:

1. Do I conduct introspection of my leadership daily?

2. Is my leadership improving daily, or am I procrastinating in making changes I know are needed in the style and substance of my management?

3. Do I have passion for what I'm doing?

4. Am I wasting time in the performance of necessary job functions?

5. Do I measure my productivity by how much is accomplished through those I lead, or do I feel like I don't get anything done personally?

6. How have my weaknesses been manifested today—in myself or in others?

7. What did I study today to keep up, stay aware, and grow deeper and wiser?

This list has seven items, a number considered perfect by the ancients. You will not achieve perfection today, nor tomorrow, and perhaps not in your lifetime, but you can achieve a perfection of effort—doing your best—in the daily attempt.

In the next chapter, as you take on full bore the daunting task of herding cats, you will need to revisit this mirror. Let introspection be a constructive refuge, not a hiding place. You must look ahead and outward to do your job, but always acknowledge the fact that building your character as a leader is a lifelong process.

CHAPTER 3

Leading the Herd

Leadership cannot be created by force of will alone. It requires mastery of aspects of management that may be new to you. In this chapter, you'll examine some of the key areas of management that you must control or else they will control you. I introduce you to the areas of your job that directly impact your ability to guide your programmers in the same direction, the central task of herding cats. I discuss administration, an area that cuts across all areas of your work life. Handling distractions that pull you off task is a key skill you must learn, in spite of how this may make you appear to others. Project man-

agement, another critical leadership skill, is put into context with the rest of your activities. Building and maintaining your staff, a group that multiplies your efforts, is also addressed. In short, this chapter is central to building the skills that make you a cat herder.

Managing Administration

Yikes! Your world has changed now that you are a manager. You have been used to dealing with a very interesting group of people as a programmer—look out! In addition to having nice conversations about the best way to build an error trap, you will also now discuss the best way to format the business requirements docu-ment so you can generate a design specification. Well, the good news is that templates for such documentation tasks abound, but what's scarce is the brain template you need to adjust to the mental mindset for doing this and similar kinds of work that may be very new to you in your management role.

Managing the flow of information as a manager of programmers is an art form unto itself. You may recall that in object-oriented (OO) analysis and design terms you need to have three perspectives when considering how to design and construct software. To aid your recollection, Table 3-1 offers a refresher.

Table 3-1. An OO Design Concept

PERSPECTIVE	PURPOSE
Business	Seeing the user's view of information and processes
Specification	Understanding the object interface's public properties
Implementation	All the internal details of an object that make it function

Map this OO concept over onto your daily interactions with the various business units that you have to deal with to get the programming/management job done. You might come up with a mental parsing routine a bit like that shown in Table 3-2.

Table 3-2. An Administrative Filter

PERSPECTIVE	BRAIN REGION	PURPOSE
Business	Eyes and ears	Knowing what information you must process to direct the programming tasks
Specification	Organization	Keeping track of what you must deliver in an organized fashion, such as by project or area of technology
Implementation	Deep thinking	Drilling down as needed to be sure the details will support what you must deliver

The primary purpose of the administrative filter I propose is to help you navigate to your goals through the data smog[1] you live in each day. This smog is created by e-mail, phone calls, requirements documentation, marketing intelligence, what Microsoft has planned for the next year, your current problem with George the slob programmer, and so on. In other words, you experience information overload on a daily and sometimes an hourly basis as you attempt to lead the herd. Every new piece of data may seem important at the moment you encounter it, but you do need a filter and you can encapsulate (another good OO design concept) the filter idea in one word:

FOCUS

1.　I "borrowed" this term from David Shenk.

Remember the first time you went to the eye doctor as a child and discovered you needed glasses? (I assume since you are the chief programmer that you have a long history of dealing with the minutiae of life, and this tends to produce the need for glasses.) Wasn't it wonderful when the optometrist put the lenses down on your eyes from that neat machine they have and all of a sudden you could actually read the eye chart? This is focus: knowing how to filter out the distractions administration always produces so that the real work can be identified.

Again, your goal is to deliver software, and anything that distracts you from this purpose isn't urgent no matter how important it may seem.[2]

> *Your goal is to deliver software, and anything that distracts you from this purpose isn't urgent no matter how important it may seem.*

Here are some typical administrative distractions:

- A power user of your software has just thought of a *great* new feature and must tell you about it right now.

- A product support team member continues to bring up the fact that the number of issues in the bug tracker is growing by leaps and bounds every week and you *must* help prioritize the list.

- A product designer needs to know if a certain desired future feature is even possible to accomplish in code and writes again, "*Please* respond to my e-mail!"

Notice the italicized words: *great, must,* and *please.* It's almost like the local evening news: "If it bleeds, it leads." The apparent distractions aren't unimportant—they just might not be urgent—but when couched in terms such as "great," "must," and "please," they will pull you off task and you will lose focus. This is your challenge. Learn to pigeonhole things until you need to act on them and keep in focus your primary responsibility of getting software out the door. A quick response to some items might be necessary so the originator of the issue will know you received their request, but your response should often be something like, "I will add it to my agenda for consideration, but I can't act on it right now due to previous commitments."

---

2. I referenced Covey's book, *The 7 Habits of Highly Effective People*, in Chapter 1. If you don't own this book, go buy it and read it. Note what Covey says about managing time and priorities.

So, what does all this talk of focus have to do with leading the herd? Well, if you want cats to follow you, because they are hard to herd, you are going to have to attract them by demonstrating leadership. This doesn't mean *talking* about leading, it means *showing* your programmers that *you* are on task and unwavering in your pursuit of a solid release of code. Of course, part of that leadership is to consider all the items, like those mentioned previously, that go into making the code complete. Focus is a matter of setting priorities for new information that might compete with assigned tasks that have already been determined to be part of the critical path for current projects.

Focus is a matter of setting priorities for new information that might compete with assigned tasks that have already been determined to be part of the critical path for current projects.

Consider how when you are writing code you can become distracted by some anomaly in an associated object you are trying to interface with or extend. It's tempting to go fix the stray object from time to time, but a good coder will just make note of it and finish the immediate procedure. Recall how easy it is to lose focus in coding because the phone rings. It can take the better part of an hour to get back on task (and into the flow of code) in these situations. Managing administration is a bit like this: You have certain tasks you must do or nothing proceeds on schedule. Be as ruthless with your administrative time as you are with your coding time.

Be as ruthless with your administrative time as you are with your coding time.

Deflecting Distractions

Don't let your e-mail inbox govern your day. E-mail is either the best thing since sliced bread or it's a tool of Satan. It's a great tool for quick communication; however, in a geographically dispersed organization, it can become the primary means of information flow. Your focus will be blurred if you allow e-mail to direct your daily priorities. Project scope creep often starts with an e-mail disguised as clarification of the business requirements. When the thread becomes longer than three strands on a single subject, pick up the phone. If making a phone call doesn't work, get some face time. If speaking face to face doesn't work, nothing will. The point is to limit your e-mail time so you can keep to the tasks already defined on schedule. If your company has invested in project management software, use it to convey information specific to a project task, but keep it out of the e-mail clutter since if it doesn't become a part of the project documentation, it may be lost in the smog.

Instant messaging is another great tool for clarification or a portal for demons from the nether world. Use it wisely. Don't allow it to be a time waster or a focus-destroying icon on your desktop. Don't try to use it to see if everyone is at his or her desk, either—no one likes feeling he or she is being watched. You have to be much more subtle in your "watching"—I talked a bit about this in Chapter 2 in the section "Don't Expect If You Don't Inspect."

As you learn to manage administration, you'll find that distractions not only affect you, they also affect your programmers. One of your primary responsibilities is to facilitate your staff's ability to focus.

> *One of your primary responsibilities is to facilitate your staff's ability to focus.*

The best way to help your people focus is to ensure they have a weekly assignment of tasks written down with priorities and complete dates affixed to each task. This list will sometimes change on a weekly or even daily basis in a volatile development cycle. Again, you're the one who must manage this task list.[3] It's amazing how many managers I have met who think programmers are mind readers who somehow intuitively know what to build. Some CEOs are like this, too. Time and again, this leads to programmers creating software for programmers, not users, and managers eventually being found of little use to corporate leadership.

If you inherit a group of programmers, one of the first things to do is get each employee to write down his or her opinion of his or her current assignments. This can be very revealing and even show you how the programmer was managed in the past. Creating and reviewing this employee-generated task list will establish a baseline for reigning in extraneous work that may be going on. Once you start managing by the method of task lists, you can't stop. Everyone will expect it, and your consistency will be an example of your leadership. One more thing: The list is just the beginning of creating directive forces for the herd. At least weekly and sometimes daily, follow up is necessary to explain, coach, and guide your people toward the desired goal on time.

---

3. See Chapter 4 for some suggestions on software that can help you create task lists for programmers. Don't turn there now—you will miss all the preparation I am doing in this chapter so you realize the real mess you are in without a good way to electronically organize your work life.

You may not be able to do much about the physical office space your programmers inhabit, but if possible insist on rooms with doors rather than cubicles. You may often lose this battle in companies more concerned with rent than productivity, but try to effect change. Some of the greatest distractions to effective programming work are created by the cube mentality of corporate planners. The movie *Office Space*, where programmers in cubes are featured "in the wild" so to speak, should be required viewing for the cube-heads that plan office environments. The impact of "worker density" was noted by Tom DeMarco and Timothy Lister in a study of 32,346 companies. They developed a chart showing a virtually perfect inverse relationship between people density and dedicated square footage of office space per person.[4] What is this relationship focused upon? Noise, distractions, and all the other negative side effects of cost cutting that lead to a decline in worker productivity.

So, let your people work from home—it's a great way to eliminate distractions and facilitate productivity. Hold on. It might be for some and one day a week might be great for others, but it takes a very disciplined worker to be effective at home. If you go this route, you'll have a more difficult job of inspecting. Only let your more seasoned and dependable people telecommute as a reward, or offer the option to telecommute on a trial basis and measure productivity carefully. If you have no choice because your company is spread out over the world, get used to 10 hours on the phone every week and lots of e-mail. A happy balance can be achieved with telecommuting—you just have to work through the issues.

Dealing with Creeps

No, I'm not referring programmers exactly since the term "creep" can sometimes be redundant in this context.[5] What I'm talking about here is the classic concept of *project scope creep*. Sometimes the business requirements analyst will insist he or she is just clarifying the scope, in which case it should be called *scope bloat*. Whatever term you use, software has probably never been specified and built without creeping requirements. This is just human nature: Everything software is supposed to do can't always be thought of the first time off the blocks.

---

4. DeMarco and Lister, op. cit., p. 56.
5. Forgive me, but I am a programmer just having a bit of literary fun.

Look at the typical process of delivering software. Whether you employ a waterfall cycle or an iterative methodology, the job always involves the following activities:

1. **Creation.** Somebody has a brilliant idea.

2. **Specification.** Bunches of people define the brilliant idea.

3. **Design.** Really smart people decide how to build the software.

4. **Construction.** Programmer-slaves labor through sleepless nights and grinding days.

5. **Testing.** People discover the resulting implementation of the brilliant idea isn't so sharp, or the idea wasn't brilliant after all.

6. Start over at step 2 until you get it right, decide it is good enough, or come to the conclusion that step 1 was an awful idea and a new brilliant idea is needed. (Then start at step 2 again!)

In view of the real-world scenario in the preceding list, is scope creep so unexpected? I don't think so, and neither should you, but among your programmers you'll hear wailing and gnashing of teeth. Show them that you are fully clothed and in your right mind by expecting creep and learning to deal with it. This is your job as the leader. Don't join in the bashing of the business units—this will not get the job done nor fix the process.

In the somewhat dated but still relevant book, *Managing the Software Process*, Watts Humphrey states a timeless principle:

> *When programmers estimate the code required to implement a function, their estimates are invariably low. While there are many potential explanations, the important point is that their optimism is a relatively predictable function of project status.*[6]

---

6. Watts S. Humphrey, *Managing the Software Process* (New York: Addison-Wesley, 1989), p. 93.

Here is an explanation of scope creep: No one really knows what it's going to take to build the next great killer app until the software is released and a project review is conducted. I've heard many programmers admit two truths about their own early estimates that are corollaries to Humphrey's principle and I posit these as axioms:

- Everything takes longer than you think it will.

- Something always comes up that you didn't think of.

Use these axioms and Humphrey's concept of "project status" to deal with creep and show your people how smart you are to have anticipated this eventuality by careful planning. Okay, "careful planning" sounds good, but what does it mean in terms of leading the herd? It means this: Go back to Chapter 1 and especially Chapter 2 and determine to make the principles there part of your character rather than a technique you try to employ. Leadership flows from the heart, not the mind.[7]

Of course, your mind does have a good bit to do with developing methods for dealing with scope creep. Consider the typical project plan you must create. You're given a set of requirements and you must develop a design solution that will be implemented with software. A simple and naïve approach would create a plan like the one shown in Table 3-3.

Table 3-3. An Unrealistic Project Plan

TASK	TIME (ARBITRARY INTERVALS)
Analyze requirements	A
Create design	B
Implement design	C
Test software	D
Fix bugs	E
Deploy software	F

This plan will get you into big trouble. You believe you will deliver in at the date equal to A + B + C + D + E + F. You will be surprised. It will not work out this way.

Consider the more realistic plan shown in Table 3-4.

---

7. Remember what Yoda said: "A Jedi's strength flows from the force." Same difference.

Table 3-4. A Realistic Project Plan

TASK	TIME (ARBITRARY INTERVALS)
Analyze requirements	A
Discuss analysis with business unit	B
Create design	C
Prototype design	D
Evaluate prototypes	E
Refactor design	F
Implement high-level design objects	G
Test high-level integration	H
Evaluate system for requirement compliance	I
Create system components	J
Integrate and test components	K
Re-evaluate system for compliance	L
Test complete system	M
Correct system faults prior to alpha testing	N
Begin alpha testing	O
Correct alpha testing bugs	P
Begin beta testing	Q
Develop deployment strategy	R
Correct beta testing bugs	S
Test deployment strategy	T
Perform final release testing	U
Deploy software	V

I won't bother to do the math here since I used almost all the letters in the alphabet. You get the picture. Please note also that this plan doesn't even account for all the phases you might need to consider for your particular project, as well as dependencies between phases of the development cycle. What this plan *does* illustrate is the reasons behind my two axioms for dealing with scope creep: lack of thinking about the details and how much time it will really take to get the software built. The more you practice identifying the details, the better you'll get at estimating project timelines and understanding that most scope creep is the result of a lack of forethought by the planners.

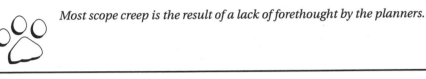

Most scope creep is the result of a lack of forethought by the planners.

You can improve your estimating skills by failing to meet project schedules over and over again until you get it right. This can be an expensive and career-threatening learning adventure. While this isn't the best way to improve, experience is a good teacher of project management. However, you can get ahead of the learning curve by taking advantage of the stories—war stories—from project management literature. In a chilling collection of essays about massive software project failures, Robert Glass notes the following reasons, in decreasing order of impact, for software development disasters: [8]

1. Project objectives not fully specified = 51 percent

2. Bad planning and estimating = 48 percent

3. Technology new to the organization = 45 percent

4. Inadequate/no project management methodology = 42 percent

5. Insufficient senior staff on the team = 42 percent

6. Poor performance by suppliers of hardware/software = 42 percent

The percentages associated with each reason for failure are estimates based on the research Glass performed about the primary cause of the runaway. Read these stories and other such collections.[9] You will be wiser for the study and gain some insight into realistic project planning and how to stop the creeps.

---

8. Robert L. Glass, *Software Runaways* (Upper Saddle River, NJ: Prentice Hall, 1998), p. 20.

9. See also Robert L. Glass, *ComputingFailure.com* (Upper Saddle River, NJ: Prentice Hall, 2001.

Gathering Strays

Not cats, but programmers. They stray when their code begins to resemble a massive monument to their own brilliance. You must conduct code reviews often enough to catch these monoliths of ego before they are erected. I discuss this more fully in Chapter 6, which deals exclusively with technical leadership. For the moment, consider this: Creativity is priceless but practical, maintainable code makes money. Your role as leader of the herd is to manage the product your people create to ensure functionality is achieved with a minimum of code. Complexity will always be an element you must contend with—and it will be necessary at times—but clarity must be accomplished in small incremental steps if you are to prevent mortal programming sins such as the following:[10]

- Lack of functional partitioning in object creation and assembly of logical layers

- Hasty creation of object interfaces

- Extravagant coupling between objects

- A love of complexity in the internal workings of objects

Use care when dealing with young or inexperienced programmers. Let them stumble forward for a while so they learn from their mistakes, but take them in hand often enough to show them the straight and narrow path. Of course, offer correction before their code becomes compiled. We programmers (and even human beings) often learn best from making mistakes, seeing the consequences, and then discovering a better way to accomplish the same functions. As long as the mistakes are addressed prior to alpha testing, you'll do fine.

> *Creativity is priceless, but practical, maintainable code makes money.*

---

10. This is only one possible list of sins. There are many others. For good examples, see William H. Brown et al, *AntiPatterns: Refactoring Software, Architectures, and Projects in Crisis* (New York: John Wiley & Sons, 1998).

Danger, Will Robinson!

One challenge you may face is leading folks with different skill sets than yourself. Let's say you're a VB guru but you have several ASP jocks and some legacy programmers in the mix. You can't conduct code review easily under these conditions, and this can lead to danger. You may have to rely on the final testing to prove their work was good. You'll most assuredly have to begin to learn enough about the other languages and methods to do an effective job and not be blindsided by a programmer who says he can do the job even if his design contains so many foreign concepts to you that you feel like a calf looking at a new gate.

Establishing a "point man" in the language areas you are not familiar with can help mitigate the risk of managing code that you're not able to read. Being able to read code, for lack of a better term, is a time-honored way of conducting code reviews. In the classic book about the human enterprise we call coding, Gerald Weinberg writes:

> *Some years ago, when COBOL was the great white programming hope, one heard much talk of he possibility of executives being able to read programs. With the perspective of time, we can see that this claim was merely intended to attract the funds of executives who hoped to free themselves from bondage to their programmers. Nobody can seriously have believed that executives could read programs. Why should they? Even programmers do not read programs.*[11]

Of course, the author goes on to say that you should read programs, and if you can't, you should find someone who can. The idea of "bondage" mentioned in the quote is what you want to avoid. Designate someone on your staff to help minimize your lack of knowledge in these areas. Even old technologies must be reexamined from time to time because they can still get the job done. Another trait of leadership is being able to seek out new (or even old) frontiers and go where no programmer has gone before. In other words, watch out for the dangers of ignorance. The greatest danger is remaining willfully ignorant; another word for this kind of ignorance is stupidity.

A willingness to learn new skills should be one of your greatest strengths as a leader and manager. If is isn't, rethink your job or get a new one, because in the bleeding-edge world of emerging technologies, you must be able to quickly grasp new ideas to judge their merit. You may not be able to become an expert, but you should be able to understand the jargon and concepts to help navigate your department through the technology jungle.

---

11. Gerald M. Weinberg, *The Psychology of Computer Programming: Silver Anniversary Edition* (New York: Dorset House Publishing, 1998), p. 5.

A willingness to learn new skills should be one of your greatest strengths as a leader and manager. If is isn't, rethink your job or get a new one, because in the bleeding-edge world of emerging technologies, you must be able to quickly grasp new ideas to judge their merit.

Building and Maintaining Your Staff

Finding good people is another management art form. The rest of your staff will judge your leadership by the new people you bring on board and the ones you throw overboard. You'll find hiring, firing, and rewarding to be some of the most difficult areas to administer in your leadership journey. They can also provide the most enriching experiences for you personally because people are the heart of software development. With the best people, you can accomplish great things; with problem people, you'll spend most of your time dealing with issues that don't advance your goals.

Hiring Practices

Choose wisely when you hire: You will have to live with your choice of a new employee and pay the price of helping that person integrate with the team. This takes a lot of time and patience but it can be done successfully if you hire smart. Some of the things to guide your decisions in recruiting are as follows:

- Administer a programming test to an applicant. Give the potential hire a problem to solve either on the spot or as a take-home assignment with a deadline.

- Conduct an oral test of the applicant's skills. Take a sample certification test, if the applicant is certified, and use this to judge his or her knowledge and ability to function under pressure.

- If you can get the applicant to agree to an online psychology assessment test, and you understand the limited use of these instruments, then do so.[12]

- Have a written job description for the applicant to review during the interview. If you haven't prepared a job description, you don't know what you want, and the applicant will tell you anything you want to hear.

---

12. Go to http://www.AdvisorTeam.com for a good one.

- Conduct at least two interviews, and if it seems appropriate, let one of your top, trusted aces interview the applicant. Beware of letting everyone talk to the potential hire, though—this will never lead to a decision.

If you must hire a consultant for a limited time (and this is the only way to hire consultants), you may not have to worry so much about team integration, but some of the preceding guidelines still apply. Beware of the dangers of consultants who seem to want to stay around forever. Committed employees with a stake in the company's success are always better than consultants whose primary concern is sometimes just their hourly rate and how long they can make the job last.

In defense of consultants, they are often needed when expertise doesn't exist in your company and you need to graft it in. Allow the graft to take and transfer the knowledge to your staff as soon as it is possible. Hire a consultant whose policy is to become a part of your team, learn your business, suggest ideas you haven't or couldn't think of, and move on. Sometimes you develop a relationship with a consultant that makes you want to offer him or her a permanent role on your team. Often this possibility is precluded by the consultant agreement, but if not, it can be a way to "try out" an employee relationship with a person before making a commitment.

Typically, consultants will not want to pass on their knowledge to you: This is job security for them. In such cases, your staff will have to reverse-engineer the consultant's code to gain new skills. This isn't uncommon, and many of us learn code from our study of the great programmers who have left examples behind in books, past projects, and on the Internet. Learn what you can where you can— just be sure you don't become a victim of a consultant who leaves you a riddle wrapped in a mystery inside an enigma, to paraphrase Winston Churchill.[13]

---

13. Churchill spoke this famous line about the future actions of Russia prior to the beginning of World War II. If your future depends on the products left behind by a secretive consultant, you will be ill prepared for the maintenance battles ahead with your software.

Cat Fight! Green Card Blues

Frank was thrilled to have the opportunity to hire a new programmer. He had inherited his current group and was eager to add his mark to the team. Having always admired those programmers from a country where chess was king, he acted on the first resume that came across his desk with the particular characteristics he was looking for. Lo and behold, here was Alex, a man who he soon discovered during the interview process could beat anyone in chess even starting without his queen. Surely he must be able to create some awesome code, even if his English was a bit difficult to wade through. So, Frank hired Alex and thus began several years of an interesting professional and personal relationship for both of them.

On most projects Alex was extremely creative. He enabled a user menu and graphing capabilities on a black-and-white LCD screen that could only display 4 lines with 80 characters each. The rest of the engineering staff was impressed. He created an in-circuit emulator for the software in his spare time that saved a lot of time in debugging. Nevertheless, Alex's English never really got better and even though Frank helped him get a green card, Alex still stayed pretty much to himself in the company.

Frank was aware of Alex's isolation from the other developers, so he gave Alex more and more projects whose scope required only one programmer. For several years this seemed to work out fine, except Frank became increasingly annoyed at the other engineers who hated to have to do maintenance on Alex's code. Frank just chalked it up to professional jealousy and disregarded all complaints.

Frank eventually left the bank and went on to greener pastures. Years later, Frank ran into Bob, the owner of a competing bank who had hired Alex based on Frank's recommendation. Bob had nothing but horror stories about his experience with Alex, who was eventually fired because no one could extend the software Alex created in a great flurry of genius and style.

No one knows what became of Alex. Both companies Alex worked for suffered losses because some of their key software products created by Alex could never be enhanced beyond version 1. It wasn't really Alex's fault—it was Frank's error in judgment that created these software monuments to suspected genius without thought for team dynamics and the need for practical, maintainable code. Frank had no sense in his hiring practice with Alex. He was fulfilling a personal mission that had nothing to do with the success of his employer. He created a schism in his team by keeping Alex isolated, thinking brilliance could substitute for clarity of design. Learn from this folks: Hire smart, don't just hire smart people.

Firing Practices

The flip side of hiring is firing, which also demonstrates your leadership. One incompetent or troublesome employee can ruin the whole team. Unless you are constrained by legal issues, don't hesitate to fire someone who has finally proven unredeemable. If you hire with a probationary period as part of the deal, don't be afraid to use it before it's too late. The longer a sour programmer stays around, the more your whole team will become infected by bad attitudes, and you'll be judged by your ability to put up with people who everyone knows should go. Lack of action is action—a bad one—and Bad Things happen to those who are afraid to make decisions when the choice is clear.

When you must consider firing an individual, plan for it ahead of time. Document the missteps and problems the employee has caused. Offer them one chance at reform. Some would suggest more than one chance, but in my experience, two opportunities to change is one too many: The cost is too high on you managing the reform, and the effect on your staff can also be costly as they cope with a difficult programmer on the team. Nevertheless, consider the potential dismissal's impact on the company. Seek help in evaluating the decision from your boss. What security issues will the firing create for the company? Does the programmer have expertise and knowledge that must be extracted prior to the firing? These questions, and others bearing on the dismissal, need to be asked and answered as part of your considerations.

You must also give careful thought to the effect of firing a programmer upon the rest of your staff. They may want to know why one of their friends was given the axe. Be careful in sharing the specifics—simply state that the programmer's performance wasn't satisfactory and his or her retention was not in the best interest of the department. A positive effect can also result from firing: Problem people are no longer around to make trouble, and everyone is warned that such individuals will not be tolerated in your administration. This is a good signal and often is one you need to send to your staff.

Promotions and Raises

I touched on money and other such rewards in Chapter 1. It will prove to be your most difficult area to administer properly. Job titles are prized by some and money by all, so what do you do? Well, in the 1960s Bell Labs had one solution: Each scientist had the title "Member of the Technical Staff," and there was no higher honor than being among this group. This can work when you have a highly competitive workforce, but it's often impractical today either due to corporate titles established beyond your control or the desire of individuals to have an impressive title. The younger the employee, the more he or she will seek the status of title. The older ones want interesting work and serious money. If an employee wants all three of these things, maybe he or she is worth it or just a bit unrealistic. No, interesting work will be a common denominator among programmers, so you'll have to sort out titles and money matters as a function of merit and experience.

Use care in promoting people before they are ready for more responsibility. Many programmers, and technical folks in general, can be happy most of their work life just doing interesting and creative work without ever getting involved in management. Learn to know when a worker has reached his or her maximum level of responsibility. That programmer may be able to handle more in the future, but most of us need to settle in for a while at a certain level of responsibility that feels comfortable. Once you see growth and comfort, it could be time to ratchet up the responsibility again. Promoting staff is often an iterative process, much like defining business requirements and prototyping: Once you prove the new level of responsibility is working, maybe an employee can handle some more.

Some people think more responsibility means more money and, to a certain extent, this is true. Be aware, however, that more money should really be offered for more productivity and effectiveness on the job, and not just for a wider scope of project activity and responsibilities for others.

If you're lucky enough to be part of a corporation that has created a technical track so programmers can reach upper management salaries, great! This eliminates the glass ceiling that often results in a technical person accepting a management position just to gain extra income. It also brings up another point: Can you manage individuals who are making more money than you are? This can happen in some organizations and isn't uncommon for those staff members who have "saved the day" for the company during their tenure. Is such a hero in your company worth more financially than you are? He or she could be, and you must learn to value the strategic employee and be glad you have that person on board. In a book extolling the value of craftsmanship, Pete McBreen addresses the issue of what a great developer is really worth:

> *Probably a lot more than they are currently being paid as employees.*
> *They are worth at least five times, and perhaps ten times, what the average*
> *developer receives . . . What was the person who 'saved' the project worth?*
> *What would the consequences have been if that person had been lured*
> *away to a different organization?*[14]

---

14. Pete McBreen, *Software Craftsmanship* (New York: Addison-Wesley, 2001), p. 61.

Keep your good people happy by rewarding them appropriately. Don't lose them because you are cheap. You've no doubt heard of the classic triangle—cheap, fast, and right—applied to software development. You can only choose two of the three. If you go the inexpensive route with people, you'll get cheap software. The other choice is a better one: Pay for quality and you'll be able to produce quality.

Grooming Your Replacement

What?! I just got this job and there is no way I'm going to train my replacement! This isn't smart thinking. Beware of the "truck factor": If you're taken out by an unfortunate act of God or other such disaster, who will replace (or succeed) you, and how will the work proceed? These considerations aren't just for calamities. They should be part of your overall plan to identify individuals who can step in from time to time and manage things as needed. This not only helps determine who is capable of more responsibility, but it also can help you figure out how much high-level administrative matters you can delegate with confidence.

A related idea to grooming your replacement is creating some depth or "bench strength" in your staff. If each person is a single project specialist, you may find yourself struggling when for one reason or the other this key individual isn't available. Cross-training works for athletes, so why not do it with programmers? It is said that the mark of a mature programmer is when they learn their second language. In the same way, a deep staff is able to switch from project to project and still maintain momentum. This will require a good bit of thinking and planning on your part, but this isn't a new concept: You always need to be thinking about your allotment of work to the staff. Some people thrive on multitasking, some crash. Learn to know your people's strengths and weaknesses and play to them accordingly.

Enough Already!

Yeah, I'm sure you're thinking this, too. Being a leader requires a lot from you. All the administrative details you must keep straight and do right can tax your soul. The payoff for effectively leading the herd, however, is large. Teams can accomplish so much more than just one individual, no matter how talented and productive he or she may be. All the areas of management I've touched on in this chapter were focused on those parts of your job that relate to effective team building. This is the goal of leadership: creating a team able to leap tall projects in a single bound. You enable this power and energy in your team by honing your herding skills.

Synthesizing this chapter into a few easy to remember concepts, a leader

- Sets priorities and deflects distractions (i.e., focuses)

- Becomes an expert in project management and thinks exhaustively about the details

- Stops bad coding before it takes root in the product

- Learns how to learn quickly in order to evaluate the merits of new technology

- Maintains staff wisely and understands that people are the greatest resource for success

In the same way I've boiled down this chapter into the previous list, you should learn to do a few things well each day rather than many things badly. Multitasking is for microprocessors, not people.

More to Come

There is more you need to do. Sorry, but if being the leader was easy, everyone would want the job. The next chapter deals with another area that will aid your leadership—namely, improving your organizational skills. Take a break. Don't read more today. Go out and do whatever gives you joy and recharge your mind and heart.

When you get back, you'll look at how to organize your administrative life so you can achieve success. In many ways, the next chapter contains methods to make the skills described in this chapter become more than theory. You'll often find that knowing what to do and doing it require taking the sometimes painful step of changing your behavior. A change in thinking must precede a change in action, but without acting on new knowledge, you become nothing more than an academic leader. Herding cats requires you to get into the field, become dirty and messy, and create order from the chaos that can reign in an unrestrained group of programmers. You can do this job—stick with me.

CHAPTER 4

Organizing for Success

Leading your team to success is the primary goal and the desired outcome of being a good manager. Some individuals in positions of responsibility for a team think of themselves as *only* managers and shy away from the task of leadership. You may feel this way because you're so overwhelmed with the daily details of your job that you don't have time to give thought to blazing new trails for your team. Now, don't misunderstand me, a manager *is*  concerned with keeping tasks on track; a leader, by contrast, while managing the productive output of his or her team, primarily focuses on the team's overall mission and is striving for more than just compliance with current deadlines. Sometimes a manager gets caught up with the trappings of management—for example, the location of the executive bathroom. A leader, however, is always developing ways to encourage and enable his or her team to achieve increasingly challenging goals. This back-and-forth struggle between managing and leading may make you feel you're walking a tightrope, trying to balance these two necessary job roles.

If you must make a black-and-white choice, leadership is more critical than management. However, if you don't give attention to what might, at first blush, appear to be the rather dry and academic aspects of management (namely, organizational skills), you won't have time to lead. Becoming more organized—personally and corporately—will help you keep your balance. An organized manager creates a working environment that allows leadership to flourish.

 An organized manager creates a working environment that allows leadership to flourish.

As you focus on your personal and corporate organizational skills, keep in mind that the goal is to make time work *for* you, rather than *against* you. When time is your ally, you can devote more energy to leadership because you are managing administration, rather than being managed by administration. If time is your enemy, one likely cause is that you feel you have too much to do and not enough time to do it. If you suffer from a severe case of disorganization, you may develop anxieties whose origin is the fear that you've forgotten the details of numerous tasks that you are expected to do.

In addition to becoming more organized personally, helping your company to organize practices and processes that directly affect software development will also benefit your department by creating expectations of your team that you can control. This is the general goal of any organizational scheme—to make success an expected outcome of the daily grind because all activity is efficient and achieves the maximum effective use of people resources.

Organize Information into Knowledge and Action

At the risk of oversimplifying your daily activities, everything you do can be considered a project of turning information into knowledge and action. One "project" might be as simple as answering e-mail, another as extensive as developing a plan to reshape your corporate software's architecture. All of these projects have details; that is, a flow of information and knowledge that must be tracked, amended, and placed into some organized pattern for the next day's follow-up work. Your desk, and by extension your computer, is typically the place where the project activity occurs.

What does your desk look like right now? It may be filled with stacks of paper and file folders—this is fine as long as they haven't been sitting there all week. A cluttered desk can hide something you should be working on right now. Cleaning up can uncover items of information that demand action on your part. You may have heard the saying, "Find a place for everything and put everything in its place." This isn't a bad rule, but the challenge is creating "the place" in the first place. Remember, you aren't trying to win the Good Housekeeping Award for your office's appearance; rather, you're rewarding yourself by having a functional work environment that keeps you from forgetting things you must do to lead your team.

Some say a clean desk is the sign of a sick mind. I don't believe it is, but your opinion may vary. What we can all agree with, however, is that if you don't have your own house in order, you can't manage the activities of others. How do you clean your house? You dust, you vacuum, you pick up things that are lying around in the way, and in general you create an environment that is conducive to living. Shouldn't your workspace be the same? I believe an orderly workspace creates an environment conducive to successful work. You know how disorderly code can create problems with software; a messy desk can create headaches for you as a manager. I define "messy" as the lack of organization of details in your daily work life that come from the improper management of information flow.

 If you don't have your own house in order, you can't manage the activities of others.

The Paper Chase

Years ago, before PCs made their way into our daily work life, the place of choice for project details was simply notebooks and file folders. Now, with computers as tools for organization, the role of paper has diminished to some extent in our daily management of project activities. However, the paperless office is still far from a reality and paper will probably be with us for a long time to come. Paper does serve an important role in organizing information, in spite of its weaknesses. Considering the strengths and weaknesses of paper, you'll probably agree with me that

- Paper is very convenient when information needs to be studied at the time and place of your choosing.

- Paper is convenient for taking notes during meetings or phone calls. It's also less rude to write on piece of paper than to type on a laptop.

- Paper is not designed well for storage, retrieval, sorting, and all the other things that software does so well.

- Many of us are more comfortable studying critical information on paper than on an electronic display.

- Our culture has predisposed us to absorbing information arranged typically on a rectangular space measuring 8.5×11 inches.

Perhaps the Tablet PC will meet all our needs, combining the strengths of paper with the power of software. I'm waiting for the LCD screen that is as thin as paper and can be written on with pen and pencil, erased, stored electronically, and reloaded with different information. I guess I will be waiting a while because I also want this thin screen to come in a ream of 500 sheets and cost $3.95.

Nevertheless, in defense of paper, for most of the twentieth century it was the main container of business information. It will probably continue to be vital. What I'm getting at, and what you no doubt already understand, is that trying to manage stacks and stacks of paper is a struggle. They get out-of-date, printer cartridges are expensive, and so on.

So, how do you handle the paper chase? You apply some fundamental skills. You can pick these up in any high school course on basic business skills, but they are worth reviewing.[1] I risk spelling out the obvious to you in this section, but I've been amazed at the mess I've seen some managers get into just by ignoring elementary principles of organization.

I suggest at least the following when it comes to organizing your paper world.

- Create a filing system. Every project should have its own set of hanging file folders or notebooks. Within the project file, keep only paper that is relevant and be sure everything is annotated with a date and source of origin. Divide the project file into sections to better organize information such as scope, design, bugs, communications, meeting notes, and other distinct project activity.

- Maintain the filing system. When a project is finished, move it to an archive location. Keep only active projects at hand and move historic information out of your active workspace.

- Every piece of paper that arrives on your desk should find its way into a relevant filing location. Stacks are not allowed. An inbox is only a temporary cache of papers awaiting your action, not a permanent storage container. If you allow things to pile up, what you are really doing is procrastinating on administrative actions that could be critical to your success.

- If you use file folders, use colors to denote relevance to action. For example, use red folders for collecting information needing immediate attention, blue folders for items you can look at later, and green folders for all things related to money. These are simple and obvious ideas, but they can make a difference in determining priorities by a simple visual scan of your files.

- Create and maintain an area for reading material. Gather professional journals in one place and vendor catalogs in another. Sort them by date and don't let the stack get too high. If only one article is worth reading from a magazine, tear it out and put it on the stack. Don't accumulate bulk just to impress yourself.

---

1. Your local office-supply store probably has all the things you need for these tasks. I've even found some business books helpful, such as *Organize Your Office* by Ronni Eisenberg (Hyperion, 1998).

You no doubt have developed your own rules for paper management, or perhaps your company has a good system in place. The main thing is to have methods for organizing paper and use them consistently. Paper can overwhelm and confuse your priorities if you don't manage the flow. If the paperless office were truly a reality, you wouldn't need printers attached to your network. If you're going to print, you must manage the output.

The Paperless Chase

Paper isn't the only thing you have to chase after as a manager. In spite of the abundance of personal information manager (PIM) software on the market, keeping track of virtual paper is still a struggle for most managers. You or your company may already have good project management software in place, and if it works, use it. I've found, however, that many organizations and especially individuals are very particular about how they want to organize their electronic world. In all my attempts to use off-the-shelf project management software, I found they all came up wanting. I will not name names here, but several products from a popular software company in the Northwestern part of the United States were either too complicated, too limited, or just plain wrong in terms of how I needed to track my administrative activities. Okay, now I will name names: Microsoft Project, Team Manager (from the MSDN CDs), and various attempts to modify Outlook via its object model just didn't work for me. Lotus Notes, ACT!, and other PIM and groupware software programs were also not flexible or appropriate for my work processes. Maybe these programs work for you. If so, you can get on about your business of leading the herd. If not, you need to consider a different approach.

So what to do? Hmm, I'm a programmer, these products that failed me were created by programmers, and I miss writing as much code as I used to. The answer was obvious: I needed to build my own project management software.

An Administrative Director

The project I assigned to myself was to create software that I could use to direct my administrative activities. I needed something that was a cross between a PIM and full-bore project management software, without the complications or constraints of either. I worked on this project at night when no one was looking, so it wasn't actually on company time. In the first 6 months of use of my software, I built over 200 executable versions of the tool as I revised, fixed bugs, and tailored the software to my needs. It has saved my administrative life numerous times. At the very least I now know how far I'm behind and don't have to live with the vague uncertainty that I'm under a pile. No, it's now possible to actually measure the pile and print out a report of how many nights I don't need to sleep so I can catch up with work.

One of the beauties of this self-imposed coding project was that I didn't have to depend on gathering the business requirements: The use-case scenarios were with me every day. On top of this, I *was* the user, so if I liked the interface, the software would meet the user's need. In other words, I had the dream project—software created by a programmer for a programmer. Beta testing was also a snap: Every time I found a bug, I just opened up the code and fixed it. This project also helped me through the withdrawal symptoms often experienced by programmers who have so much management work to do that they find little time to code. It's hard to let go of the keyboard, isn't it?

Here we go. The next few subsections will give you an overview of a software tool that is, in my humble opinion, an effective way of organizing for success. If you like it, or if you think you can make it better suited to your needs, see Appendix A for the details and information about how to obtain the source code.

The Task Object: A Central Organizing Principle of the Administrative Director Software

If you think about the nature of software development and all the associated administrative details derived from it, the work is all about performing tasks that are related in three fundamental ways.

1. **Projects.** Tasks are associated with a project, a convenient grouping construct for organizing related activity that has one goal: Ship good code out the door and make the company some money. Some projects might not necessarily be related to a shippable product, but if you're focused on your company's success in the marketplace, you'll be sure that any project you create does eventually contribute to your team's ability to create successful software.

2. **Sources.** Tasks originate from a person (yourself, often), a process, or usually (groan) a committee. Relating tasks to their source is very helpful when you have to own up to your promises, especially those made to your boss.

3. **Assignments.** Tasks are assigned by your humble Lord and Master (this is you) to the folks who work for you. You remember these guys, don't you? I spent the last three chapters talking about them, but now you're getting into the more comfortable region of intimate objects that don't talk back. In my case, I have a text-to-speech engine on my PC, so they *can* talk back. Not to digress too much, but this is part of the struggle with programmers promoted into management. We are basically "thing"-type people rather than "people"-type people.

Okay, enough small talk. A picture can substitute for many words, so look at Figure 4-1 for a visual representation of the preceding concept.

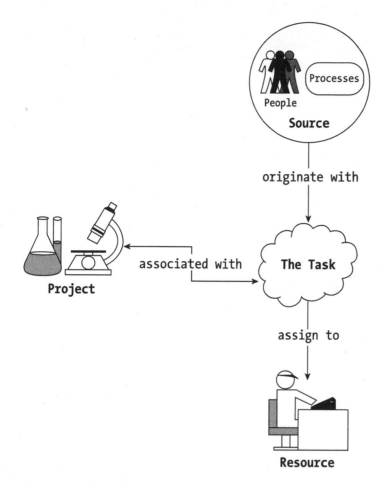

Figure 4-1. The task

As promised, this image shows the three relationships of a task to the flow and process of administration.

The next step after accepting the preceding task concept is to implement it in software. In the tradition of a classic two-tier,[2] fat-client, MDI application—true retro in these days of Web applications[3]—Figure 4-2 shows a GUI that implements this idea.

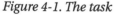

2. Two physical tiers, not logical ones.

3. I tried the Web type but my programmers would not play well with it. I don't blame them— my job is to assign, and theirs is to do. The limited richness of the Web interface also didn't meet my needs.

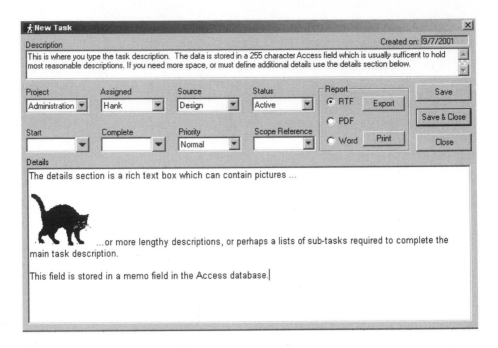

Figure 4-2. An implementation of the task concept

I built the window in Figure 4-2 to gather all the data needed to identify and track a task. The three key relationships—source, assigned, and project—are supplemented by typical parameters you would expect, such as status, start date, complete date, and priority. My version also includes a scope reference entry[4] that, depending on your organization, might be helpful. Other nice-to-have features include the ability to create a document version of the task item and, of course, the ability to actually save the collected information to the database. I used a rich-text box for the details section so graphics could be pasted in from other places. Sometimes a picture is worth a thousand words to a programmer.

Displaying and Organizing Tasks

After capturing task data, you obviously want to display it in a helpful way. If you think about your role as a manager, what you need every day is a list of things you must do today as well as a way to monitor what you expect of those to whom you've assigned time-critical work.

---

4.   This assumes a scope document exists with enumerated items for the features of the product you are building.

My solution was a primary MDI child interface that would gather everything critical to "today" in one place for easy access. If you remember and agree with the well-worn phrase "seize the day," you can understand my reasoning. Again, to relate this software to its purpose, if you don't keep on top of your work and the work of your staff every day, you aren't doing your job. Recall the clever phrase I stole from some college professor in Chapter 2: "expecting without inspecting." This phrase was the driving force for the screen shown in Figure 4-3.

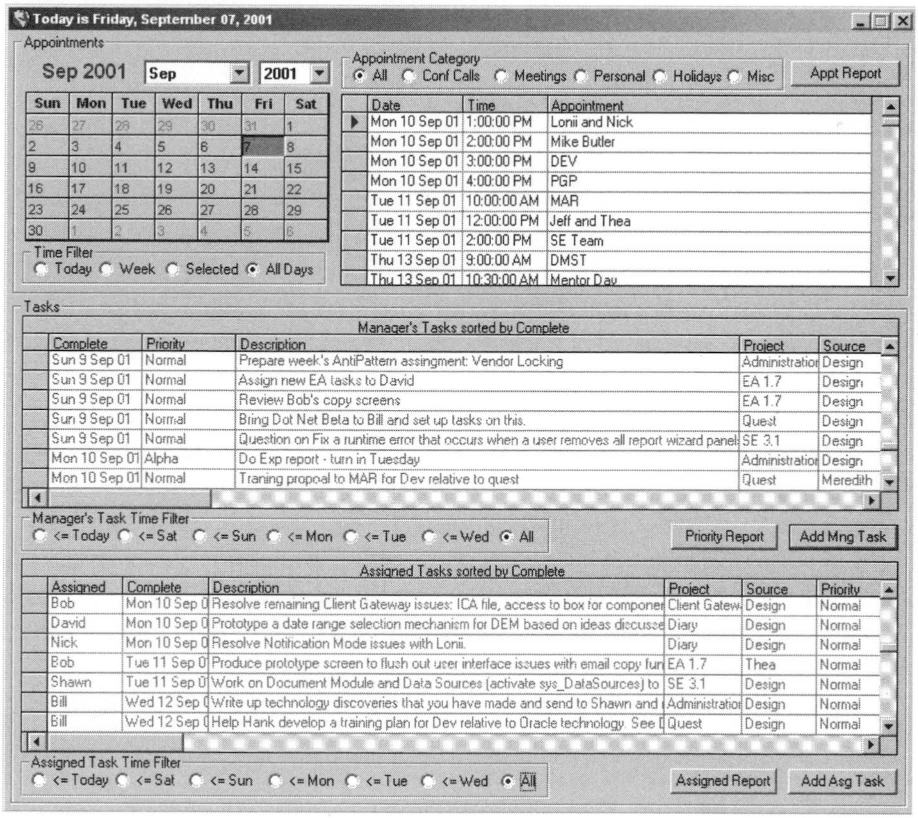

Figure 4-3. The Today screen

Included on the Today screen is a calendar so I can remember what day it is after many long nights catching up on work, as well as an appointment entry area that supplements the task concept. To be academic, an appointment is simply a task that involves talking to or meeting with people. Because my system is always on, I put in a timer control to reset the view of the Today screen at midnight.

Reports for the manager's tasks, appointments, and lists of assigned tasks can be generated for printing or exporting. Each task list allows filtering on the complete date as a function of today's date: The radio buttons allow quick choices for "today and past due" (<= Today), up to 5 days from the current date, and a view of all tasks. The timer on this form resets the filter captions at midnight so they always are presented with a range of 5 days from "Today."

To add a task with the Assigned combo box preselected for you, simply click the Add Mng Task button. To create a new assigned task, click the Add Asg Task button.

In Appendix A, which is entitled "Caring for Your Pet: The Administrative Director Software" (this software became my pet project), you can see more details about the software and some of its construction techniques and components.

Customize Your Administration

I've described number of administrative solutions for organizing the flow of information across your desk. You shouldn't use my methods unless you find that they meet your particular administrative needs or can become a good starting point for creating your own techniques. You probably know how to file papers, so I won't belabor this point. Perhaps you're already using an off-the-shelf project management product that works the way you need. Great—be consistent in using it. However, chances are any tool that isn't flexible will force you into a process that doesn't fit well with your daily activity. I've found that flexibility in the tools I use for organizing often contributes to success. Obviously, being able to program your own tool grants you the maximum flexibility for organizing administration. The main goal of your organizational efforts is to customize your administration to fit the specific needs of your job. Your success depends upon this and you may find it necessary to reevaluate your organizational methods frequently as conditions warrant.

No doubt a massive project involving many interdependencies among tasks could not be managed by the simple software I presented in the last section. You be the judge of this. More important, evaluate and judge how you are coping with all areas of administration in your department. The origin of the word "administration" is "added ministry." In some sense, administration isn't primary to the actual work you're employed to do. It's the amount of effort required to cope with the details of administration that's the core issue. Recognize that there will always be tasks added to your daily work life that must be done in order to get down to actual work. Organizing helps you minimize the time required to get to the significant tasks on your desk and get them done.

The term "actual work" can be misleading. Administration is real work and necessary work, but for a programmer-cum-manager it may seem like a bad dream. You might draw a parallel here between coding and commenting. Code without comments is hard to follow. Managing without administration is unfocused and often misguided. The central point of this book is that you must lead your department, and effective and organized administration plays a key role in both the perception and reality of your leadership.

> *Effective and organized administration plays a key role in both the perception and reality of your leadership.*

You can draw another analogy about administration from the role of an orchestra conductor. It's the orchestra that produces the music, but without the conductor the symphony can become a cacophony. If you've ever watched an orchestra tune up prior to a performance, you understand what a cacophony is. An administrator is like a conductor—strive to be a real maestro. Note also that a conductor tailors his or her directions based on the nature of the orchestra to be led. If you're leading experts, administration might be a minor task each day; if you're leading novices, administration will need a formal organizational structure to guide their efforts.

Organize to Control

To control or not to control? Hamlet struggled with a verb similar to control, one with more serious ontological consequences. Your struggle will not be, shall we say, as life threatening, but many processes in your company will affect your success. Some of these processes will be in your control, some will not. This is why your own organization of the processes that *are* in your control is so critical. Being personally organized can help you cope with chaos that might exist outside your department. You'll find others in your company struggling as you do with administrative details, so look to them and share ideas.

Consider the list of control issues in Table 4-1.

Table 4-1. Control Issues

YOU CAN CONTROL	YOU CAN'T CONTROL
Your methods and efforts to sort and categorize information.	Other people's need to flood you with information.
Your staff's specific task assignments.	Your choice of projects to work on. You must do all you are asked to do, not just the ones you like.
The architecture of your software.	The business problems you're asked to solve.

Table 4-1. Control Issues (continued)

YOU CAN CONTROL	YOU CAN'T CONTROL
How many hours you put into the job.	How many hours you're expected to put into the job.
Your expectations of your own performance.	The expectations of others about your performance.
Your attitude toward difficult people.	Difficult people that don't work directly for you.

You can add to this list as you see fit—it could go on for many pages. I just want to raise your consciousness about control and help you see that organizing for success is about gaining as much control as you can over your work and thus success. Drilling down on these control issues will demonstrate why.

Information Flow

We live in an information age where being able to wrap your mind around a business problem is critical to producing software solutions. This wrapping process involves gaining knowledge from the information that flows within an organization related to particular business needs. You don't have all the answers and so you need facts from others. Often you'll be overwhelmed with the sheer volume of data that comes your way. This was the major point of the previous sections about organizing project details.

Modern science emerged from myth and superstition because the scientific method began to be consistently employed to the study of nature. Nature is filled with information and the first step in any science is classification. This has a direct parallel to your organizational techniques. You may not understand all the data given to you, but if you at least classify it into relevant topics you are well on your way toward gaining knowledge.

You can't often control how much information you are given, but you can control the methods you use to organize it. Perhaps you might feel like a librarian from time to time, but this isn't a bad analogy for being a good manager. If you know where to go to look up a needed piece of data, at least you are better off than the manager whose disorganized style obscures the needed information.

When faced with a new bit of information related to a project, ask yourself the following questions:

- How does this new data affect the project scope, design, or deadline?

- Is the source of this information authoritative, or can it be ignored?

- Do I have to act on this information now, or can it wait until another time?

- Where or how do I store this information for retrieval when I need it?

- What is the expiration date of this information? When will it no longer be relevant?

- How does this information relate to what is already known about the project?

Questions like these are geared toward organizing information so you control it rather than it controlling you.

Assignments

It would be great if you could work only on projects that are personally interesting. This wouldn't work out in the long term, however, because your business often needs answers that don't always resonate with you emotionally. Thus, controlling assignments carefully becomes your best method of keeping your staff (and you, too) interested in the work. Some individuals are better suited to certain projects than others. Chapter 1 covered this concept during the discussion on programmer breeds.

There will be a limit, however, to your ability to give everyone interesting work. All the projects assigned to your department must be accomplished if you want to keep your job. You'll have to work on some problems that just aren't your cup of tea. How do you overcome the lack of enthusiasm that often accompanies the beginning of a dreary code maintenance project? One way is to vary the assignments so no one person is stuck with all the boring tasks. This is in your control. Use your ability to manage your staff's daily and weekly assignments to create variety. Variety is the spice of life for many, and I believe programmers crave and need variety to keep our mental engine working at peak efficiency.

Knowing your staff's individual likes and dislikes is critical to keeping them happy. Happy programmers create good code. Disciplined programmers create even better code. You may not always be able to create happiness—this isn't your job—but you can build your staff into a disciplined group ready to handle tough jobs by controlling the variety of work they do each month.

Architecture

As the technical leader for software development, system architecture is largely in your domain to control. The problems you solve with your architectural solutions may not be completely in your control, but this is to be expected in business. As I mentioned previously, you aren't given your job for your own personal intellectual satisfaction. What is satisfying, however, is the ability to craft a solution using your best technical skills and turn business needs into market share for your company.

Chapter 6 focuses in depth on your role as the technical leader. For now, you need to recognize that controlling your company's software architecture is vital to your success. What do organizational skills have to do with architecture? A lot! The techniques you apply to managing administrative information flow apply to software design. How do you classify software requirements so they can be implemented by code objects? Isn't encapsulation of code similar to creating a file folder for a project? Improving your organizational skills in one area can help you in another.

It's often said that programmers are left-brain people, all logic and analysis. We certainly can't do without this side of the brain in our line of work. Organizational abilities are closely related to programming logic, so don't think that straightening up your desk is a mindless activity. In the same way, creating good software architecture relies heavily on organization skills and control of abstract ideas.

Working Hours

Here is a tough area to control. So many factors affect your ability to control the number of hours you work that you probably think working longer than the standard 40 hours per week is a given in your job. It might be. When the PC revolution began, we all thought it would lead to greater productivity, which would lead to more manageable workweeks. Well, the revolution is over and we have inherited a mixed blessing. We do enjoy greater productivity using computers, and this often means we can get more done in less time. However, my experience has shown that being able to get more done leads to doing more, which inevitably means working longer than might be healthy to the rest of your life.

You'll influence your staff toward working longer hours if you do. This can work for you and against you at the same time. Perhaps you don't have any family responsibilities and so working longer hours doesn't affect your personal life adversely. Longer hours will, however, adversely affect those on your staff with families to care for and you need to consider this as you set the tone by your example. Overtime is often a reality in the software business, but you eventually reach a point of diminishing returns when you work continuously without a break.

Learn to balance the need for overtime with liberal use of compensatory time. Manage overtime by being well organized, so extra hours are seldom needed. This is another goal of a well-organized administration: to make normal work hours efficient so extra hours are rarely needed.

I know the reality of the workplace today flies in the face of a standard 40-hour workweek. This doesn't mean you can't buck the trend. Few people on their deathbed regret not having spent more hours at the office. Keep this in mind as you schedule overtime, and be careful to manage the signs of burnout in yourself and your staff. Recovering from a season of continuously overworking takes a lot more time than becoming well organized as a manager.

> *Recovering from a season of continuously overworking takes a lot more time than becoming well organized as a manager.*

Expectations

You no doubt set high expectations for yourself. This is probably one of the reasons you are in a leadership role. Don't stop setting these grand goals, but temper your ambition with realism. Being real means knowing you will fail from time to time. Being real means that you can't control what others expect from you unless you've made unrealistic promises. Beware of what you promise—this is what sets the expectations of others with whom you work. You'll begin to control the expectations of others if you're judicial with your promises. Richard Carlson, who has made a franchise out of the title *Don't Sweat the Small Stuff*, writes the following about promises:

> *Think about some of the promises we make to others that may not even seem like promises, or that we make semi-unconsciously. Statements like, "I'll call you later today," "I'll stop by your office," "I'll send you a copy of my book next week," "I'd be happy to pick that up for you," or "Call me if you ever need me to take your shift." In a more subtle way, even innocent comments like, "No problem," can get you into trouble because this can be perceived as an offer to do something that, deep down, you may not really want or be able to do. In fact, you have just allowed that person to ask you to do even more for her because you told her it's not a problem.[5]*

---

5. Richard Carlson, *Don't Sweat the Small Stuff at Work* (New York: Hyperion, 1998), p. 74.

Some individuals will expect more than you can deliver. You can't control these kinds of expectations. Some bosses have a mindset that expects the world from you but they never fill you in on the details. This isn't your fault, it's the fault of your boss, and you can't be a mind reader. I'll have more to say about working with your boss in Chapter 9, but for now use your organizational abilities to fend off unrealistic expectations. Know what you're expected to deliver; if your boss doesn't make his or her expectations clear, press him or her until they are clear. You can't build software successfully without a clear set of deliverables. Being organized about the process is the best way to guard against version 1 being an unexpected and unwanted surprise to the business units.

Attitudes

You've probably heard the popular advice, "You can't control the problem but you can control your attitude toward the problem." I've heard it until I now truly believe it. Do you believe this advice? If you don't, you'll be in a losing battle with difficult people. Being organized is more than just filing papers and keying in data for your project management software, it's having methods for dealing with problem people. Larry Constantine, a leader in managing software people problems, wrote:

> *Finding a way to make difficult situations better begins with questions. In my experience, asking the right question is the greater part of getting a useful answer. Instead of wondering why some person is so difficult, I find it more useful to ask myself why I am having difficulty with that person. It is, of course, usually far easier to spot the mote in a colleague's eye than to see the macaroni in your own, but every frustrating encounter with a difficult person is an opportunity to learn more about yourself. Over the long term, you may find yourself meeting fewer and fewer people who are difficult for you to handle.*[6]

What methods do you employ to solve people problems? The one suggested in the preceding quote is excellent and should be as much a part of your administrative talents as keeping your desk organized. Because people create the most powerful and far-reaching forces that can lead to disorganization, developing constructive attitudes toward people problems is a core skill in organizing for success.

---

6. Larry L. Constantine, *Beyond Chaos: The Expert Edge in Managing Software Development* (New York: Addison-Wesley, 2001), p. 4.

Because people create the most powerful and far-reaching forces that can lead to disorganization, developing constructive attitudes toward people problems is a core skill in organizing for success.

Helping Your Company Organize

Up to this point you've focused upon your personal organizational skills with the idea that good organization leads to effective management. This is even truer in the corporate arena. You and your staff are part of a larger organization in most cases, so the impact you have upon the company is a function of how well you are organized to achieve shared corporate goals. And, if software is the primary product of your company, your department can be either a bottleneck or a wellspring for corporate success. The choice is up to you, the leader, working in conjunction with other leaders in your company.

What is the primary reason your department exists? The answer should frame any scheme of organization that you employ to accomplish your goals. Let's explore some possible reasons for your team's existence and determine the logical implications of these reasons on your organization of software processes and procedures. Table 4-2 groups possible reasons for further exploration.

Table 4-2. Raison d état

REASON	IMPLICATION
Make money for the company by creating outstanding products.	Work to minimize overhead by the efficient and effective use of people and resources.
Have fun with technology.	Buy lots of software tools and wander aimlessly building stuff that's fun.
A stepping stone to greater personal ambitions for myself.	Work hard so I can be promoted, or use my position to play politics and gain a promotion by whatever means fulfill my ambition.

Only the first reason in Table 4-2 is valid—the others are secondary or wrong. You'll become acquainted with the third reason in Chapter 7, which deals with the dark side of leadership. For now, consider that ambition isn't bad as long as it doesn't prevent you from serving the company first and yourself second. The second reason—fun—is hopefully a by-product of the first reason.

Exploring the first reason more deeply should give you a clue about how to help organize your company for success. The first and most obvious area that must be organized is the process by which you create and manage software development. This may not be yours to completely control, but you obviously have a key role in the creation and management of the activities.

While this book isn't a formal text on project management, you must become a good project manager to be a successful leader. This area, of course, is the topic of many well-thought-out books in the marketplace, and the Bibliography contains a number of suggested readings in this area. You'll need to become a student and master practitioner of project management, especially the techniques designed to manage software projects. The authors of one of my favorite books on the subject write, "The primary cause of software development failure is the lack of appropriate project management."[7] Note the key word, "appropriate"—this has many implications and successful organizational skills geared to control projects is a crucial factor. At first reading, the quote might seem overly simplistic. The many reasons this statement is true, however, are worth exploring as you read the literature and the proposals for project management I recommend.

Product Management

You're concerned with developing a product, or software service, that is defined by the business needs of the company. While you manage the development, who manages the definition, specification, marketing information, and all the other aspects of what you're building? No doubt you have an interactive role in the product specification, but your primary job is to build it. Others more in tune with customers and business intelligence should have the overall job of managing the product, including deciding what goes in the next version, what bugs have a priority for fixing, and how the user experience of the product should be improved or modified. You'll have something useful and decisive to say about all these areas, but another group should initiate and manage the process.

In the past several decades, some programmers were capable of doing everything from product conception to rollout. This is rarely the case in corporate America today. Software is no longer produced in a garage or bedroom, much to the regret of some developers (mostly of the cowboy persuasion). The day of the killer app created by one or two coders is over. We have entered an era where software is no longer a novelty but a necessity.

---

7.   William H. Brown et al, *AntiPatterns in Project Management* (New York: John Wiley & Sons, 2000), p. xxi.

> *The day of the killer app created by one or two coders is over. We have entered an era where software is no longer a novelty but a necessity.*

If your company is small, having a department of product management may be difficult or cost-prohibitive. Nevertheless, the function of this department must still be performed. Perhaps this becomes another part of your job. If so, you have my sympathy and empathy: I've done both and it's challenging to juggle the roles. Ideally, you need to keep your staff's focus on the development rather than the definition. This doesn't mean that a programmer can't understand the business needs through and through; on the contrary, the more a programmer understands, the better. Keep in mind, however, that you're expecting the programmer to be concerned with implementing the definition, not redefining the product. In my experience, programmers can create scope creep without any help from other people or departments. A carefully defined product is the best one to build, and it will be a more manageable project than reigning in a wide-eyed coder dreaming up ad hoc features.

What is your proximity to the product management group? In a word, it should be close. At every phase of the definition, you, or one of your key staff, must be involved with the business experts. Not only does will this facilitate the transfer of knowledge between the two groups, but it will also lead to a better specification because unreasonable or impossible features will be weeded out from the beginning of the process. Nothing is more ineffective than having the due date and business requirements tossed over the cube partition to you. The classic waterfall process should be dammed up so everyone in the company can swim in the same river of business problems and solutions.

> *The classic waterfall process should be dammed up so everyone in the company can swim in the same river of business problems and solutions.*

Project Definition

Notice that this section's heading isn't "Project Management." You can't manage a project that hasn't been defined. Once the product is defined, it's time to define the project. You'll have something to manage in this case. You may recall from the last chapter the difference between an unrealistic product development cycle and a realistic one. The key difference between an Alice in Wonderland project and one that really delivers a quality product is the organization of the details. Definition leads to specification, design, prototyping, and many other iterative processes that make up the phases of the project. It might all be considered development, and it is, but the context of the various pieces of the project is important to mapping out the whole cycle.

Focus on organizing the project based on your experience with past projects, whether they were successful or not. Sometimes failure is the best teacher. (Success ain't bad, either!) Be careful about adopting the software engineering approach. It has a valid area of application to certain large projects, but craftsmanship is more critical than engineering when it comes to software. This is my opinion, which is shared by many, so take it for what it's worth. After all, you *did* buy this book, so you paid something for my opinion. All kidding aside, if your group and the business sponsors can agree on defining the project phases, coming up with a due date won't be an arbitrary shot in the dark. We often consider the release date of software a moving target, but you can take effective aim on uncertainty by knowing that the rollout can't precede comprehensive testing. Obviously, testing comes after coding, coding comes after design, and so on. Again, I'm not trying to force you into a procedural straightjacket for every project; rather, I'm reminding you to consider how to define and organize the project activities before you begin to build.

If you're new to leading a team of programmers, read widely (that's what you're doing right now) and consult with your boss frequently. Organizing a process to develop software requires more than just technical skill; it demands management experience and business wisdom. You may not have all that it takes. Learn to be a team player with the other teams in your company.

Process Management

Change is the only constant in the universe. How many times have you heard this? Basic physics teaches that an increase in entropy in closed systems is to be expected. Then why are we here reading books, writing code, and engaging in many other organized activities? Because something, or Someone, imposed order on the natural tendency of the universe to become disorganized. What am I saying? Should you be the "God of Process Management"? Yes. Call it the "Czar of Change Control" if you want a fancy alliterated title. Whatever you call it, do it: Manage the process of product and project definition as part of your overall organizational strategy.

Change comes in two basic flavors: deliberate and emergent. The former is usually planned, the latter typically unpredictable. Organizing for success means conducting careful deliberations so emergent change can be optimally managed.

If a product must be modified, what impact will the change have on network infrastructure? How about the change in the user experience of your software when version 2.0 is rolled out? Have you thought about these implications? You don't code on an island. Thomas Merton said, "We are warmed by fire, not by the smoke of the fire. We are carried over the sea by a ship, not by the wake of a ship."[8] Too often we create software without considering the impact of our technical choices and the "smoke" and "wake" of our efforts destabilizes our company.

> *Change management must be considered at every phase of a development project, from conception to completion.*

In less poetic terms, change management must be considered at every phase of a development project, from conception to completion. If no one has created even a basic template for gathering the impact of a requested (or unexpected) change, you're going to be in deep trouble throughout your development efforts. A simple set of questions can uncover the hidden dangers of change. Ask the following questions for every request for product modification:

- How will the change affect system architecture and maintenance?

- How will the change affect network infrastructure to support the requested change?

- How will the change affect the user's ability to work with the software effectively and efficiently?

- How will the change affect the departments that must manage the effect(s) of the change?

When you get to the answers of these questions, you will have organized a process of managing change that will inform many decisions about the activity of software development. I recommend weekly change management meetings with the leaders of other departments who are stakeholders in your company's success. As you coordinate change through an organized process, you'll gain control over the destiny of your products and your ability to support them. Instead of putting out fires, you'll create a policy of fire management that will allow you to plan for the future instead of being caught up in emergency meetings every week.

---

8.   Thomas Merton, *No Man Is an Island* (New York: Harcourt Brace Jovanovich, 1955), p. 117.

Testing

You've heard Java described as "Write once, run everywhere." The reality is "Write once, test everywhere" and this should be applied to all languages. Don't rely on your staff to do the final testing. Organize a testing group if you don't have one, or at the very least, let your staff members test each other's code. Allow junior programmers to do as much testing as coding during a development cycle. This will help them gain valuable experience about the more seasoned coders in your group.

The danger of allowing a programmer to certify his or her own code as "good enough" is the variability of the meaning of "good enough." A test script written by a business expert is far more effective in uncovering bugs than a programmer exercising functions that he or she created. The effects of collateral software changes to a product can't be measured by any one person. A test group, who also manages deployment, is critical to organizing for success. Become best friends with the testers—they aren't your enemies but your allies in releasing a solid product. They are also the first line of defense against a GUI flow that isn't well designed.

Facility Management

You might think that the physical environment in which you work each day is secondary to your success. Think again. In Chapter 3, when I discussed deflecting distractions from your programmers as one of your herding skills, I briefly mentioned office space. Cubes aren't for programmers. Hand-me-down computers aren't for programmers. Fighting with the network engineers to gain access to needed system resources is also a disruptive tactic for programmers. Everything you need in terms of physical facilities to lead a successful programming staff costs money—it can't be done for free. If you compare the cost of productivity (time and money) for performing in a poor work environment with that done in an adequate facility, you'll find that spending money on your physical plant is worth the cost.

Organize Collaboration and Solitude

Programmers need time to talk and time to think. Some claim to be able to do both at the same time very well, but I have my suspicions, born from years of observation, that time alone and time together must be managed carefully for successful programming to occur. Every programmer should have his or her own office with a door that closes. The ideal square footage is obviously a function of how much money you have to invest, but if you get much smaller than about 130 square feet, you're asking for trouble. How did I come up with this number? It is about the size of the average teenage American's bedroom. If teenagers can spend most of their adolescence in this space and flourish, so can your programmers.

 Time alone and time together must be managed carefully for successful programming to occur.

You need a bit more space only because you must engage in frequent collaboration on a one-on-one basis with your staff in private. You don't deserve a larger office just because you're the boss—you need it to better perform your job. A conference room with a printable whiteboard is also required for the entire staff to meet comfortably for days on end, if need be. We've all heard tales of high-tech legends engaging in group video-game frenzies. Throw in a little physical recreation space if you can, or share it with other groups if you can't have your own private facility.

Working from home, also mentioned in the last chapter as a good way to ensure minimal distractions, can help solve your solitude issues, but it does very little to foster collaboration. E-mail and the telephone are poor substitutes for face time when building software. Balance telecommuting with the needs of the group to work together. Decisions can be made in minutes when you are all in one place versus hours or days when you are dispersed.

Offer the Best Tools

A typical programmer needs a fast machine with the maximum memory and storage space. He or she also needs a test machine that duplicates the typical user environment. Your company may have some type of network infrastructure to support its products (Web servers, Citrix Metaframe, and so on) and you need mirror images of these facilities to test your development work. These facilities can often be shared with the testing group, but isolating the development and test environments from production is crucial. I've seen companies that unwisely allowed the programmer to directly update the Web site via remote downloads—this is the worst method to employ. It's convenient, but it's also very dangerous.

Laptops are often the best choice when mobility of your staff is required (or extra hours working at home), and today's technology has made a laptop almost as powerful as a desktop, so don't be cheap. Programmers have needs far beyond the average computer user. Your company's PC policy may have to be adjusted for your staff. Your programmers should be able to modify their machines at an administrative level. If they create configuration trouble for themselves, they should be trained to repair the damage. Calling in the network folks should be a last resort. Programmers who don't know how to modify the operating system or set it up from scratch aren't fully trained. They should be able to speak TCP/IP as well as the infrastructure engineers.

At the End of the Day

I know you expect me to tell you to clean off your desk and put everything in its place. I could say this, but what is more important to say is that in spite of the best organizational skills, you may still feel overwhelmed from time to time. The very nature of the kind of work you manage will lead to this. Creating software, managing and leading people, and all the other art forms you practice in your profession will sometimes make you feel like things are a mess. Nevertheless, to sum up, and in the spirit of organizing for success, keep the following list at hand.

- Is your personal work environment conducive to turning information into action? If it isn't, organize your affairs according to the best practices that will enable you to do more than just manage (i.e., lead).

- Spend your time on things you can control and don't fight against the ones you can't.

- Become a force and energy source for organizing your entire company by your interactions with other departments. Get and keep your department in order as an example for other leaders to follow.

Break up large tasks into manageable pieces so you can begin to attack the whole. By manageable, I mean create subtasks that can be accomplished in one contiguous block of time. This way, you organize your time effectively, getting at least one job completely done at one sitting. Nothing will build your confidence more quickly than having an organized plan to get work done and actually doing it. Confidence has many offspring: success, a lessening of harmful stress, and the personal satisfaction that comes from leading others to great achievement.

Next on the Agenda

The next chapter focuses on your role in meetings. The organizational skills you bring to meetings will help shape their success. You want meetings between yourself and another group, and especially those with your staff, to be organized affairs with clear goals and expected outcomes. As you progress through this book, keep in mind that you can't take in everything here in one sitting. You also can't stuff the book's contents into neatly defined pigeonholes in your head. You need to reorganize the topics presented here so they fit into your way of working with your job. Go ahead, cut and paste to your heart's content—I won't be offended.

Managing Meetings

Why should you manage meetings? Because when you put programmers in a group meeting, you best be thinking of all the interpersonal dynamics that can take place and possibly wreck your goal for the meeting. If you've been used to writing code day in and day out, you may have some uncomfortable apprehensions[1] about leading a meeting for the first (or fiftieth) time. Not to worry. This chapter is devoted to the subject of meetings and should raise your consciousness in this area; it is your conscious brain that must be fully engaged to lead a meeting effectively.

Often, technical people like us have a disdain for meetings. We sometimes think they waste time and we should all just have our heads down at the keyboard pounding out code. As the leader, you do want your folks pounding at the keyboard, but you also want to control what they write. Meetings are central to coordinating the outcome of your efforts and you must not view them as a necessary evil, for they aren't. Gathering to discuss technical ideas as a group provides opportunities for the very best ideas to mingle until everyone on your team has a clear picture of your strategy and tactics.

The Weekly Staff Meeting

I recommend a staff meeting at the same time each week, even if you feel there's nothing new to talk about any given week. The truth is there will always be something to talk about if you establish the following simple agenda for each week:

- What did you do last week?

- What are you going to do this week?

- What problems are hindering you from accomplishing your assigned tasks on time?

---

1. Perhaps this is redundant—all apprehensions are uncomfortable. Nevertheless, don't feel alone, your group may be feeling similar uncomfortable feelings with you as the leader. I guess this truth doesn't help, but it's the price of leadership.

Have each of your people answer these three questions each week with their task list in hand. You're creating tasks list with due dates, aren't you? It's essential that you provide written goals for your programmers even if each task is simply a high-level description of a new feature they're adding to an existing product. It may be that each task implies many other subsidiary tasks, but they need a place to start and your job is to remind them of what they must deliver. Depending on the level of project management you enforce or encourage, the task list could be as simple as a description and a due date or as elaborate as a project timeline chart with drill-down subtasks for each major project deliverable. The last chapter gave you an example to start from. Construct your own method of producing task lists; make it fit your organization and style of leadership. The task lists serve as the focal point of the weekly staff meeting.

Enforce the concept of *deliverables* during the staff meeting—these are features or products your programmers must produce for public consumption. Shy away from the vague assignment couched in terms such as "fix the bugs" or "add some enhancements."

Enforce the concept of deliverables *during the staff meeting—these are features or products your programmers must produce for public consumption. Shy away from the vague assignment couched in terms such as "fix the bugs" or "add some enhancements."*

If you have a strong product definition group with good marketing inputs, your job will be made much easier. Again, the purpose of the staff meeting is to promote the delivery of the software, not to just have fun talking about code. Of course, having fun with code can help deliver good products, so avoid becoming a tyrant.

The beauty of the previous meeting agenda is that it's simple, it encourages dialogue, and it will keep you knowledgeable about any stray tasks your folks may be pursuing. By having programmers articulate what they've done and what they expect to accomplish on a week-by-week basis, you also enforce the mindset that they work to deliver a product. Another important function of this simple agenda is that you want your people to think of all the supporting tasks associated with a high-level task as they dig into the details of implementation. You'll find it helpful to establish high-level goals for a project, such as "implement a module to accomplish function X," and then let the assigned resources develop the supporting dependent tasks. This will become additional data for you to track in your administrative processes. It would be great if you could think of every last detail that would achieve one particular software feature, but then you wouldn't be making the most of the power of delegation nor taking advantage of other minds and technical approaches. To balance this last statement, you should try to think of all the details, but if you have good and properly motivated people, they'll help you do the job. Ultimately, this is the group's function, and it's your personal responsibility to encourage and track the result.

One agenda item I've added for a period of time is a book review. Pick a good book on programming techniques, design principles, or something related to the future of your industry and dig into it together. Make assignments to your team members with oral presentations during the meeting. Create a brief atmosphere of a graduate seminar and have some academic fun. Encouraging learning can be greatly fostered with this technique.

You'll no doubt add to the simple agenda as needed, but don't get too ambitious or detailed because any staff meeting that goes over 45 minutes may be counterproductive. The staff meeting is a good time to grow team cooperation and help those stuck with particularly difficult tasks to benefit from the shared wisdom of the group. You'll also put some needed pressure on those who procrastinate by having them explain to the group why they missed a deadline. Don't overuse this group dynamic: Public humiliation is rarely an effective tool in correcting bad performance, so be careful with your criticisms and be lavish—in public—with your praise.

The staff meeting will take on a particularly important role near code-complete time. This is when you must really focus the group's attention on stubborn tasks and last-minute programming—these items must always be handled with care. The predictable weekly nature of your staff meeting will help to maintain focus as you enter these critical cycles of the development process.

Your leadership skills when conducting the staff meeting will be on display each week. Another reason for having a meeting each week is that you may need the practice! Remember, half of life is just showing up. Seriously, and with apologies to Emerson,[2] consistency is rarely foolish. As your group interacts week after week, you'll begin to form a real team if you look for ways to foster cooperation. Also, allow competition to have its natural place. This will require a delicate balancing act on your part. You may have to stifle some programmers gently and encourage others when needed. If you really *know* your people, you'll sense when these corrective actions are needed on your part. It's a bit like being a parent of teenagers, a subject I'm glad to not be writing about.

---

2. "A foolish consistency is the hobgoblin of little minds, adored by little statesmen and philosophers and divines. With consistency, a great soul has simply nothing to do . . ." —Ralph Waldo Emerson (*Self-Reliance*, 1841).

Leading a Design Meeting

You may be the smartest programmer in the group, but you probably don't have all the skills, not to mention the time, to design every new feature that comes your way from the business units all by yourself. Even if you had the time, it's a bad idea to design it all yourself because none of your programmers will have any sense of ownership. This leads to the sometimes dreaded design meeting, where the socially dysfunctional group[3] you manage needs to turn into a happy, motivated, and empowered team eager to design and build cool new software features on time and with few bugs. How do you create this kind of team using the people you have on hand? Magic or bribes might work but aren't practical. What you need is the mind of an experienced psychologist and the heart of a career diplomat. Welcome to the wild, wonderful world of team dynamics.

 It's a bad idea to design all the software by yourself because then none of your programmers will have any sense of ownership.

So how do you become this great design team leader if you aren't already? You don't without a lot of hard thinking and practice. Consider the dynamics and issues involved in a typical design meeting:

- You need to get all the features designed correctly so they can be built with quality.

- Each person on the team may have a different design for the same feature.

- Programmers want to design the things they know how to build or want to build.

- Some programmers have a hidden agenda that may be hard for you to discern and could result in the meeting being sabotaged.

- You don't want everyone to endorse your ideas unless they are the best.

- Consensus in design is the goal—a tough thing to accomplish but worthy of the effort. Compromise might seem more realistic but will foster resentment when someone's pet idea didn't get the vote.

---

3.   I don't mean to imply that all programmers are socially dysfunctional, but we're somewhat peculiar and this is what gives us our edge and makes long hours of heads-down programming possible. These peculiar traits lead to interesting group dynamics.

It can get worse, or it can be a wonderfully rewarding time. It depends on you as the leader to make the critical difference. Your job is to take the people you have and the requirements in hand and produce workable specifications that can lead to good code.

This is a tall order in most organizations, and thankfully this book is only a guide and doesn't pretend to have all the answers. Whew—got out of that one!

Just kidding, here are some guidelines:

- Know the strengths and weaknesses of the team members, including you, the fearless leader. This is what the first three chapters were all about.

- Break out the requirements document into sections of functionality that are related and small enough in scope to be attacked by object-oriented (OO) design principles.

- Take good notes. Use a printable whiteboard if you can afford one. Video-tape the session and digitize it for review by the team as the first design specification draft is created.

- Have a laptop connected to a large monitor for reviewing existing code as examples to embrace or avoid.

- Don't have a phone in the room that you intend to answer unless you need to conference in someone for ideas.

- Work in a comfortable and quiet location, and take enough breaks to keep the bodies in the meeting supportive of the minds.

- Have an agenda for each day and revise it as necessary to accomplish all the design work needed for the project. Set aside the last day to review and summarize the results of the meeting.

Taking good notes was previously described as a necessary activity. This may be a problem if you're often at the whiteboard creating design ideas. You may have to designate someone on the team to be the official note taker. Nothing is more discouraging than having a great meeting one week and then forgetting what you decided the next. You might create a template for the note taker. Figure 5-1 shows an example of a realized template design.

Some comments about this template. Most of the information you capture is self-explanatory. The large Notes area is intended to be free-form so you can draw a block diagram (if the printable whiteboard is on the blink) or just jot down raw ideas that often come out in meetings spontaneously. The Design Impact section is fairly important. Anything you design will more than likely affect existing software or some other aspect of your organization—try to note the effects. The Actions Needed area is intended to assist in tracking what to do next to realize the design. A meeting without follow-up actions is a waste of time. You'll also want to provide a written summary of the meeting that can serve as a knowledge base for the team. This will be especially useful for those who weren't present at the meeting or those just joining the team who need to get up to speed on the history of the project.

A meeting without follow-up actions is a waste of time.

Try to keep the template to one page in order to promote clarity of focus. If you need to expand a particular design to more than one page, use a second template sheet and number it appropriately. I think you get the general idea, and I'm sure you may think of a better method—*just be sure you do have a method other than memory* to help you in the next phase of design: writing the design specification. Now, I'm off the hook for this one because this book is neither a full-fledged project management book nor an OO monograph.

Okay, I may be off the hook for more detailed ideas about software design, but on the people side of the issue, consider this: You may not be the best architect in the group even if you are the leader. Programmers come in many flavors, often many flavors all mixed up (recall the discussions of Chapter 1). If your strength isn't in big-picture architecture, identify the ones in your group who have this strength and let their contributions take center stage. You may feel that you must take part in the creation of these ideas, but if you can manage to foster the best ideas, you will have done your job well. Being a facilitator of good ideas is just as good as being the creator in many cases. This is where your diplomacy skills will come into play.

What did you say? You don't have any diplomacy skills? Well, begin to learn. Diplomacy is the art of listening before speaking, thinking before proposing, and striving to achieve consensus.

Diplomacy is the art of listening before speaking, thinking before proposing, and striving to achieve consensus.

Product/Version_____ / _____   **Date** _____

Feature/Function_____

Notes

Design Impact

Associated Software	Infrastructure	Other Departments

Actions Needed

What	Who	When

Figure 5-1. Template design for the note taker

A big assignment, no doubt, but that's why they pay you the big bucks. I could recommend a number of books on the subject of team building (see the Bibliography), but if you have a strong desire to succeed with your group during the design meeting, you have the one most essential ingredient for a good outcome. A desire to succeed as a group should be put ahead of any motive on your part to win arguments; no one wins an argument. In a team either everyone wins or everyone loses.

I've touted consensus as a goal of the design meeting. Achieving this is not a matter of taking votes on the candidate ideas. Democracy, while a good thing for nations, doesn't map well onto technical design.[4] If you compromise the ideas of one person in favor of another, you won't have the best ideas. Consensus is reached via a synthesis of ideas, not a wrangling over "You can have this feature if I can have that one." Synthesis means the best ideas win out as the implications of the competing ideas are worked out. This takes patience and persistence on your part as the leader since you're trying to get to the best design possible. It's the price you must pay for success. In a great collection of essays on peopleware, Larry Constantine notes:

> *A synthesis is something original that incorporates essential features of each contributing idea or proposal . . . Not only does a consensus based on synthesis incorporate the best of the alternatives, but new features or capabilities typically emerge from the combination.*[5]

Cat Fight! The Outsider

Paul was a real corncob to work with. He always rubbed you the wrong way. I didn't like him, and the fact that the CEO had hired him from our chief competitor, gave him a larger salary than me, and then told me to manage him didn't help the situation. So what if he had a Ph.D. in physics and had single-handedly created a killer piece of software that had kicked our rear end in the marketplace? He was impossible to work with; he always thought he was right and the rest of us were amateur programmers. Of course, his idea of brilliance was one object serving as a switchboard for every function a program had to perform. He had no concept of component development or team programming. I had a mission impossible: Use Paul to create the next generation of software and use his ideas to motivate the existing developers while still managing to make them feel they had a sense of ownership in the design.

---

4.   I love what Gene Hackman said to Denzel Washington in the movie *Crimson Tide*: "We are here to preserve democracy, not to practice it." In a similar way, you should lead the meeting to preserve the best thinking, not simply choose the idea of the moment, no matter how passionately promoted.

5.   Larry L. Constantine, *The Peopleware Papers* (Upper Saddle River, NJ: Yourdon Press, 2001), p. 10.

I set to work planning the first design meeting in which Paul would interact with my other guys. I devised an agenda that would show the architectural approaches we had employed in the past as a bridge to the future. Paul had other ideas. He said to me, "Ralph, do you really think you can create a revolutionary product built on the tired ideas of the past?" It was a rhetorical question, of course—at least I had enough smarts to figure this out. It was also a hint of what the week of design meetings had in store: judgmental comments from Paul while the others looked to me for help. I was not disappointed. The week was a disaster, and the best I could do was let Paul go build the software alone and hope it all turned out okay.

After a month I told the CEO that unless I had full authority over Paul's work life (salary, promotion, threat of being fired, and so on), I could not manage him and would not take responsibility for his work products. Unfortunately, the CEO agreed, and then I realized what a fine mess I had gotten myself into. There was now no one to blame but me if I didn't help Paul succeed. Another problem was that Paul began to like me because he thought I let him work alone because he was good, not because I had no alternative due to his abrasive personality. As it turned out, Paul wasn't that good. He had been lucky once and, as I discovered after many long lunches with him, had many jobs and careers over the years. He was the peripatetic outsider.

This story of Ralph and Paul ended unhappily. Ralph finally had to fire Paul because he could never get his next miracle product out of alpha testing. The rest of the team turned inward and felt neglected; they were correct to feel this way. Ralph had little time for anything but keeping Paul away from meetings and any other interaction that provided Paul an opportunity to criticize the work of others. Several lessons are apparent in this story.

- Teams can't be successful based on the past successes of any one team member.

- Only a team leader can build a team. The leader must have the confidence of his or her boss to assemble the team.

- Check out a person's job history to validate their worth, not just their latest achievement.

- Some people can never work on a team—don't try to make them. They may not even belong in your organization.

The One-on-One Meeting

You'll find it helpful to have meetings with each of your programmers alone from time to time. You may need to spend regular hours mentoring a novice or helping a pro who is stuck on a particular project. These meetings should be given the same thought as any other. Have an agenda, take notes, and consider all the dynamics of the two people involved. Leave the meeting with an action plan, not just good feelings.

One-on-one meetings should be given the same thought as any other. Have an agenda, take notes, and consider all the dynamics of the two people involved. Leave the meeting with an action plan, not just good feelings.

If you can discipline yourself—and you must consider that discipline is one of the traits you need to grow the most in your leadership skill base—set aside one day a week to spend extended time with each of your people. Not everyone will want or need this one-on-one time, but as you invest yourself in others, they will in turn invest themselves in your goals and consider their role important enough for you to give your valuable time to them. You want your goals to be their goals, and sharing time is the best way to foster a sense of group ownership about the mission of your department. This is best done one on one.

Your greatest resource is people. They can also be the source of your most troubling problems. Thus, building solid and professional relationships with your staff is crucial to your success as a leader. Be wary of making relationships with employees too personal. This can be a challenge, since all interactions between people are personal, but you must maintain a professional tone for the relationship to benefit your position as leader. Friends will do a lot for you, but you can't often rely on this dynamic in business: Too many other things are in play, such as the fact that you control the livelihood of your staff. If you ever reach the point of having to dismiss an employee, having centered the relationship on a business rather than personal foundation will make the task a bit less personally disturbing.

The one-on-one meeting is also the only venue for an employee review where salary increases or promotions are considered. If your company has a formal review procedure, this can offer you some hope of objectivity. Realize that all reviews are at their core subjective, but this doesn't invalidate the process. As the leader, you should be noting performance all year long, not just trying to recall an individual's achievements or failings when the time for review pops up on the calendar. One way to track employee performance (either by paper or electronically) is to gather data as work occurs week to week. If you have a personnel file, drop a note in for each staff member as they do something good or cause a problem. Candidate data is e-mail, missed or achieved deadlines, design contributions, and problem solutions.

Another useful function for regular one-on-one meetings is tracking project progress and problems. You can even formalize this process by having a standard survey or status form that is completed each week by team members. Call these forms opportunities to send up smoke signals when things are going badly. As you review these forms, bring in the originator and have a meeting to discuss ways to resolve issues that are hindering progress. Solving problems early on is a much better method than having your project devoured by unaddressed issues you failed to notice.

Meetings with Other Groups

Now that you have this neat new job, you'll begin to broaden your social horizons. Dilbert informs us here, especially from your perspective in the driver's seat (see Figure 5-2).

I hope you aren't as afraid as the poor programmer pictured in the cartoon. We techies are sometimes a bit uncomfortable when we have to engage groups outside of our normal circle of influence. "Normal" will now begin to change for you: Not all your meetings are going to be with programmers. They'll begin to include an array of nontechnical people, as well as those with technical skills you may not fully understand or appreciate. Those responsible in your organization for generating business requirements, support and testing staff, quality assurance, finance, and other key areas will be demanding your time.

DILBERT reprinted by permission of United Feature Syndicate, Inc.

Figure 5-2. The newly promoted programmer

How will you handle yourself in these meetings? You may have to dress up for some of them, so be sure you have at least one good suit in your closet. Remember, they expect you to be a little weird. Just keep the weirdness restricted to what's expected of a creative individual, but still acceptable to those more concerned with bean counting than Boolean logic.

Always present your department in the best light. Never blame your failures to deliver on time on your team. No one will respect this and it will add fuel to the fire in our industry, where programmers are wildly unrealistic at estimating and keeping deadlines. We may think that programming is an art (and it is), but your boss may expect it to be a science with all the attendant predictability this term entails. If you receive praise, count your lucky stars, bow humbly and graciously, and give all the credit to your team. You can boast in private.

You'll gain respect among your staff for successfully working with the rest of the company. This will be especially true if they can avoid the long and sometimes tedious meetings that you must endure.

Never blame your failures to deliver on time on your team. No one will respect this and it will add fuel to the fire in our industry, where programmers are wildly unrealistic at estimating and keeping deadlines.

One of your key roles with other groups is assuring that business requirements are delivered to you in the fullest possible state of completion as possible. Scope creep starts with poorly defined requirements, accelerates when programmers have to invent things to make up for a bad product definition, and only goes downhill from there. You may begin to spend as much time in the product definition phase of a project as you do in the design and programming cycles. This can work out for the best because the smarter you are about the business side of your company, the better you can deliver what is needed to create market share.

Another word about the requirements side of your business. As a programmer, you enjoy building software because you take an idea and make it a virtual reality. There's something magic about creating a well-defined user interface that's actually hooked up correctly on the back end. The best software product you probably created was the one where you understood the business problem very well; you probably had the most fun as a programmer building this application also. Take this love of fun over across cube land into the product definition group and help them know what's possible as the requirements are being gathered. Your technical skills will stop a bad idea before it gets started, and their business smarts will help you come up with some really good ideas. Learn to marry technology to business, but be aware that business is the dominant partner in this union. You might not like this as a technologist, but it's reality and it does pay the bills.

Project Retrospective Meetings

Let's hope you don't call these meetings "project post-mortems." They aren't intended to be gripe sessions, but rather a formalized way of learning by experience. Norman Kerth wrote:

> *For a retrospective to be effective and successful, it needs to be safe. By "safe", I mean that the participants must feel secure within their community—to discuss their work, to admit that there may have been better ways to perform the work, and to learn from the retrospective exercise itself. Safety must be developed and maintained. While safety is ultimately the responsibility of all the participants in a retrospective, the facilitator needs to initiate, monitor, and control the safety. Part of being safe means knowing that there will be no retribution for being honest (such as begin given a negative evaluation during the next performance review). Trust must be established and maintained during a retrospective.*[6]

---

6. Norman L. Kerth, *Project Retrospectives* (New York: Dorset House Publishing, 2001), p. 7.

Creating a safe meeting format can help you glean much from a recently completed project. Use this knowledge to improve your development process. Safety in the meeting is important because you'll often ask some hard questions as you deliberate.

Typical questions to research during the retrospective meeting include the following:

- Was the product specification clear or did it require so many iterations to revise that the design phase was delayed by an unacceptable amount of time?

- Did you have time to prototype your design before you began coding?

- Was the existing architecture easy or hard to extend for the new features?

- Did the project leader build a foundation for success by being available, knowledgeable, and organized?

- If you had to write the code over again, would you do it the same way?

- Did you have all the software tools needed to complete your work?

- What would you change about your development process if you could?

The last question, obviously, opens the door for a wide range of topics to be introduced. This is fine as long as you keep it relevant to the project under review and encourage constructive comments.

Conference Calls

Conference calls are meetings, too—they're simply meetings devoid of body language and hopefully conducted with a clear agenda and good acoustics. The absence of body language, however, is a great hindrance to an effective meeting. Geography may nevertheless dictate telephone meetings and they're very common in our industry today. If visual items must be examined during a meeting, ensure everyone has a copy and reviewed it prior to the meeting. Don't make a meeting an occasion to read a document to adults: This is a waste of everyone's time.

One protocol that might get you into trouble in a conference call is the "silence is agreement" rule. In other words, when you make a decision or relate information, if no one has a comment, what has been said becomes accepted. In general, this is a good way to proceed because it forces others to be proactive in the meeting. Since you can't rely upon facial expressions or body posture for communication, often silence is truly agreement. Enforcing this rule depends upon the group dynamics. If you're meeting in a conference call with people you've never personally met, this rule isn't a very good idea. It will take work to make an audio meeting between strangers effective, so if you can afford video conferencing, you should make this the medium for the meeting.

Limit conference calls to an hour at the maximum. If the meeting takes more time, the agenda is either too long or not well organized. Start the meeting at the agreed time and don't wait for all the participants to dial in. They'll learn from experience when they miss key items by their tardiness. Be sure you don't begin the meeting late, however; this is not only rude, but it's also unprofessional and sends the message that the meeting isn't really that important.

Your voice is the only way you have to lead a teleconference. Use it wisely and considerately. Take good notes (or have someone else take them) and distribute a record of the meeting with action items as soon as possible after you have concluded your business. Try to avoid unnecessary chatter during a phone meeting; some banter is fine, but too much simply lengthens the meeting.

In Between Meetings

Now, don't get too wild at my next suggestion: Foster a "myth" about yourself. Be sure the myth is founded in truth, but don't discourage others from extending or amplifying your devotion to the job. Don't encourage them either—just let your performance speak for itself. What is this myth? Nothing less than the fact that you practice principles of effective leadership consistently.

Don't confuse devotion with bad planning. If you're like most managers, your job may often require more than the 40 hours a week most people expect. Working overtime doesn't necessarily mean you're devoted. It could mean you're not very well organized and can't get the job done in a reasonable amount of time. In addition, if you neglect to have a life outside of work, your myth may simply be seen as that of an individual wound up a little too tight about work. If you put in extra hours, others will feel they have to also. Sometimes this will be necessary. But if you make it a habit, you're not consistently working on your leadership skills and your staff will suffer. As I mentioned in the last chapter, you're in control of your working hours as well as your ability to make the job fit into the rest of your life.

I know I'm getting personal here, but an effective leader does leave a mark on his or her people. I'm just trying to raise your consciousness about what kind of mark you make. The legacy you want to leave behind at work should be almost as important as that you leave with your family. If you're true to yourself, your public persona will be a reflection of your private one. I'm not advocating taking an ego trip—just recognize some of the realities of being a leader and try to take advantage of them. This whole chapter on meetings was aimed at making you aware of your need to focus outward toward others.

Meeting for Consensus and Action

I've discussed a wide range of meeting types in this chapter. The goal of any meeting is to reach a consensus among the participants and leave with an agenda for action. You'll foster this by always assuming a professional role in meetings, no matter how informal the setting. What does "professional" mean? Webster's lists one dimension of professionalism as "making a constant practice of something." Your consistency in leading meetings will, over time, result in successful gatherings. Meetings should be designed to debate until the best ideas are adopted. Your expertise—another shade of meaning of the term "professional"—must come to the fore in the discussions planned to lead to action.

By way of summary, keep these ideas in mind as you review your role in all the meetings in which you either participate or lead:

- Don't allow your staff meeting to become a social gathering. Make it a working time to kick off the week.

- Have a well-planned agenda when you engage in days of design meetings. Keep group dynamics in your heart as you lead from the head.

- When meeting one on one with members of your team, employ all the techniques of a larger meeting: Strive to reach consensus and have an action plan.

- When you meet with nontechnical staff, you're the technical representative, so speak in such a way to convey complex ideas simply. Impressing accountants with acronyms won't gain you respect. Take on the role of teacher in these meetings, but do it with forethought and avoid any trace of condescension.

- Don't use project retrospective meetings to bash other departments. Focus on what your staff could have done better.

- Keep conference calls to a minimum if possible. Keep them brief by careful preparation and a focused agenda.

Our Next Meeting

A lot of what you've been working on in this book is fairly personal—nothing is more personal than your leadership role in meetings. In the next chapter, I'll discuss your role as the technical leader. This involves aspects of group interaction, but you'll be moving into an area that you might feel more comfortable about because you probably have more experience with technology than people. This isn't to say that you've lived in a basement all your life away from people; it's just that the core skill you bring to your job is your technical expertise. Don't stop reading now, because it's going to get really good in the next chapter!

CHAPTER 6

Philosophy and Practice of Technical Leadership

As I discussed earlier, you may have been promoted to management because you're a brilliant technical person. While technical skills don't necessarily translate to management expertise, for the purposes of this chapter you're sitting pretty. Much of what I talked about in previous chapters may have been new to you—the material in this chapter will more than likely not be. Of course, you still need to read this stuff; otherwise, I wouldn't have included it! Also, you may appreciate the look at technical issues from your new perspective as technical leader. No longer are you just the "technical lead" on a team, you're  the leader with a capital "L" for the whole department. When choices have to be made, you're the one in the hot seat. In addition, you'll have to live with the long-term consequences of your choices upon the software you're responsible for building, so making the best choices is of paramount importance.

To help you make the best choices, in this chapter you'll survey technical principles and focus on the philosophy behind the details that should spur you on to action. The goal is to develop a way to *practice* leadership in our technology-driven profession based on a correct philosophy about the technical dimensions of leading programmers. Philosophy must be determined first, but without actions that put it into practice, you won't fully exercise your leadership and successfully herd cats.

Seize and Hold Your Technical Role

Your role as technical leader is to manage architecture and design. They're two different things, architecture and design. Often as programmers, we think of them as almost synonymous, but they most assuredly are not. As you lead your department, you'll quickly determine that designing an application's components is very different from determining its overall architecture. The goal of architecture is to promote design reuse. Ideally, an architectural concept will be prototyped before a system is assembled from all its constituent components. Contrast this with OO component construction, where the goal is code reuse. These are very different things, and in my humble and correct opinion, design reuse is more important.

> *The goal of architecture is to promote design reuse.*

The power of OO technology, without regard to the language in which it's implemented, is its capability to create objects that tie together application data with user interactions. It does this while hiding the details, so objects can have a public interface that works within the program structure and process flow, rather than acting directly on the data or user interface layer. You can thus assemble components that fit together with properties and methods that have names meaningful to the problem domain rather than the solution domain. For example, a method called "ShowAppointments" can populate a GUI interface property "Appointments" while hiding the details, such as "Select * from Appointments where Date = Today". This makes the program understandable when viewing the problem you're trying to solve.

It's this heightened level of understanding that makes OO methods truly great stuff and has moved us a long way from the functional decomposition and structured techniques of earlier decades of computer programming. Where OO technology falls short, however, is in its applicability to creating the overall system architecture. Certainly, OO techniques are useful in architectural analysis, but you can't directly map the skills gained in creating a component to those needed to create an overall system of components. There's a missing piece in the OO skill set and this is where architectural considerations must be applied and come to the rescue. Your role as the technical leader is to focus on system architecture before you decide on a technology of implementation or the underlying details of the components from which a system will be constructed.

Consider the following analogy. The Greeks and Romans launched Western civilization's great tradition of classical architecture. For over 2,000 years, classical buildings have been like great novels, offering a simple message when viewed externally. For the observant inspector of these structures, however, layers upon layers of creative detail were found within the inhabitable spaces. Software architecture can offer the same wonder of outward beauty enclosing wonderful complexity, but it has only been with us for about half a century. We've a long way to go before anything we create will be called "classic." Your role as technical leader is to lay the foundations upon which your team and others will build. We may live in an age where popular art is proclaimed an instant classic, but only validation through time can grant this distinction to the works of our minds as we labor at the keyboard.

Construct or Plant?

The graphic at the head of this chapter was intentionally chosen so you would feel the comfort of a traditional metaphor—that of construction. How often have we used this term to describe what we do? Often, I've observed. Even as children, we played with erector sets, if you're from my generation, or LEGOs, if you're from Generation X. This familiar idea of constructing software describes the day-in and day-out activity of programmers in a commonsense sort of way. If you take the metaphor literally, what does it mean to add features to an application? Can you add ten floors to a skyscraper and be sure the foundation will support this new addition? I don't think so, and neither should you. A new metaphor is needed—that of gardening. When you plan and plant a garden, you expect that from time to time you'll uproot some plants and put in new ones. Note what Andrew Hunt and David Thomas say concerning this metaphor in their excellent book on pragmatic programming:

> *You plant many things in a garden according to an initial plan and conditions. Some thrive, others are destined to end up as compost. You may move plantings relative to each other to take advantage of the interplay of light and shadow, wind and rain. Overgrown plants get split or pruned, and colors that clash may get moved to more aesthetically pleasing locations. You pull weeds, and you fertilize plantings that are in need of some extra help. You constantly monitor the health of the garden, and make adjustments (to the soil, the plants, the layout) as needed.*[1]

This gardening metaphor is a much more appropriate paradigm for software development. It enforces the idea that all software is temporary and the architecture must be established to account for new structures being implemented upon a flexible foundation. When it comes to architecture, stovepipe systems are constructed, whereas living software is planted. We need to move to an organic approach to software development in order to meet the needs of twenty-first century business.

---

1. Andrew Hunt and David Thomas, *The Pragmatic Programmer* (New York: Addison-Wesley, 2000), p. 184.

We need to move to an organic approach to software development in order to meet the needs of twenty-first century business.

The underlying concept expressed by the gardening metaphor is the difference between the organic and the synthetic. Organic entities are grown; synthetic ones are assembled from constructed components. True, we build the components and they're synthetic by their very nature, but where we plant them must be a living framework that allows the whole to be more than the sum of the components. It also supports the needs of changing business requirements and technological evolution.

Keep biology on your mind as you read ahead and put the construction industry in the back corners of your thinking machine. Realize that the use of metaphors is simply to give you a mental hook for holding up abstract ideas to the light of technical scrutiny. You can't write code based on a metaphor—you need the gritty design details. But all these details form a pattern. It's this pattern that can be viewed from the perspective of a metaphor in terms of its appropriateness as a software solution to a business problem. You haven't forgotten about thinking, have you? As you've weaved your way forward in this book, thinking wide and deep has been a primal force that you must use to do your job. Keep it up, it's good for you.

The Primacy of Architecture

A growing body of work, both academic and practical, has emerged in the past decade to address the need for good architecture in software development. Authorities who have studied the subject insist that a very large percentage of application development efforts fail due to the neglect of architectural soundness.[2] Stovepipe systems are the result, and evolving such systems to meet changing business requirements is very costly in terms of time, personnel, and intellectual capital.

The management of risk in the design of any system should be your overriding concern. What kinds of risk should you manage? The kinds that can hurt your business as you need to add features never envisioned in an existing product because the competition already has it online; the kinds that make the maintenance of your product a nightmare, because too many subsystem components

---

2. See works by the authors of the pattern and antipattern movement, such as Brown and others who are referenced in the Bibliography.

are tightly coupled or not flexible in their configuration. Another risk is unwarranted complexity at the higher levels of the architecture that makes learning how to fix the underlying components a nightmare for coders who didn't create the system. All these concerns relate directly to time and money, two things your boss would like you to minimize.

Architecture requires an active creation process that goes beyond sitting at the keyboard typing out business requirements and thinking up code components that could meet these needs. You must step back from the machine and become intimately familiar with the problem. The machine—software—may be the solution, but unless you fully understand the problems your business faces, any product you create will likely fall short of having a long or productive life. Marc and Laura Sewell, writing about the role of architects, list a number of essential activities that must be performed prior to any design plan.[3] According to these authors, an architect must have done the following:

- Mastered the arts of listening, asking, and observing

- Acquired sufficient knowledge of the client's domain, such as banking, government, education, health care, retail, or racetracks

- Developed a strategic worldview of the client's enterprise, rather than a mere tactical or operational one

- Possessed a wide-ranging knowledge of technology, so a full spectrum of strategic choices can be brought to bear on the architectural plan

- Communicated effectively to the client and builder

- Monitored, inspected, and protected the client's vision and the design

Following through on these tasks may seem outside the scope of your little old job. I recommend you broaden your scope, if you think this way, and consider how many products you've created over the years that never went beyond version 1.0. We have all created our share of short-lived products. I would posit that the lack of a thorough understanding of the problem resulted in a tactical solution that looked good coming off the floppy disk, but didn't really stand the test of time.

An architect must walk around the problem, keeping in mind two domains of concern: design forces, which drive all software decisions, and analysis viewpoints, which enable you to make the decisions design forces demand.

---

3.   Marc T. Sewell and Laura M. Sewell, *The Software Architect's Profession* (Upper Saddle River, NJ: Prentice Hall, 2002), p. 68.

Design Forces in Architectural Planning

Because formal software architecture design is a relatively new field, there are a number of competing schools of thought. Malveau and Mowbray,[4] two experts in the area, list the major approaches: Zachman Framework, Open Distributed Processing, Domain Analysis, 4+1 View Model, and Academic Software Architecture. Wow! That was a mouthful; perhaps your palate is not familiar with the taste of each. Not to worry? No, you *should* worry and you must begin to become a student of these ways of thinking so you're equipped with the best tools good minds have devised for creating reusable system designs.

Once you begin to dig into architectural ways of thinking, you'll soon discover that all share a common goal: controlling design forces that influence all software decisions relative to architecture. Design forces are the factors that must be considered when software is conceived from the ground up. These forces pose at least the following list of questions and issues that must be addressed by your architecture.

- Will the system provide a good user experience and perform as expected?

- Will the system function as designed and be capable of change and maintenance as business needs and technology change?

- Is complexity minimized in the high-level architectural features of the system?

- Whatever is built will change over the next few years and paths to the future must be built into the foundation.

- Solutions will be implemented in hardware and much thought must be given to infrastructure creation, configuration, and maintenance.

- If new technologies are used, can your staff gain the expertise needed to maintain the system? If older technologies are used for construction,[5] will they still be up to the job years down the road?

---

4. Raphael C. Malveau and Thomas Mowbray, *Software Architect Bootcamp* (Upper Saddle River, NJ: Prentice Hall, 2001).

5. Notice how easy it is to slip back into old ways of thinking. If I had said ". . .older technologies are used for planting . . ." would you have known what I was talking about?

Be aware of these questions and issues, and make them publicly known to all members of your design team. Knowing the correct questions to ask is often more important than having the correct answers. Well, maybe that's a bit of an overstatement, but you get my general point. There are often many ways to do the wrong thing. What you want to ask first is, "What's the correct thing to do?" Asking the right questions will guide your team toward sound, strong, and long-lasting architecture.

Analysis Viewpoints: Managing the Forces

You'll successfully manage the issues that result from design forces if you consistently think about the different viewpoints involved in any enterprise-level architecture. A *viewpoint* is simply an analysis perspective you adopt in considering how to address the design decisions. This viewpoint or perspective changes as you move around the conceived system in design space, driven by the strengths of the competing design forces. All schools of architecture emphasize at least the following viewpoints described in question form:

- How will our users interact with our systems? (*Use cases* is a common name for this viewpoint.)

- What components will we assemble to enable the system to function?

- How will our components work together to enable the system to perform?

- What technologies are the most appropriate to create the software?

- How will we deliver the system to our customers?

Are you asking these questions about the software you conceive in the design meetings discussed in the last chapter? You must or else you'll have architecture by coincidence, a deadly antipattern. Refactoring architecture is much more difficult, and potentially more destructive, than rebuilding components. Keep this risk factor foremost in your mind as you design.

 Refactoring architecture is much more difficult, and potentially more destructive, than rebuilding components.

At some point in the preceding discussion, you were probably asking yourself, "Do I really need to know all this stuff?" I believe the answer is "Yes" if you want to be an effective technical leader. If your language of choice is fourth generation (i.e., a 4GL such as Visual Basic) rather than say C++, even more thought must be put into the system architecture. You can create bad architecture with C++, but it's much easier with a 4GL. 4GLs certainly give you the user perspective right out of the box, but this is just the skin of your system. The term *rapid application development (RAD)* from the early days of Windows-based software development was originally used to describe the great speed in getting products to market using a 4GL. Today, "fast" has often come to mean bad software is delivered quickly. Perhaps RAD now stands for "rotten application development"? You must be concerned with the skeleton, nervous system, and internal organs to use organic terminology; otherwise, you'll contribute to the "fast and bad" school of architecture.

Some companies are so concerned with speed that they'll live with the long-term consequences of bad architecture. Maybe you're in such a company right now, near the end of a development cycle and new bugs have just been reported to you by the support group. You're trying to add new features, but you're forced to go back and fix bugs that may be a result of the fast and bad school of thought. If you had time to consider the underlying causes, you would soon conclude that "fast" really means you'll get into trouble fast with poor architecture. Building software isn't a 100-yard dash, it's a marathon. A pace that supports endurance is critical for quality production.

 Building software isn't a 100-yard dash, it's a marathon. A pace that supports endurance is critical for quality production.

How do you keep your focus organic, rather than synthetic, and create sound architecture, thus avoiding connecting fast with bad? You think organically by taking a new look at design principles and the sequence of steps you follow in the design phase of development.

A Fresh Look at Design

To differentiate design from architecture, think of yourself as a god who wants to create a living, conscious, and adaptable being. I hope this isn't too much of a stretch for you; if it isn't, you'll need to pay close attention to the next chapter on the dark side of leadership. Anyway, you can't design an organ without a framework into which it's placed. For example, your lungs wouldn't work well if they were hanging off your left arm—they're better situated in the chest cavity. I think you can guess where I'm going here. Design assumes the architecture is already established so the place for each component, which implements a system function, is known. This makes design the "fleshing out"[6] of the architecture and the appropriate development phase to pick a technology of implementation.

What? I'm a VB programmer and that's what I'm going to use in any application development program![7] Rethink, reboot, and look again. Can you say "silver bullet" or "golden hammer"? Every problem you face isn't a nail, so the tool you need isn't always going to be a hammer. Now, I know this falls back to the construction metaphor, and it works fine in this context. Remember, metaphors and analogies are but mere illustrations: Their function is similar to opening a window shade in a dark room so light can reveal the furnishings. In other words, an illustration isn't identical to the real thing; mapping from the illustration to the problem domain isn't one to one, to use a concept from topology. In an analogous way, design choices can only be made after the architecture is established.

In the sections to follow, you'll examine some of the steps you need to make in order to bring your carefully grown product to the harvest stage. I could be misleading you here. Is it a step-wise process?

Design Step 0

So, you have a great architecture and you're ready to design components. Great. Now polish up your OO skills and have at it. The first thing you want to do is prove the architecture, which I refer to as step 0 in order to emphasize its priority within the total scope of design efforts. This means prototyping in a new way. Rather than creating an extensive GUI, build enough low-level components with interface stubs and return values to prove the system architecture works from top to bottom. Any GUI you create should be just enough to stimulate the system or kick off a few processes. You wouldn't build a human without first proving that the brain can talk to the heart, would you? This is why cosmetic surgery is usually elective while brain surgery is not. Again, proving the architecture is primary. It may take more time than you'd like, but the benefits will pay handsomely if you do this up front. Sure, you'd rather be building the real system components, but what good would that be if when you hooked them all up, they didn't fit right or function properly?

---

6. See how well the organic metaphor works!

7. I've been using VB since version 1.0, so don't think I'm prejudiced against VB. For those who need help with VB-related architectural and design issues, see Billy S. Hollis, *Visual Basic 6 Design, Specification and Objects* (Upper Saddle River, NJ: Prentice Hall, 1999).

Your first responsibility in design is to prove the architecture.

I'll leave the details of this "proof of concept" exercise to the vast body of literature on architecture and design. Don't you, however, leave the proof of your architecture to someone else or, heaven forbid, beta testing. This is your job to accomplish through your team and the whole point of this book is that you can't shirk your responsibilities. Your first responsibility in design is to prove the architecture. This is why step 0 in the design process is to test your architectural plans for soundness. If you can answer yes to all the following questions, your gardening plans will *probably* bear good fruit.

- Does the architecture allow for subsystems of functions to be identified and not couple to other subsystems? Have you built objects that can stand on their own without too many helper objects?

- Is the "bird's-eye" view of your system plain enough that a salesperson, after being given a brief tutorial, could use it to demonstrate to customers how the software they should buy will work?

- Is hard-coding of system configuration parameters eliminated? For example, if a server name is changed or the domain in which it exists is renamed, will your software require a recompile or simply an edit of a configuration file?

You may have noticed the italicized word *probably* in the sentence preceding the list. The word was chosen because you must think through the forces that will affect your system 1 or 2 years out. No one can come up with a foolproof checklist without understanding your business environment. Again, if you know your business, you're the best forecaster of your software's future.

Why did I choose to use the term "forecaster," rather than "prognosticator"? My reasoning is as follows. "Prognosticator" is composed of two Greek words: *pro,* meaning before, and the root *gnosis,* which means knowledge. You can't really have true knowledge about the future, but like weather forecasters, the more you practice prediction, the better you'll get at anticipating the future. Remember, software is an art form emerging into a science. The first stage of any science is phenomenology. Relative to software development, this means you observe and document all the things that are happening to the process and look for patterns. You may soon develop theories about why things go right and why they go wrong.

Eventually you'll be able to establish laws for this thing we do called coding. When you get to that point, name them after yourself, publish a book, and enjoy your fame. Of course, this is what the design pattern and antipattern movement of the last decade was all about, so you've probably been preempted in your chance at fame.

No, seriously, you may not achieve international recognition, but within your company, you'll grow in stature if you can at least figure out what's broken in your approach to producing moneymaking software. Maybe your company doesn't have this problem. Great, more power to you. Most of us, however, haven't reached software nirvana yet and need help. You're the only one as technical leader that can give help where it's needed.

Design Step 1, 2, 3, 2, 1, 4 . . .

Okay, you're ready to really crank up the design machine. The rest of the work is uphill from this point on. Wait a minute, I meant to say *downhill*. No, I'm full of contradictions—design is a roller coaster, just like life. Enjoy the ride, relish the thrills, and keep on coming back. I believe the best design process can be likened to a roller coaster running along a spiral rather than a circular track. There is a beginning and an end, but you view the same territory from time to time. Contrast this with a waterfall ride: You go down a river, shoot out into space, have a big splash, and hope to emerge alive. Which kind of amusement park do you work in?

No, strike that; the word "amusement" comes from two other Greek words: *a,* meaning not, and *muse,* meaning to think. I insist you think about your design process and so does your boss. I'm just trying to give you a few word pictures to contrast the old waterfall development cycle with the highly touted iterative one. Obviously, I believe in the iterative method, even if sometimes it feels like an endless cycle. Nevertheless, what you must do, if you're to proceed productively along the design roller coaster, is constantly use the architectural plans for guidance while you move forward with the gardening project. Many books and seminars offer to teach you the "correct" design methods. Some of them are very helpful. The best design method is the one you and your team have proven over time to be successful in meeting your corporate goals. If you haven't had much success, don't take it too personally. We're all struggling. Some of us are getting better, and those that aren't usually are missing in action after a few years. It's a dog-eat-dog world, so buck up and determine to take a big bite out of your competition by improving your methods.

I just used a traditional Darwinian metaphor in the last paragraph alluding to survival of the fittest. This is a strong, nineteenth-century idea that we often apply to business culture and practice. Sometimes these ideas are appropriate; however, let's not forget other ideas from evolutionary biology, such as adaptation. An emerging twentieth (and now twenty-first) century approach to adaptation is currently being proposed by those who study complex systems behavior and the principles of self-organization in such systems. Stuart Kauffman, one of the leaders in this field writes, ". . .both biological evolution and technological evolution are processes attempting to optimize systems riddled with conflicting constraints."[8] Kauffman proposes the term "arrival of the fittest" to describe, in a more meaningful way, how organisms survive and thrive at the edge of chaos associated with complex systems. Others have taken up this insight and mapped the findings onto software development processes and practice.

James Highsmith's book, *Adaptive Software Development*, is a perfect example of applying complex systems theory to software development. Highsmith proposes an iterative cycle he calls the "Adaptive Development Life Cycle," which contains three chief components: collaboration, speculation, and learning. He states the following benefits of following this cycle:[9]

- Applications evolve in response to periodic feedback, resulting in a close match to customer requirements.

- Changing business needs are accommodated more easily.

- The development process adapts to the specified quality profile of the product.

- Customer benefits are generated earlier, for example, because the customer gets the application more quickly and can use it to increase revenue.

- Customers gain early confidence in the project.

What does all this have to do with design? You have a method in your company that works well, needs improvement, or is broken. Perhaps you need to throw it out and graft a new one in. You make the call. And this is my point: You must make the call, study your design processes, and adapt them to what works.

Descending now from the heights of theory—very good theory, I might add—I offer in the following section my humble opinion of some practical guidelines that I've found to work well for me in my particular corner of the software development world. I believe they're general enough that you can use them with any team or programming language.

---

8. Stuart Kauffman, *At Home in the Universe* (New York: Oxford University Press, 1995), p. 179.

9. James A. Highsmith III, *Adaptive Software Development* (New York: Dorset House Publishing, 2000), p. 40.

Guidelines for Design

If we insist on organic architecture, shouldn't we also have organic components? How in the world do you grow a software object? You do have to write some code—objects don't just spring into existence from some seed of an idea you whisper into your computer microphone. Actually, the seed idea isn't a bad one, if you consider a seed to embody a concept for coding that involves at least the following:

- Follow programming standards[10] appropriate for your language. This will ensure that the construction techniques of objects dictated by your architecture won't vary widely from programmer to programmer. (Yes, you can use the construction metaphor in this context.)

- Encourage strong cohesion within your objects. Objects aren't just containers for a bunch of procedures, they're organs that perform a specific function. The heart doesn't try to breathe and the lungs don't try to pump blood.

- Discourage coupling between your objects. Unless you have a significant other, coupling isn't a good thing because it makes maintenance a nightmare.[11] When objects are coupled, divorcing them later costs time and money.

You'll want to add to the preceding list as you gain experience from managing projects over time. It takes a while to uncover and establish best practices in the software business. I'm sure you have your favorite authors that have guided your software career, so stick with them if they've helped you. The Bibliography contains a good list of helpers if your library is short on books. You need to learn from those who've gone before you or who are traveling with you. You've chosen me as your companion today. I'm here to guide you into thinking about the reasons behind the principles and why they should be promoted by you, the technical master among many journeymen.

---

10. "Programming standards" are two words that speak volumes. They range from how to build a good procedure to insisting on only one exit point from a subroutine. The list could go on and on. My main point is this: Have standards and live by them.

11. A nightmare for a programmer is to be awake all night fixing your code because you changed one thing in one object and it broke three other things in several other objects.

A Guideline for Success

A fully stocked library is no guarantee of success for your technical leadership. It's a necessary condition, but not a sufficient one. You can line those fancy volumes up on your shelf to impress yourself (or others) all day long and this won't make you a better leader. What you must have is a mental library full of volumes of determination to be wise with your design processes. Wisdom comes with experience that has taught you to learn from mistakes. That's why my dad always told me to "chalk it up to experience" when I made a mistake. Of course, some mistakes led to a serious word of prayer, but often knowing that it was okay to make mistakes was a relief.

You must have a mental library full of volumes of determination to be wise with your design processes.

Are you afraid to make a mistake? Don't be so arrogant to think that you can lead a software team without making errors in judgment along the way. Mistakes will happen and you may pay for them dearly when deadlines pass without success. As your experience sharpens your skills, however, you'll begin to meet deadlines and the other departments will throw roses at your feet. Majestic music will play as you enter the building, and glorious choirs will sing your praises. Well, maybe this is a bit of an exaggeration. What will happen if you improve your department's performance is that you'll feel a sense of confidence about your job and grow in your passion for the work. Passion is contagious and it's something you should spread within your company.

Now to a specific point: What is this singular "guideline" I'm proclaiming? The same one I've promoted all along in this book: *focus and lead*. This chapter addresses the focus part and you must address the lead part. After all, you do have the "lead role" in your development organization, so act the part, be the part. Taking a cue from Shakespeare's *As You Like It*:

All the world's a stage,

And all the men and women merely players:

They have their exits and their entrances;

And one man in his time plays many parts,

His acts being seven ages . . .

It's the fifth age that Shakespeare describes that you should focus upon: ". . .justice . . . with eyes severe and beard of formal cut . . . full of wise saws and modern instances . . ." He describes here the mature leader, the person you must be to focus and lead. Knowledge is the beginning, wisdom must be pursued as experience hones your skills, leadership must be seized and maintained with consistency.

Cat Fight! Asleep at the Wheel

Greg was sort of a slob. I'm not just talking about his eating habits, though these were often an object of contention during late-night coding sessions. No, his carelessness in code matched his lack of concern for his body in many ways. His idea of a quick fix was to down a bowlful of nachos and salsa while he created yet another global constant to pass information back and forth between objects. Of course, none of us knew much better in those days, having spent the DOS decade doing whatever it took to make a program work. Object orientation was not in our vocabulary.

We had just begun creating a new serial communications program and the sales guys needed it to ship as soon as we could get it working. Back in those days, there was no testing department, just coders doing their best to meet sales driven deadlines. Greg had done a pretty good job for a number of years, so he was used to the pressure. At least I thought he was used to the pressure. He was even considered a valuable resource, mainly because he was the only programmer who knew how to maintain all the old code in applications that were no longer being sold.

The whole department was feeling the pressure back then. Windows 3.0 had just been released and we were doing our best to create applications while trying to master the idiosyncratic nature of the Windows API. We had it pretty good, though. Each programmer had his own office with a door that could be closed. This is where Greg got into trouble.

One day, while the CEO and vice president of sales were showing customers our facility, they wandered back to the engineering department. They were being introduced to the various engineers, and when it came time to meet Greg, they had to open his door to find him. And, boy, did they ever find him. He was sound asleep at his desk, feet propped up, junk food containers opened, and the place looking pretty bad. Needless to say, it was a bad scene. I wasn't there at this particular moment, so I only report what I was told.

And I was told a great deal. The VP of sales insisted that I fire him on the spot. The CEO agreed. I had little choice. I gave Greg the bad news in short order while he begged for forgiveness and a second chance. I told him it was out of my hands and how sorry I was, but before lunch, his desk was cleaned out and he was out the door.

An obvious lesson here is to not fall asleep on the job. This would be only common sense, of course. The deeper truth is that some programmers, sadly, just aren't cut out for the pressures of the job. When business moves at a fast pace, we have to keep up or get out. A hard lesson, but it really did happen. I hope Greg is doing well; I haven't seen or heard from him since.

The Code Police

Let's jump now from the fifteenth to the twentieth century when Elliot said, "This is the way the world ends / Not with a bang but a whimper."[12] Don't let this be an epitaph for your software. You'll avoid this by assuming the role of a code cop. In familiar terms, conduct frequent code reviews to ensure compliance with the architectural foundation you've laid and the design principles you've established. Recall a principle from Chapter 2: You can't have good expectations without frequent inspections. This is the reason why code reviews are necessary.

The challenge you face in doing consistent code review is twofold. Time works against you, and programmers can be very touchy about their code. We all have just 24 hours in each day. It isn't about making more time, it's about using what you have wisely. The topics of Chapter 4 on organizing for success should help you manage your time more effectively.

With regard to touchiness, your programmers just have to get over it. You're doing your job. Don't view a programmer's sensitivity about his or her code as a bad thing. It shows a sense of ownership and this is critical for quality software. If your team members don't react with a little emotion to your constructive criticism, do they really care about their product? It helps to have a thick skin as a technical leader. If yours is thin, just wait awhile and the bruising you'll take from not correcting faults will toughen you up.

Enforce the Laws

You and your team should be working as if engaged by the terms of a contract. The business specifications combined with your architectural vision are the contract's outline, and the design principles and techniques are the terms of the contract. As a software cop, you must monitor and correct software as it grows from the embryo to the fully formed adult. Maybe software never becomes an adult; it's probably better described as a teenager, considering the state of technology today. Perhaps we've moved to young adulthood, I don't know. Each

---

12. T.S. Elliot, *Collected Poems 1909-1962* (New York: Harcourt Brace Jovanovich, 1971), p. 82.

organization is unique and there are models to assess your software maturity.[13] Many good books have been written on measurement principles for software engineering. In *Applied Software Measurement*,[14] Capers Jones states that the companies most successful at bringing software development under control share six characteristics.

1. They measure software productivity and quality accurately.

2. They plan and estimate software projects accurately.

3. They have capable management and technical staffs.

4. They have good organization structures.

5. They have effective software methods and tools.

6. They have adequate staff office environments.

Of these six characteristics, Jones points to number 1 as the most significant. This is where code reviews have their affect.

You know the laws. You probably wouldn't be in your position as leader if you weren't good at following the rules for creating good code. Code reviews should be about sharing your experience with others less seasoned. Reviewing isn't like school, where a grade is given and you have to go home to mommy and get her to sign off on it. No, reviews should be like a graduate seminar, where keen minds are looking for the best ideas and weeding out the bad ones. Anyone who can't profit from correction isn't fit to stay in our profession. This may sound harsh, but if you allow the laws of development to be only theory, then you'll have to live with some pretty harsh software.

Common Violations

In this brief survey of guiding design principles, I've touched on three areas: standards, cohesion, and coupling. Look for violations related to these topics. The following are some brief examples.

---

13. See Humphrey, op. cit., p. 5, or The Software Engineering Institute's Capability Maturity Model for examples.

14. Capers Jones, *Applied Software Measurement* (New York: McGraw-Hill, 1991), p. 1.

Violation of Standards

Are comments in all the right places so someone new to a module can see who's been in the code? If you're trying to verify that a bug has been fixed, can you tell by the trail of comments how the bug was fixed? Comments should explain the why and how of the code, with major emphasis on the why. The code itself documents how, but comments help explain what was in the mind of the coder as he or she created the objects. To pick up after someone else, you must know why he or she went down a particular path. Comments are the guideposts.

> *Comments should explain the why and how of the code, with major emphasis on the why. The code itself documents how, but comments help explain what was in the mind of the coder as he or she created the objects.*

Naming conventions. Have they been followed? Can you tell right away the scope of a variable by just looking at the name? It can be maddening to debug code where you have to spend 30 minutes just trying to figure out the scope of a suspected bad parameter. Are the procedure names so long that they make you wish Windows never supported long filenames? Are they so short that you need a glossary just to decipher the routine names? Balance is obviously needed, and perhaps a lesson in grammar that shows the difference between a verb and a noun. You may be tired of always seeing routines that retrieve data begin with "get" but you'll never be mistaken that they're getting something. The same could be said about "set." Often, simplicity is elegant and practical.

The purpose of naming conventions and code comments is to provide a common language and a guide as we write code. In a book of poems about a common language, the great American poet Adrienne Rich writes:

The technology of silence
The rituals, etiquette

The blurring of terms
silence not absence

of words or music or even
raw sounds

Silence can be a plan
rigorously executed

> *the blueprint to a life*
>
> *It is a presence*
> *It has a history a form*
>
> *Do note confuse it*
> *With any kind of absence*[15]

Don't allow your team to engage in a "technology of silence." Make those cats comment and name things correctly. Sometimes the comments are missing not through haste, but because they aren't sure why they did what they did—they may have just copied code from a library and hoped it would work. Perhaps they leave in the comments from the author of the copied library. This should be a warning sign to you. Of course, the most obvious reason for missing comments is sloth and a lack of pride in what has been built. It will take more than a few "code tickets" to correct this. This might reflect an underlying problem with the coder that should be dealt with on a more serious administrative level.

Other common violations of standards include routines with multiple exit points and, if your language supports it, the use of the dreaded "GoTo." (VBers can be forgiven here until .NET makes Try, Catch, and Finally a part of their vocabulary.) Lack of frequent error handling is another common mistake in programming. Some coders think they're so good that error handling is a waste of their time. Perhaps an error trap at the top of a call chain is enough in some cases, but a failure to anticipate potential sources of errors reveals a lack of strategic thinking on the part of the coder.

Recalling the programmer personality traits described in Chapter 1 should help you identify other areas of transgressions specific to each of your coders. The list could go on and on depending on your programming environment[16]—my purpose here is to remind you that as a code cop, you must also take names of those who violate your list!

Weak Cohesion and Strong Coupling

You can link these two areas of violations together, because one usually results in the other. As you trace through a procedure, do you find yourself branching hither

---

15. Adrienne Rich, "Cartographies of Silence" from *The Dream of a Common Language* (New York: W.W. Norton, 1978), p. 17.

16. For VBers I recommend James D. Foxall, *Practical Standards for Microsoft Visual Basic* (Redmond, WA: Microsoft Press, 2000). For other languages, you have many resources from which to choose, including the following "classic" for C: Steve Maguire, *Writing Solid Code* (Redmond, WA: Microsoft Press, 1993). See the Bibliography for more listings.

and yon? A typical term for this is fan-in and fan-out, a description of the coupling between procedures. If the degree of fan-out is large, a procedure must use many others to perform its function, which is not desirable. On the other side, fan-in is good because it reflects good encapsulation. You can sum up violations in the cohesion and coupling arenas by measuring the general lack of compliance with OO principles in general.

Can you create a block diagram of object hierarchies from studying the code? Does it look like a logical relationship or do the arrows go all over the place? Can you determine the parentage of objects? These are the types of questions to ask and answer during code reviews. Again, note the weaknesses and then do something about them. Don't try to fix the code yourself. You'll be tempted when it's close to a deadline, but your team members will benefit greatly from you making them correct the problems. This does take more time up front, but by now, you've certainly learned that if you don't have time to do it right, when will you have time to do it over?

Go to Jail, Go Directly to Jail, Do Not Pass Go

When you discover violations, coding should stop until they are corrected. The longer you allow violations to persist, the quicker your code is headed toward the compost heap.[17] If other coders see that someone has gotten away with poor code, human nature will lead them to do the same. If gun control means using both hands, code review means using your position as boss to stop violators in their tracks.

Writing and reading about code review is easy, but doing something about it is hard. We all know the things that break code and make maintenance a royal pain in the neck. If you're new to the job of managing and leading, you'll find it hard at first to act when you know you should. Your reluctance will stem from your lack of confidence as a leader no matter how technically skilled you are. It's one thing to sit around with a group of peers and discuss code problems; it's an entirely different thing when you're the boss. You'll be expected to take action when the whole team knows the code is weak. Sometimes, the anticipation of finding problems, knowing you should take action, will make you look the other way. I've said plenty in these pages about what *ought* to be done when problems arise. Turning the *ought* into *will* is not going to happen just because you read this book on management. Something else has to happen in your character for this transformation to occur. This is the topic of the next and last sections in this chapter.

---

17. See Hunt and Thomas, op. cit., for a great metaphor related to software entropy called "Don't Live with Broken Windows." I'm trying to persuade you here to buy their book—it's one of the good ones.

Philosophy in Action

A correct philosophy is sterile unless practiced. Attitude and action should fit together like a hand in glove. In a phrase, *follow through* on what you know to be correct. Many people, and this includes programmers and managers, often know the correct principles to follow but just don't act on their knowledge. Is there a secret to putting philosophy into action before the consequences of inaction sneak up on you? I believe there isn't a secret, but there is more dialogue we can have that might persuade you to get up off the couch (my term for being lazy) and do something. If I were to list the consequences of inaction based on the principles described in this chapter, would that help?

Follow through on what you know to be correct.

Bad architecture, or architecture by accident, leads to the following:

- Maintenance nightmares and time delays (see dollar signs here) in adding new features.

- Programmers who don't want to do code maintenance because the system is hard to understand and they aren't sure where to start when fixing bugs or adding new features.

- Bloated code as objects grow like lava flows. Executable file sizes increase while performance decreases.

Poor design leads to the following:

- Every object looks like it was created by a different programmer because standards were not followed.

- When you change one thing you break two others.

- Duplicate code is found in many places. To change one function means searching for all the other instances where things must also be changed.

I could add to each of the previous lists, but, folks, this is getting real scary, isn't it? Are you frightened enough to take the actions recommended in the preceding pages to prevent these Bad Things?

Maybe you are and maybe, if you're like me, you need to think a bit more about this subject. After all, the world is filled with people with all the correct intentions but still performing all the wrong actions or just being passive.

A Case Study of Philosophy in Action: Leonardo da Vinci

While I'm not a big fan of the positive thinking school, a work about Leonardo caught my attention a few years ago. It was a book that promised to teach you how to think like Leonardo. Now, Leonardo is so famous that we just use his first name. Bill Gates paid a bunch of the money he earned from us for software to purchase a number of Leonardo's original journals. Need I say more? Leonardo was one smart guy. If you study Leonardo's life, and to do this you have to do more than just read a self-help book, you'll find that he had a philosophy of life that guided his creative genius. His philosophy was summed up by Michael Gelb as follows:[18]

- An insatiably curious approach to life and an unrelenting quest for continuous learning.

- A commitment to test knowledge through experience, persistence, and a willingness to learn from mistakes.

- The continual refinement of the senses, especially sight, as the means to enliven experience.

- A willingness to embrace ambiguity, paradox, and uncertainty.

- The development of the balance between science and art, logic and imagination. "Whole-brain" thinking.

- The cultivation of grace, ambidexterity, fitness, and poise.

- A recognition of and appreciation for the interconnectedness of all things and phenomena. Systems thinking.

---

18. Guess what, I did read this self-help book. Michael J. Gelb, *How to Think Like Leonardo da Vinci* (New York: Dell Publishing, 1998), p. 9.

Perhaps Leonardo would've made a fine software architect. He certainly was a great artist and engineer. These principles are admirable and thought-provoking, worthy of emulating.

If you review Leonardo's contributions to the technology of his day, you'll be mightily impressed. How could one man create all the things he drew about in his journals or actually built in reality? He obviously did it by following through on his philosophy. What was it about his philosophy that produced action? I'm convinced it's not any one thing in particular, but rather the ways the various tenants of his thinking were balanced against each other.

Note, for instance, his quest for learning as compared with his willingness to tolerate uncertainty. See how he believed experience was the best teacher and at the same time worked on improving his "vision" in order to increase his powers of observation. Leonardo was also a great teacher of younger artists and he spent much of his time inspecting the work of his apprentices. Observe how he was perhaps the first to employ systems thinking, something we try to do every day in software design. This means envisioning the plan all the way through to its completion. This relates directly to why a system's architecture must be proven before it's fully realized in all the glory of its component subsystems.

In other works on Leonardo, you'll discover that he was an extremely fit man physically. He didn't let his body slow down his mind. I can only get so personal here, but is your body up to the task your mind knows must be done? If it isn't, you may need to work on your physical state while you improve your mental one. You're the only one who can determine what in your work life is keeping you from acting on a correct philosophy.

I recommend that you study Leonardo on your own for inspiration to help focus your mind on following through on what you know to be the correct course of action. Stories of many other modern leaders in our industry and others can also spur you on to action.[19] As you read outside the software industry, you may be surprised that other leaders have faced challenges exactly like the ones you face every day in your job. Biographies might just be a nice supplement to your nightstand reading selection. It certainly will balance out your current reading, where authors of books such as ADO 2.1, MTS MSMQ with VB and ASP, and HTML 4.0 apparently think that acronyms on the book spine are a catchy marketing technique.[20] Who knows, maybe the biography of Judy Garland will remind you that you aren't in Kansas anymore as a programmer who leads other programmers.

---

19. See the excellent book on the unfolding of the power of ambition. James Champy and Nitin Nohria, *The Arc of Ambition* (New York: Perseus Books, 2000).

20. I guess it is a good marketing ploy, because I bought them.

A Dose of Reality

You must acknowledge that you'll fail to put into action every time those principles of technical leadership you know to be correct. Leonardo, when he died, felt that his life's work was unfinished. This is reality. Nevertheless, I challenge you to improve upon your reality by striving to put into practice a bit more each week those philosophies you've concluded are correct. Knowing and doing always create the greatest polarities in our work life. It isn't just a contest between epistemology and ontology, either. It's the very fact that we're predisposed to inaction until we finally say, "I've had enough of all these problems in my code!" to finally do something about it.

A Bird's-Eye View

Rising above the details and viewing the results of your technical leadership, are you satisfied with what you've helped create? The following list is a summary of what we've surveyed in this chapter. It gives you an opportunity to evaluate the effects of your role as technical leader.

- Have you consistently maintained your role as technical leader? This doesn't mean your ideas were always the best, but rather that you worked to bring the best ideas to the fore and act on them.

- Has the architecture of your products proven to be extensible and maintainable? The answer to this question can only be determined after version 1.0 is out in the marketplace and you evaluate the effort required to produce version 2.0 and its success.

- Have your designs produced reusable components? Can any one of your staff pick up the work of another and perform maintenance or enhance the functionality? The answers you give to these two questions measure how successful you've been in leading and managing design efforts.

- Do you address code deficiencies immediately during the development phase of your projects, or do you have a backlog of code that needs refactoring?

- Have you seen improvements in your staff as you corrected their short-comings?

- Do you talk a good talk or walk the talk? Pardon the cliché, but without action, philosophy is idle babble.

In the spirit of managing the manager, ask yourself these questions frequently. Of course, you have to answer them too. Technical leadership is grown from the soil of your knowledge and nourished by your willingness to learn from your mistakes as you rejoice in your successes.

 Technical leadership is grown from the soil of your knowledge and nourished by your willingness to learn from your mistakes as you rejoice in your successes.

Leading to Excellence

Putting philosophy into action can be hard. In the next chapter, as you look at the darker side of leadership, you'll be reminded of the consequences of having the wrong philosophy of leadership. It's amazing how sometimes those with the wrong ideas can accomplish so much trouble. At least they figured out how to put their philosophies into action. Again, I urge you to rethink your thinking and measure your leadership by the degree of "follow-through" that you accomplish on any given day.

CHAPTER 7

Leadership in Eclipse

Yoda said, "Beware of the dark side." He gave a fair warning: Leadership can have a dark side or, to put it in terms that matter outside of the realm of science fiction, leadership can be ineffective or destructive. In my experience, I've seen leadership become dark—that is, shedding no light for others to follow—due to styles of management that create an environment where leadership can't take root. The results of these inappropriate management practices leads to what might be called an eclipse of leadership, and it can affect or afflict you, or, heaven forbid, your boss. These styles creep up on leaders like shadows, sometimes dancing around an otherwise strong leader and affecting his or her judgment. Effective leadership then becomes eclipsed by the shadows cast by bad management styles.

The tone of the preceding chapters assumed that you could change practices that lead to ineffective management and learn new techniques that enable you to become a strong leader. Sometimes, people can't change, and we must learn to cope with them like a used car: as is, no warranty, no money back. I don't believe you're one of these unchangeable people, or else you wouldn't have made it through the pages of this book where I've challenged your assumptions about management and leadership. Nevertheless, we all suffer from some degree of stubbornness or a lack of willingness to change, and this can lead to failures in our job. Yoda's opinion was that fear leads to the dark side. Maybe he was right. I do believe that fear of failure is behind the shadows I discuss in this chapter. Realize that fear can be conquered and doesn't have to result in you employing tactics that mask this fear with a counterproductive management style.

The Face of Darkness

If fear leads to darkness, a truly dark face of leadership was demonstrated during the awful reign of Hitler, where the noble German idea of "The Leader" (der Furer) was perverted into a sick and sadistic nightmare for Western civilization. I take from these grim pages of history a lesson: Destructive leadership can lead to horrible consequences for people. In a similar way, though not of such historic proportions, leading a group of developers down the wrong path can hurt their productivity, ruin your company's software, and poison your staff's ability to act on the goals you lay out for them to accomplish. The ancient Jews had a proverb you may have heard: "Where there is no vision, the people perish." The Hebrew word translated as "perish" in older, less informed translations has the more accurately translated meaning of "being unrestrained and without leadership."[1] This is what happens when you lose your way as a manager. People metaphorically scatter and, to herd cats, as I said in Chapter 1, you must strive to get them moving in the same direction. This is why leadership is the central theme of this book. To have a dark face as a leader is to cease to be a leader.

I encourage you to examine the dark styles of management presented in this chapter and watch for similar patterns in your own administrative activities. These styles are the shadows that will eclipse your leadership. Sometimes just recognizing the problem is half of the solution. The other half takes a bit more digging, but you can improve your style when you realize how damaging to you and your staff these bad traits can be. Becoming motivated to change will lead you to the other half of the solution: acting to correct your behavior. I believe you're motivated because you've persisted with this book up to this point. Stick with me—I have to deal with the shadows from the dark side every day myself.

Antipatterns in Management

In Chapter 1, you had fun looking at various facets of programmer personality types. This chapter takes a similar approach, although I don't think you'll have nearly as much fun. The method will be like antipatterns in psychology, for those of you familiar with antipatterns in design. Examples of what not to do are the theme of antipatterns. If you recognize yourself in these antipatterns, stop it. If you see your boss, beware without being judgmental. This advice may seem simplistic, but it will have to do for now. I'll have more to say in a while about coping and corrective strategies in the context of the problems this chapter analyzes.

Many managers, who should be leaders, may exhibit a mixture of the styles described next with varying degrees of intensity. I'm not talking about true evil in discussing bad leadership styles; no moral judgments are being made. What's important is that for whatever reasons, within certain individuals, destructive styles of management emerge and are a reality in the workplace, and they all

---

1.   Compare the King James version for Proverbs 29:18 where "perish" is used with the New American Standard version where "unrestrained" is given as the translation of the Hebrew. The original Hebrew, transliterated as "para," is always used in the context of leadership.

eclipse leadership. Your job, in recognizing these antipatterns, is not to become a member of the helping profession, but rather to become adept at spotting and coping with these types of managers. Well, I do encourage you to help yourself. The purpose of this book is to prime you for leadership; just realize you can't fix other people. This one simple fact will help you immensely in dealing with difficult people.

> *Realize you can't fix other people. This one simple fact will help you immensely in dealing with difficult people.*

Adapting several ideas from the antipattern movement,[2] I weave the following topics in the presentation of dark management styles:

- **Symptoms and consequences:** Taking a phenomenological viewpoint, you can't get inside the head of someone who exhibits these patterns, but you can note his or her behavior. You can get inside your own head if you're afflicted with one of these antipatterns, however, and I encourage you to do so.

- **Variations:** This topic refers to the fact that the pattern may have several manifestations, but at the root, the problem is always the same: a style of management that eclipses leadership.

- **Exceptions:** There will be few exceptions, but when there are I note them. Can you every really excuse or permit a management style to persist that doesn't create an environment for leadership to govern? Only in rare cases will this be true, as you'll see later.

- **Solutions:** This topic explores how to bring some light to the darkness. This may only apply to you, since you can't fix someone else, but understanding how to "refactor" your style is critical to getting back on track as a good leader. More general solutions are discussed in a later part of the chapter, but I point out some quick corrective actions you can take in the context of the specific dark style being discussed.

2.　See Brown et al, *AntiPatterns in Project Management*, op. cit.

Each antipattern style described begins with a heading that describes the "face of darkness" in a concise manner. I've placed these antipatterns as stand-alone sections in this chapter; they're of such weight that they can be studied within their own context.

You'll notice several plays on words in the section titles that follow. While attempting to hold your attention, I also believe shadows, light, darkness, and eclipse all lend themselves to illustrating one central fact: A manager who can't lead sheds no light on the path his or her team must tread.

The Shadow of Micromanagement

A variety of individuals exhibit the much-maligned practice of micromanaging. It's maligned for a very good reason: Micromanagement is the polar opposite of good management where delegation with inspection is the theme. Micromanagers can drive themselves crazy, in addition to those who work for them. We all have a tendency to be like this under certain conditions. For example, near the end of a development cycle you've found out that old Joe forgot one task. You'll be tempted to do it for him if the hour is late and you're the only one around. Is this a forgivable exception? Maybe, but if you allow it, it teaches those who work for you that if they don't get their job done it's okay, because the boss will fix it. You'll set a bad precedent under these circumstances.

Part of the challenge for technical leaders is that we're usually very good at the "down in the trenches" work and may believe we can get the job done better and faster than those to whom we've assigned the work. After all, many of us were promoted into management because of the very fact that we were good at software construction. However, coding isn't our primary job. A manager's first priority is to accomplish work through others. A leader's first job is to create an environment where management by delegation really works. The micromanager fails at being a leader and a manager. You may note that I didn't use the term "microleader" because you can't call a micromanager any type of leader—he or she doesn't have time to lead. Micromanagers are too busy minding other people's work. Call them "microscopic leaders" if you want. It will take a microscope to find any evidence of the marks of their leadership.

 A manager's first priority is to accomplish work through others.
A leader's first job is to create an environment where management by delegation really works.

This "face of darkness" is the most common in the workplace. Several variations of micromanagers are as follows:

The Know-It-All. This manager believes he or she knows everything there is to know about the work, the company, and your specific assignments. The know-it-all considers him- or herself a polymath, a term that can no longer be applied since about the seventeenth century. Now I wish I could be a polymath, and so do you, but it isn't possible today: The scope of accumulated technical knowledge is too deep and broad. Some think that being good at Web surfing makes them smart or informed. Certainly, the Internet is a tool for knowledge, but while the information age has arrived, the knowledge age isn't here for everyone. Don't mistake your grasp of technology or your superior puzzle-solving abilities as reasons for doing everything yourself.

The Dictator. "My way or the highway" is this manager's mantra. The dictator not only wants to tell you what to do, but how to do it. Of course, we all have to watch out for this tendency. Part of leadership is to show your team how to accomplish a task, but not often at a level that creates a loss of ownership about the work. The danger of a dictator is that he or she creates such an atmosphere of dread that no one can perform to the best of their abilities—they're too busy watching out for the boss' latest edict or the consequences of having shown some independence. Leading by dictatorship has rarely proven successful politically—do you think it will work for you in business? You shouldn't. Leadership means creating an environment where programmers want to take pride in their work, and they must be given latitude in how they accomplish their tasks for pride to lead to excellence. Setting limits on the latitude given is part of good management. Stifling freedom is the job of the dictator.

The General. This manager is the master of the "command and control" school of software development. Very much like the dictator, but a little bit more standoffish. This is the way all business was conducted at one time, based on the military model. It might work in the military context, where everyone wears uniforms as an affirmation of being part of a vast human machine to be commanded. Many large software projects, usually conducted for giant corporations or the federal government, have employed this methodology. The origin of the software engineering approach to development occurred in this environment. In my opinion, this approach doesn't work well for managing or leading today's programmers because herding cats is a different task than commanding troops. They don't wear uniforms (other than ratty T-shirts, sometimes), and they love to flaunt their independence. If you think of yourself as a general and your programmers as soldiers, your battles will be between you alone and the enemy. Your troops will probably be off in a corner somewhere, having a café latte. "Collaboration" is the current buzzword for countering this style, and it has currency because it's the correct approach. In time of war, there's rarely time for collaboration; however, there's never a time in software development when collaborating is unwarranted.

The root cause of micromanaging is a belief on the part of the manager that no one can really do the work as well as him- or herself. Combine this belief with a fear of failure and you can understand why some leaders fall into this trap. Sure, you want to succeed, but at what cost to yourself or your staff are you willing to manage every detail of your employees' work? Why did you hire your staff in the first place if you're going to do their work for them? You'll reach a limit of productivity if you attempt micromanagement for very long. The limits will be measured by your own ability to do everyone else's job, as well as yours, and the limit of your staff to live with the knowledge that their talents aren't really needed.

Table 7-1 shows a comparison between a micromanager and a good leader.

Table 7-1. Micromanager versus Leader

MICROMANAGER	LEADER
What do I need to do today?	How do I help others succeed today?
What happens if I fail?	How can I involve others to help mitigate the risk of failure?
Why can't my staff follow my directions?	What can I do to give clearer directions?

You should be able to think of other characteristics that distinguish a leader from a micromanager as you examine your management style. We all fall into this pattern from time to time. Notice the focus of the "I" pronoun in Table 7-1. The micromanager turns inward, while the leader turns toward others in a constructive way. Move out of the shadow of micromanagement into the daylight of leadership by considering the value of using others without the bridles on. You have a staff; let them do their job.

Cat Fight! The Owner Who Couldn't Let Go

Once upon a time, about a decade ago, a small software consulting company made a good living for its owner. The staff was small, loyal, and enjoyed their scope of work and solving problems for their several clients. The owner wanted more. No one blamed him for wanting a larger company with more clients. "Grow or die," he thought. He began to bring in consultants who could expand his business. Things did begin to grow, even though the owner was slow to expand his staff. He had high standards and not just anybody off the street met his criteria for a loyal employee. Finally, he found a consultant willing to become an employee and take over the day-to-day management of development so he, the owner, could be the visionary entrepreneur. A sound plan, and, on paper, it looked like a winning combination.

The new manager took to the job with delight and began to learn the existing business, and become familiar with the staff and their various projects. The owner began to dream of expanding the horizons of the company and sought out new clients. Everything was looking good for a few months, and expectations were high.

The new development manager instituted weekly staff meetings after a few months. This was a new feature in the company. The new manager also created an internal software product for tracking programmer tasks and project deadlines. The developers seemed responsive to these new initiatives and showed signs of liking the new procedures. In the past, the owner simply directed the staff by the seat of his pants, so to speak. This had worked well for many years, but growth dictated that a more formal approach be adopted. The owner, of course, sat in on the staff meetings every week. This is where the trouble began.

Many decisions or processes the new manager put into place were questioned publicly by the owner during staff meetings and often overridden in private. After a few months of staff meetings that ended up never accomplishing anything, the new manager felt like a fifth wheel. Deadlines were still being missed and the programmers were confused as to who was in charge of their work life.

During this time of change, several new employees were added to the staff. The hiring process was a real nightmare. When the new manager found someone he liked, the owner inevitably didn't agree. Bending to the owner's wishes, these new people were brought on board but they didn't last. One thing the owner was happy to leave to the new manager was the firing process. The new manager at least had an area in which he could act.

Soon, greener pastures beckoned the new manager. After a very minor struggle, he left to go where he could make a difference and feel that his talents could be fully exercised.

This story is one of the classic micromanager, in this case the owner of the company. It illustrates the effect of micromanagement upon those underneath the leader who's afraid to relinquish control. People will leave an organization if they feel they aren't needed and they aren't able to exercise their skills and judgment.

Advice for the Micromanager

Are there any exceptions to micromanaging your staff? Perhaps only when a deadline looms, it's late at night, the code is due in the morning, and you can make a quick fix. Any other time you engage in this style you'll find it limiting your opportunities to lead. Leadership attempts to create self-motivated staff. Part of this process is to create ownership for success and failure, and opportunities for creative expression. Micromanaging thwarts these areas.

How do you fix yourself if you're afflicted with this style? One thing to examine is why you feel you must micromanage. Is your staff truly incompetent and not capable of performing their assignments? If this is true, you need to replace them. However, if your fear of failure makes you look over everyone's shoulder, you have deeper areas of personal expectations to inspect. No one wants to fail. We all do sometimes. This is reality, and once you accept this you'll be on your way to a more balanced work style.

How do you adjust your expectations to accept the possibility of failure? I believe you must examine your efforts to succeed as thoroughly as you do the results. It may be human to fail, but a good leader usually fails when his efforts to achieve success are less than what is required. A lack of effort isn't a forgivable sin, while a failed result may be. Put your efforts into motivating your staff to be productive, rather than contaminating your staff with your anxieties about failing. Motivate them with the goal of how good success can be, rather than how dreadful failure will feel. No one really needs to be reminded that failure has bad consequences. You aren't telling anyone new things when you do this. Focus on the goal of success and trust your staff to work toward this end.

 A lack of effort isn't a forgivable sin, while a failed result may be.

Trust—a difficult word in the context of software project deadlines often so rigid that the smallest slipup can result in disaster. The deeper issue about trust is contained in the answer to the question, "Do you trust your staff?" You may have hired competent programmers, but only time and experience can build trust. Trust entails risk: risk of failure, risk of disappointment, and other such unpleasant emotions. There isn't any way to make the building of trust an easy job, but it's the most critical factor in eliminating your need to micromanage. These matters take time, time you may not feel you have. The alternative to micromanaging, however, will ultimately lead to more time, and time that's wasted.

Building trust between you and your staff is a two-way street. You must earn their trust by being dependable, supportive, and always available for their needs. Going the other way on the street, trusting them begins in small steps. Establish a "baby-step" plan: Give them a small, noncritical task to do all on their own and see how they do. As they accomplish more and more independently, without your direct supervision, your trust of them will grow and their feeling of being needed will blossom. As I said, this takes time but the benefits are well worth the cost.

Radio Shack has an interesting principle they teach their staff: Do what is right, even when no one is looking. This is what you're after: a staff that does the right thing because they're properly motivated and responsible. As trust grows between you and your staff, you'll have programmers who do the right thing because they've learned that this leads to the best results for them and the company. A leader is always working to create this kind of environment; a micromanager destroys such an atmosphere at work.

How do you respond to your manager if he or she is a micromanager? You have two choices: Let them crash and burn all on their own, or try to demonstrate to them that you can really do the job. Maybe you never have a chance to prove your abilities—this would be a rarity if you were hired to do a specific job and never given at least one opportunity to prove your worth. When your micromanaging boss gives you a task, excel at it beyond their expectations. Outstanding efforts and results will catch the attention of most micromanagers. They're struggling with the fear of failure, so if you show them the glory of success, you may assuage their fears. If you can engage in an open dialogue with your boss, suggest that you'll help him or her out by working hard and he or she really doesn't have to look over your shoulder. Anything you can do to demonstrate to your boss that you're competent and working to make him or her look good will help fend off micromanagement.

Dimming the Light: Unfocused Managers

This antipattern in management reveals a lack of organizational skills, coupled sometimes with a shortage of applied intelligence. Some might say the manager is ditzy or, to be a bit more descriptive, an airhead, a bit silly, one sandwich short of a lunch, with a room to rent upstairs, and so on. The manager might also appear to have his or her mind on something other than work most of the time in spite of a keen intelligence. Sometimes the lack of focus is the result of inexperience. You might find this individual a bit entertaining, but put him or her in charge and no one's in charge: a dangerous idea for software developers.

I've seen several forms of this unfocused style. More no doubt exist, but my personal observations bring to mind these variations:

The Scarlet O'Hara. In the classic 1939 movie *Gone with the Wind*, this character was fond of repeating the following line when faced with an immediate difficulty needing resolution: "I'll think about that tomorrow." I'm not talking about women in this antipattern; in fact, I've worked for more men who are Scarlets and, in my experience, I've never found a woman with these characteristics in management. These individuals are unable, or unwilling, to focus on the immediate tasks and decisions at hand. They either consider them too complicated or are so afraid of making a mistake that they make no decision. As you've no doubt learned, making no decision is often the same as letting others make it, or worse, letting the consequences of indecision force a choice.

The Just Passing Through. A ladder climber. Someone on his or her way to bigger and better things and just doing time in middle management. They might spend most of their time relating their ambitions to you rather than focusing on the project you're working on. When asked to make a decision, they'll usually ask, "What do you think?" Certainly, it's okay to ask for opinions, but a real leader has strong opinions because he or she is focused on the mission of the moment as well as the long-term goals. Those passing through will seldom invest themselves in you or the project of the day. This is a contradiction for these managers. They want to succeed so they can move on, but they'll never succeed unless they focus. Daydreaming about the future doesn't make it come any faster. Realizing that your work each day is your life's work will make an imagined, bright future a reality.

The New Kid on the Block. An inexperienced leader, one who is so new to managing others that he or she doesn't know what to do first. These managers aren't even thinking about becoming a leader; they're just trying to cope with the overwhelming administrative details of their new job. They may even believe they're a leader just by virtue of title, rather than reputation. Setting priorities for new kids on the block is tough because all tasks seem of equal weight. They sometimes end up like an airplane climbing too steeply without sufficient power—that is, they stall.

The consequences of the unfocused style are many—among them, missed deadlines and a staff uncertain about the details of their assignments. Often, the unfocused manager will establish so many new initiatives that by the time you're halfway through one project it's already obsolete. Sometimes, a general lack of seriousness about work afflicts this manager. I've seen these unfocused leaders tell great stories on many topics (usually unrelated to the day's work), and I've enjoyed the storytelling but left with the feeling, "What was that all about?"

There's a time to have fun at work, but if it takes the place of clearly directing your staff, in the end no one is going to be having any fun.

In the excellent work, *AntiPatterns in Project Management*, Brown, McCormick, and Thomas write:

> *. . . many project managers do not have leadership experience and assume that management is a proscriptive activity. A project death spiral can occur when a critical event is not managed properly, either due to the inexperience and lack of skills of the project manager, or because someone who has not been empowered to make significant decisions acts a conduit for higher management decisions in the absence of any knowledge of project reality. Software development plans and processes cannot predict all the possibilities that can occur and therefore cannot be followed to the letter to overcome unpredicted problems. A project manager and other managers need to be flexible to ensure that when risks are identified they can be tackled in a flexible, pragmatic, and effective manner. Once chaos starts it is very difficult to restrain.*[3]

The unfocused manager contributes to the "death spirals" by allowing decisions to occur without forethought tempered by experience. Procrastination is usually a hallmark of unfocused managers, and chaos is their legacy.

Procrastination is usually a hallmark of unfocused managers, and chaos is their legacy.

Are you unfocused? Is it because you're afraid of making a decision, or are you just confused about the details of what your job is about? These are common concerns, and they can be addressed with careful attention to the organizational aspects of your administrative life. Review the materials in the preceding chapters again. I've been building a foundation into which you can plant your leadership roots. Give yourself time, but be unrelenting in your efforts to grow, and you'll begin to get a handle on your job.

If you're passing through the ranks of management, realize that the road to the top is paved with success and this only comes from a care and concern about the job at hand. Schemes and hopes won't lead to your future promotion. A solid performance record will, and as you learn to do your current job well, you may find your ambitions moderated or more manageable. Very few organizations promote based on eagerness to climb the corporate ladder.

---

3.   Brown et al, *AntiPatterns in Project Management*, op. cit., p. 39, 40.

I can think of no reason to excuse an unfocused management style. There may be reasons why it exists and sure, from time to time we all feel a bit fuzzy about what we should do, but regaining focus is critical to being a great leader. The "regaining" part can be tough; it may require a break to recharge your batteries, so to speak. A vacation or "mental health day" might even be in order. Whatever can clear your mind so you can get back to the necessary command of the details is worth the effort.

How do you work with your manager if they are unfocused? Try applying micromanagement in reverse. Suggest good solutions to problems. Do those tasks you know need to be done, especially when your assignments are unclear. You may have a lot of time on your hands anyway if your manager is not on task. Use this time wisely. Who knows, maybe you'll be promoted. Of course, this isn't the main goal, but getting your department's job done well is the goal. If the boss isn't up to the task, the staff can make the difference if they care about the company.

The Blinding Light of Misapplied Genius

Somewhat common in our industry is the situation where a very good programmer is promoted to management but has zero aptitude for management or leadership. This programmer can sit at his desk all day long and churn out great code, but try to get him to impart his skills to someone else and he's at a complete loss. In a design meeting, this manager is brilliant at the whiteboard and often unable to make others understand the concepts he diagrams with such ease. His working definition of consensus is that everyone should agree with his ideas.

Genius comes in many flavors, and while I won't delineate the variations because there are so many, I must point out that all geniuses have one thing in common: a unique ability to focus. They usually focus on the technology rather than the peopleware, and this is where the problems in leadership arise. You have to do both as a leader of programmers, but your primary focus must be on the people who work with the technology. Code doesn't magically appear when you insert the programming language installation CD. It requires a fine mind freed from the intellectual tyranny of a manager.

The genius as manager will often create an entire programming framework for the team to use in the creation of any product. It may often be complicated and difficult to apply to simple projects, but he insists that it must be used so "our code has a common foundation." The framework will be unique to his genius, even if commercial products that could accomplish the same functions with good documentation and flexibility are available. I've worked for these geniuses in my career and often learned some good technical tricks from them. I never learned a useful thing about management from these individuals, other than the truth of this antipattern of the misapplication of great intelligence.

I worked for one genius in a past job where his software framework required a call chain of 15 procedures before you could unload a user interface. The framework had been built for a previous product and he insisted I use it for a new product, even though it didn't really fit the needs of the solution. I spent more time learning how the framework functioned, and ways to get around it, than writing new code to get the software to alpha stage. Others on my team had similar experiences. We were blinded by the brilliance of our manager's intellect and unable to avoid the embrace of his imposed methodologies. Most of the products we created never made it to beta because they took too long to build, and the business need had evaporated by the time we were almost done. He was one smart guy, but not a good manager of people or process.

This type of manager will usually contribute to the disintegration of any administrative processes that have previously helped the department achieve success. Their genius often views administration as a job for "other people" and beneath their station in life or not worthy of their time. Managers higher up the food chain may view your genius manager as a great leader because of his brilliance. The more removed you are from the daily process, the more prominent the genius appears, and it blinds you to the mistakes that result from the ineffective use of people or the disregard of administrative procedures.

 Their genius often views administration as a job for "other people" and beneath their station in life or not worthy of their time.

Does this describe you? If it does, your intelligence isn't being applied to the correct problem domain. Don't give up your focus on technology; begin to apply your genius to the peopleware needed to get the job done. Consider the comparison in Table 7-2.

Table 7-2. Genius versus Leader

A TECHNICAL GENIUS THINKS . . .	A GOOD LEADER THINKS . . .
What software technique will solve this problem?	How can I use others to develop good techniques for solving problems?
How many new language tools can I learn this month?	What training does my staff need to become more productive?

Table 7-2. Genius versus Leader (continued)

A TECHNICAL GENIUS THINKS . . .	A GOOD LEADER THINKS . . .
Complexity is only dangerous to the unintelligent.	Complexity is only warranted if all involved understand the details and have contributed to the creation of such a system.

It's possible to broaden your horizon and place people center stage in order to solve business problems. They will use technology, and your genius will be needed here, but unless you focus on your people, you aren't leading anyone anywhere.

If you work for one of these genius managers, the only way I've found to survive is to ratchet up your own intelligence and show that others have good ideas also. It may become a battle from time to time, but the boss is the boss, so what can you do? I'm not advocating open intellectual warfare, but saying "Yes, sir" isn't always the best response to these managers. A "Yes" followed by a "but have you considered this . . ." can work if you say it respectfully and with all the facts at hand. Don't try to argue from a position of ignorance: You won't gain the respect of the genius manager with this style.

I've seen situations where a misapplied genius had an effective administrative assistant who picked up the slack for the boss. This is a difficult management combination, but it can work. We do need smart people in leadership in our industry; we just need the smartness to extend beyond technology to the users and implementers of technology.

Dark Empire Builders

Mr. or Ms. Political might also be a name for dark empire leaders. While office politics is a reality in most corporations, it doesn't often result in success when it comes to creating great software. The empire builder will seek to build a staff loyal to them, but not necessarily to the goals of the company. They may be great to work for in the short term, showering their staff with "toys," but their focus isn't on building a cooperative team; rather, it's on accumulating a group of yes-men and yes-women. Leaders who only want to hear yes aren't leaders—they're aggregators of personnel and position. Posture is more important than performance for these managers.

The empire builder will seek to build a staff loyal to them, but not necessarily to the goals of the company.

I once worked for a company that had software development teams working in two different cities. After a number of successes and failures for each of the teams, one team began to dominate the corporate development activity. Their leader had the ear of the other decision makers and was able to secure very good facilities for his team. The developers had 21-inch monitors, good laptops, the latest PDAs, and any training they desired. They also were better paid than the other team. Friction arose whenever the two teams would collaborate, and the manager in charge of all development was continually frustrated trying to coordinate corporate development. He had one team leader speaking in each ear and the noise was deafening. Eventually, the empire builder's team was usurped by yet another would-be empire builder. The company struggled during these years to deliver any good product due to the infighting of the teams.

Empires are good when they deliver quality products and don't only serve their own ends. Microsoft, in my opinion, is an example of an empire that has brought some unity to our industry. Your opinion may differ with regard to Microsoft—you may spell their name "Micro$oft"—but they have come to dominate the desktop and created a de facto standard by their efforts. The dark empire, however, is out to serve the personal ambitions of the leader and only benefits its clients as part of its agenda; a hidden agenda is always to grow the empire, no matter what the cost. Even if you violently disagree with my opinion of Microsoft, you can't value the following characteristics of the leader of a dark empire.

- The job is about him or her. Personal power and prestige are critically important to the leader.

- If you're in this manager's favor, you can do no wrong.

- Loyalty is valued more than performance.

- Rewards (pay, equipment, and so on) are given to influence and are not solely based on merit.

- This manager has an "us versus them" mentality, and anything that threatens his or her power is vigorously challenged.

What kind of empire are you building today? Is it one that seeks to serve your clients, and not just your personal ambitions? Don't misread me: Ambition is a good thing and the personal dimensions can't be ignored; indeed, it often serves a good end both for you and for those who work for you. The darkness is what needs to be avoided in an empire—that quality that makes the development team look out for its own interests and growth at the expense of the larger corporate needs.

If you're managed by an empire builder, there may be little you can do to escape the downsides when (and if) they come. They may eventually come your way. The best you can do is to perform with integrity—this will help you weather any storms ahead. My opinion is based, of course, on a belief that the best interests of the company are being looked after by upper management and that they'll only tolerate tin gods for a limited amount of time. An empire builder who performs well, however, may be tolerated because it benefits the bottom line. It isn't a perfect world; dark empires have existed as nations for many years in history. They'll no doubt exist in the corporate world if they have a useful and profitable function.

Empire building runs counter to building consensus in technical matters. A leader more concerned with position won't often tolerate competing ideas. Competition of ideas leads to consensus; thus, dark empires often have a weak technological foundation. This should be a major concern for your leadership style. You want to be a strong leader; strength means being able to endure certain stresses and not capitulate when pressure builds. The pressure imposed by evolving technology and changing business requirements means you must be fleet of foot. Flexibility and empire building aren't comfortable companions. Consider these issues as you build your staff in numbers as well as quality.

> *Empire building runs counter to building consensus in technical matters. A leader more concerned with position won't often tolerate competing ideas.*

Flirting with Darkness

You may find yourself pushed into the dark side if you don't heed the warning signs. After working for six straight weekends on a project with a team and worrying about all the details, you may get to the point where you say, "I don't care anymore." This is a warning sign and all too human. Balancing work with the rest of your life is an ever-increasing challenge in our always-connected world. You can't dance in the darkness and hope to come out unscathed. Don't flirt with danger: Learn to see the following warning signs.

You've Reached Your Limit

You keep working longer and getting less done. You find yourself short-tempered with your staff and have outbursts of anger or unwarranted criticism. Code reviews become less frequent, and you can't stay focused long enough to generate constructive and instructive feedback. Your own sense of frustration becomes contagious and the team's productivity plummets.

It's time to back off and admit to the other groups involved in your project that you're operating at the maximum level of activity and missed deadlines can't be avoided. This is a hard thing to do, but you don't have any other choice when you reach a limit of productivity. Pushing the limit will only result in a more dramatic failure.

You're over Your Head

The job is too much for you. You can't seem to understand the complexities fast enough nor manage the people adequately. You feel out of control. You dread driving to the office. You look for excuses to miss work, or you daydream about another job. You avoid making decisions, hoping the situation will resolve itself on its own.

Ask other managers for advice. Turn to your boss for help—this is why you have a boss in the first place. Slow down the pace of work if possible and confer with your team to come up with strategies and tactics to regain control over the development process. Admitting weakness early on and asking for help is preferable to having your failures become plain for all to see at the end of a project. It may be time to bail out if you can't regain control. Only you can determine if you aren't really cut out for a leadership position. Better that you figure this out before someone else does.

Criticism Pushes You to Rage

Usually you'll become enraged as a result of ignoring the two previously mentioned warning signs. Rage is an irrational response to feelings of powerlessness or a sense of failure. Watch this sign carefully because you can burn your bridges at work when this happens and never regain the respect you might otherwise have earned. Criticism, in the best sense, is designed to improve performance. It becomes a source of irritation when you already believe you've done your best.

Doing your best becomes harder and harder when you operate at maximum capacity for weeks or months on end. Add to this inexperience or a bad fit with your job description and you may become a time bomb waiting to explode. It's hard to pick up all the pieces after a bomb goes off—it's a little bit like unringing a bell or having complied and distributed a bug-ridden executable.

Surviving and Emerging from an Eclipse

This is a book about practical matters. In theory, if you follow the best advice (mine, of course), you'll avoid the shadows that can eclipse your leadership. Reality, however, often makes a liar out of theory. You can count on lapses in your leadership occurring for a variety of reasons, many of which I've described in this chapter. Thus, coming out of an eclipse and getting back on track is a necessary management and leadership survival skill.

What relationships has your journey into darkness damaged? Can they be repaired? What do you do about the failed projects and missed deadlines? Where do you begin repairing the damage? These are questions you must ask and answer if you're to reclaim lost ground as a leader.

Start with people first. Seek out those who've been directly affected by your errors and openly apologize. Don't make excuses and admit your faults. Don't get sentimental or dramatic, just express regret and move on. People generally expect excuses and when you admit failure, they'll usually respect you for your honesty. The goal of the repair is to reestablish a foundation for leadership, not just to create warm feelings. When you have to do this with your staff, it will be difficult, but most welcomed. If you've been a good leader, they'll expect an apology. Don't disappoint them, and don't apologize via e-mail; a personal touch is required when the offense is personal, and you don't need to document your missteps.

Damage to processes, while a bit less personal, can be just as hard to correct as damaged relationships. If the errors on your part were a direct violation of some company policy, practice, or development methodology, the best repair policy is renewed compliance with the expected behavior. Put yourself on a personal remediation plan to review all the relevant company polices that govern your work. Polices are written for a reason: to ensure uniform performance and quality. We developers, because of our love of independence, can often treat these polices lightly. As a manager and leader, if you don't regard policies seriously, you can expect your staff to do the same.

Avoiding Eclipses

The best situation you could be in as a leader is to avoid eclipses altogether. A firm grounding in leadership principles, the topic of the next chapter, will help you reestablish your roots as a leader. Our look at the dark side in this chapter was designed to expose you to some of the default styles of management we often inherit or emulate because we don't know any better. As promoted programmers, we don't usually have the benefit of a formal education in management or leadership and thus tend to take over any administrative strength we have as programmers into our new role. Some of these skills can be transferred, but not the majority.

By way of a summary, and as a synthesis of the topics presented in this chapter intended to help you avoid shadows from the dark side, consider Table 7-3.

Table 7-3. Summary of Shadows

STYLE	CAUSES AND SYMPTOMS	CONSEQUENCES	REMEDY
Micromanagement	Focus on self-effort, lack of trust in staff, fear of failure	**For the manager:** Overworked and anxious **For the staff:** Loss of ownership in the product, feelings of uselessness and powerlessness **For the product:** Has mostly the efforts of the manager, thus maintenance will be difficult	Turn outward and use your staff, build trust, and mitigate your fears by collaborating with others.
Unfocused management	Procrastination, mind elsewhere, inexperience	**For the manager:** Backlog of decisions to be made **For the staff:** Chaos, everyone does what he or she thinks is right **For the product:** Deadlines missed, product doesn't meet the specifications	Focus on the job at hand, organize, and seek help from other managers.

Table 7-3. Summary of Shadows (continued)

STYLE	CAUSES AND SYMPTOMS	CONSEQUENCES	REMEDY
Misapplied genius	Lack of focus on peopleware, overly concerned with technical methods	**For the manager:** Frustration with lack of staff buy-in to his or her ideas **For the staff:** Afraid to challenge technical ideas from the boss **For the product:** Has mostly the ideas of the manager implemented, thus maintenance will be difficult	Hire an administrative assistant or gain training in leadership and management.
Empire builders	Self-absorbed with position and power, focus on politics	**For the manager:** Never satisfied, always want a greater empire **For the staff:** Isolation from and friction with other departments in the company **For the product:** Accomplished often by force rather than cooperation	Learn to let others succeed and stop playing politics.

In Table 7-3, note that all the dark management styles lead to severe consequences for the manager, the staff, and the product. There is no focus on leadership in these styles, other than leading the wrong way or not at all. Knowing these consequences will help you avoid exhibiting the symptoms. You must examine yourself for the personal causes, however, because a remedy that doesn't get at the source of the affliction will only be a symptomatic cure, not one that destroys the disease.

Moving On

The next chapter zeroes in on the core qualities of leadership. You'll want to contrast and compare the dark styles described in this chapter with the ones presented in the next as essential to quality leadership. Knowing about the negative aspects of leadership while viewing the positive can lead to an epiphany. We all need these moments of revelation and inspiration, and I hope the next chapter will contribute to growth in your confidence and skill as a leader.

CHAPTER 8

Leadership Redux

After the last chapter, considering all the shadows that might hinder your leadership, I believe a refresher course in leadership is warranted. Seeing all the problems that can occur might make you believe there is no way to "get it right," but this just isn't so. Becoming a good leader is more than being a great manager. Leadership, while fostered by appropriate management styles, requires efforts beyond those of just managing the people and processes. Leaders are required to be "out front" and blaze new paths for the company using the most appropriate technology.

Sometimes you'll be all alone, waiting for others to follow. If you have charisma, something I'm not sure can be taught, you may already have staff ready to follow you. If this is the case, knowing where you're going is even more important.

Leadership, like software, is built upon a foundation: For software, the foundation is the architecture, for leadership, it's your character. A very specific type of character, I should add. It is character focused upon awareness that you're responsible to lead the company in technical accomplishments, and your staff in the implementation of these shared goals. In the sections ahead, I'll expose the foundation so you can see the cornerstones and build upon it for greater accomplishments in your job.

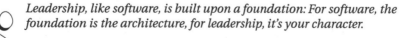

Leadership, like software, is built upon a foundation: For software, the foundation is the architecture, for leadership, it's your character.

Foundations of Leadership

First, a test question, a bit like the chicken and egg question: Which came first, the leader or the follower? Give up? Yeah, it was a trick question—I'm just laying the groundwork for excavating the foundation. What's on my mind is this: Leaders require followers if they are to be called leaders and a good leader will create his or her own followers. This creation process helps illustrate five foundational corner-stones that I consider the content of a leader's character. In Figure 8-1, I've arranged these cornerstones in two different ways: The first way illustrates the sequential nature of the function of the cornerstones, and the second way displays the cyclic nature.

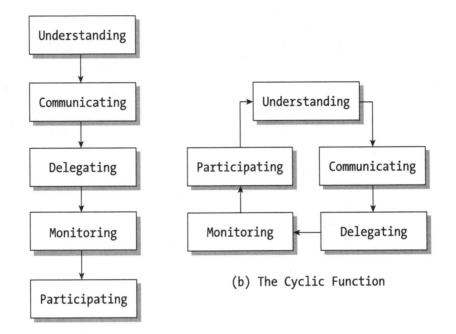

(a) The Linear Function

(b) The Cyclic Function

Figure 8-1. The cornerstones of leadership

The substance of each cornerstone is critical for its cohesion and purpose in supporting the foundation of leadership. In the same way that a building's foundation must be its strongest part, so too must the cornerstones of your leadership be strong.

Understanding

Before you can begin to lead, you must have a clear picture of where you're headed. Climbing to the top of Mount Everest requires more than a map. It often entails studying the journeys of those who've already reached the top and returned safely. You must know the conditions along the way, the risks, the challenges, how to use the necessary equipment, and the purpose of the journey. In the case of a mountain, often the purpose of climbing it is "because it's there." I think there's often a deeper purpose: Humankind needs to conquer things perceived as greater than themselves, just as business needs to build products and services to conquer competition and win market share. Perhaps my analogy is a bit strong, but the market is a wild place of competition and struggle, and the ultimate goal of our job as software developers is to put out a product or service that will win some of these battles. Marketplace battles will only be won by leaders who understand the nature, methods, and goals of software development warfare.

> *Marketplace battles will only be won by leaders who understand the nature, methods, and goals of software development warfare.*

You must first understand the depth and breadth of your company's needs in order to communicate them to your staff. This understanding starts with a bird's-eye view, but those of us in development often have to drill deep to comprehend the whole picture. Seeing the forest and the trees is a necessary skill for a leader. As programmers, we often get lost in the trees and don't realize the topology of the forest in which we're working. A leader of programmers can't afford to be lost: The cost to the staff and product is too high.

Until you cogitate, incubate, and contemplate a business requirement all the way through to the "eureka point,"[1] you don't have understanding. Hoping your staff will read the product specification and grasp enough to implement it correctly can be a vain wish. Unless you first see the path to implementation, you can't lead others toward the goal nor monitor their progress. Time and persistence are again required. The former you never believe you have enough of, and the latter is a matter of how seriously you regard your responsibility as leader. With respect to time, we all have the same amount but some use it more wisely than others. With regard to responsibility, experience is the best teacher about neglecting this fundamental aspect of being put in charge of people and product.

---

1. The moment you say, "I've found it," as Archimedes did when he discovered a test, based on the principle of buoyancy, for the purity of gold.

If the requirements can be thought up, they can be figured out. This is an inelegant way of saying that where there's a will, there's a way, a good cliché once you realize "will" involves study until understanding reigns. A plan for understanding consists of the following tasks:

1. Read requirements twice: once for breadth, and the second time for depth.

2. Map the requirements to know techniques of implementation and identify those areas of functionality that will require new development.

3. Develop a preliminary plan for prototyping projects that will flush out the unknowns in the requested features.

4. Flag those requirements that are at high risk and develop a mitigation plan in conjunction with those who generated the requirements.

5. Turn the requirements document into a checklist for guiding the task generation plan. This will enable you to map a requirement to a set of tasks that will ensure you don't miss implementing a feature.

From understanding come solutions. This leads to your next role as leader: communicating your understanding.

Communicating

The first time I heard the term "evangelize" was as a child, in church. This usage has a very specific religious purpose: Spread the good news. The first time I heard the term used in a secular context was from Microsoft, where the term "product evangelist" stuck me as an appropriate term for the young man who so enthusiastically taught a programming course I attended. Communication (or the lack thereof) is the second cornerstone of leadership. It has often been said, "Those who can, do, those who can't, teach." I consider this a false aphorism and posit a counter: Those who can't teach don't understand. I believe this is behind failures to communicate adequately in business: A lack of understanding leads to timidity and a wish for others to grasp by osmosis the tasks they must do. Osmosis might occur if you use the business requirements document as a pillow for a few nights, but it will never take the place of clear communication.

The goal of communicating is to impart the same level of understanding you have about the requirements to your staff. How did you reach your level of understanding? The steps you took are the ones to teach, in sequence, with the wisdom of hindsight. A good communicator is a good teacher; all other communication is an act of performance. While it's true that a good teacher needs students willing to learn, you have an advantage as a leader of programmers: These folks work for you and they're a captive audience. Perhaps they don't always listen, but you have methods as a boss to enforce learning. Of course, encouragement is better than enforcement, but sometimes whatever gets the job done is required. Back to the main point: If communication is synonymous with teaching, what makes a good lesson plan? At least the elements described in Table 8-1 are required for effective communication.

 A good communicator is a good teacher; all other communication is an act of performance.

Table 8-1. Elements of Effective Communication

FORMAL ELEMENTS OF COMMUNICATION	FUNCTIONAL ELEMENTS OF COMMUNICATION	STYLISTIC ELEMENTS OF COMMUNICATION
Introduction. An overview of the subject, exposing the scope and plan of the presentation.	**Explanation.** Clarifying technical terminology and simplifying concepts.	**Voice.** Formal or personal, depending on the audience, venue, and urgency.
Discussion. Describing details, topic by topic, striving to make each point self-contained and yet part of the whole.	**Argument.** Persuading by the power of logic and truth with the instrument of language.	**Tone.** Serious, but not dramatic; appropriate for business. Humor helps.
Transition. Tie together all the pieces and show relationships between topics.	**Application.** Moving from theory to practice, how to implement what you are learning.	**Rhythm.** Variation in voice and tone helps make all the points stick.
Conclusion. The logic of the communication must lead to a plan of action.	**Illustration.** Analogies or metaphors that cast the subject in a different light to aid understanding.	

Many leaders are overly concerned with style—sometimes it's because they're fuzzy on the substance. Concentrate on the content and the presentation details can be refined as you gain experience communicating to your staff. The elements of communication in Table 8-1 are important to observe in verbal and written mediums.

One thing to keep in mind is the difference between intentional communication and casual conversation. As a leader, your casual remarks may be understood as formal directions to your staff. We spend most of our lives communicating without intention, delivering unprepared statements that arise out of the context of the moment. Be conscious of these differences between casual and formal ways of talking; sometimes a causal remark in business can have destructive consequences you didn't intend. Learning to control the battlefield of communication will help you win the war of understanding.

> *Learning to control the battlefield of communication will help you win the war of understanding.*

For programmers, a partially functional prototype is often the best means of communicating requirements. At least capturing user interfaces can go a long way toward creating understanding. Don't neglect the underlying architecture, however. As you learned in Chapter 6, you must plan out the garden in which you grow software objects before you start planting for the harvest.

Using UML, PowerPoint, or Visio is also a time-honored way to facilitate communication. Your organization may already have a process for generating requirement and design documents. Embrace it or change it to suit the needs of the project. Be aware, however, that software generated from documents isn't the last step. Prototyping and reviewing the preliminary implementation concepts is often a neglected part of the communication process. Do you miss coding as a manager and leader? Then here is a realm where you can get back to your first love and still fulfill your job description. We often want to say, "the code is self-documenting," but this is rarely the case. Prototypes, however, can be constructed as a means of communication and thus address two issues at once: your love of coding and your need to impart your understanding of the problem solution.

Delegating

You've explained what needs to be done, now it's time to get it done. Delegating is an art and many of the earlier chapters of this book delved into the reasons why this is your primary job function. Knowing who to delegate tasks to is part of the skills you must refine as a leader. I touched on this in Chapter 1 by identifying the traits of programmers—these traits, as applied to your staff, should inform your decisions about who gets particular assignments.

Ideally, you would like to split up a project into units of work that can be spread out among all your developers. This doesn't always work in practice. Some of your people will be better at certain or even all parts of a given project. You may want to pair up programmers in certain situations where two minds can be better than one. The software development methodology called "extreme programming"[2] emphasizes this practice heavily. Another technique related to this trend is delegating to a team of two where one writes the code and the other tests and reviews it on a daily basis. I've seen this be an effective delegation scheme with the right people, especially a senior and junior programmer pair. With the wrong people, the innate independence of programmers can thwart this otherwise great idea. Part of your skills in delegation is to know what staff pairs can work well together.

Keep in mind the classic rule that adding developers to an already late software project only creates more delay. You can delegate tasks, but not speed. If you find yourself having trouble splitting up the project into discrete slices of development, it may be the fault of the design. Perhaps more modularity is needed in the construction plan. Often, at the start of a project you'll find it easy to delegate. Then, as the work proceeds, some of your staff will complete their work early and others will be late. This is often a result of an inadequate view of how long certain tasks take to complete. This all relates back to your design. A good software design, assuming your architecture is sound, will lend itself to delegation by modules.

 Keep in mind the classic rule that adding developers to an already late software project only creates more delay. You can delegate tasks, but not speed.

Adapting your delegation plan during the course of the project is a learned skill. Knowing that adaptation will be needed should be assumed and come as no surprise. You'll feel that you're shooting at a moving target as the project moves from the beginning stages toward a conclusion and this is why experience is so vital to the leader. If we could create a firing range for software leaders, where they could practice hitting moving targets, we would all be better off. Unfortunately, you must practice in the real world and often you'll miss a few deadlines. The more you practice, the better you'll become. Delegation is your best weapon for these targets. Try to take them all on by yourself (i.e., micromanage) and you'll soon be out of ammunition before the target is destroyed.

---

2.   See the Bibliography entry for the book entitled *Extreme Programming Explained* by Kent Beck.

Monitoring

Our old friend, "expecting without inspecting," comes to center stage in this cornerstone. After delegation, the obvious logical task is to monitor the progress of the work. This isn't micromanaging—this is inspecting. Conducting frequent builds of components, prior to code complete, is the best way to ensure you'll meet your deadlines. It also ensures that you haven't gone down the wrong path and run into a dead end in design. Nothing takes more time than having to start over as you near the end of a development cycle because the design is flawed. Daily monitoring is recommended during most of your routine work, and as a deadline draws near, you must conduct even more frequent inspections.

Effective monitoring is like conducting a continuous code review: You look for compliance to the design as well as to your coding standards. The longer you wait to review, the more you'll have to do and if you wait long enough, there won't be time to do much about code that has gone astray.

Consider using these techniques for monitoring:

- Visit your staff daily and ask in general how their assignments are going. If you can't do it in person, use the phone or as a last resort, e-mail.

- Every several days, test modules of code that are complete. This turns you into a tester, but you should think of it as a prime leadership responsibility.

- Practice integrating the components into the system and test for architectural soundness periodically. Here you get to "play" with code. It also ensures you don't overlook mistakes in construction efforts, nor fail to understand the techniques used by your programmers to accomplish their work.

- Use the weekly staff meeting (described in Chapter 5) for project status and brainstorming. This is a supplement to the daily visit and allows for the group mind to address common problems.

- Employ staff members who've finished early with their assignments to test the work of other programmers. Use care here, but don't let anyone say, "Testing isn't my job." This will not do. Programming is more than writing code—it's proving it really works.

- Request programmers to document their new code modules and gather these documents into a form of internal release notes that can be passed on to the testing department. This will help you and your staff to validate your progress and compliance with the requirements.

Don't let anyone say, "Testing isn't my job." This will not do. Programming is more than writing code—it's proving it really works.

The preceding techniques and others you develop will make monitoring a productive and constructive endeavor, not one of just criticism. Leaders must monitor their followers or else someone will be left behind, which means the product will not be done on time. The whole team needs to reach the summit of your development mountain or the expedition will be in vain.

Participating

You're the leader but often you'll participate in the coding. If you balance this with delegating and monitoring, you'll do fine. Guard against micromanaging, as discussed in the last chapter, but participating in the "dirty work" can be an effective way to demonstrate your leadership. Many times your staff will feel it's nice to have the boss help out; however, realize you're on a slippery slope coding as a manager. Depending on the size of your staff, this may be necessary, but writing code and managing the writing of code require different parts of your brain. Switching from one to the other can be a challenge. Administrative matters don't often require as much concentrated and uninterrupted focus as programming, so maybe you can afford the inevitable break induced by the phone or e-mail. For coding, however, you already know how disrupting interruptions can be.

If our minds were really like microprocessors, where an "interrupt" preserves the state of the system, we could truly multitask. We might brag about being able to multitask to others, but often what we really mean is that we do several things poorly at the same time. Our work demands focus, and trying to accomplish only one thing at a time is a good practice for software development.

As I mentioned in the "Monitoring" section, your participation in the coding efforts often takes on the role of testing. This is a valid exercise of participatory leadership. There will probably be no one else available in many corporate organizations to do the integration and testing prior to the alpha stage. Your technical skills will be challenged and your time will feel compressed. You must pay this price and rise to the challenge as the leader. More than 40 hours a week will often be required of you if you fully participate in the development efforts. You may run into danger here: Recall the warning signs I described in the last chapter that are often summed up in the phrase, "I don't care anymore." When you reach that point, it's often too late. You must monitor your own level of stress very carefully so you can remain available to your staff during the real "crunch" times of the development cycle. I've said software development isn't a sprint, it's a marathon; pacing yourself is critical to the whole team's health and endurance. Marathons are won when the runners have a measured pace, concentrate on placing one foot in front of the other, are focused on the immediate terrain, and hold in their mind the thrill of crossing finish line with a good time.

On a personal note, I was an avid cross-country runner during high school and college. After these years, marriage, the military, children, and pursuing the American Dream resulted in my exercise routines falling by the wayside. Decades later, I began to get back into shape. I can no longer run 5 consecutive miles in 30 minutes as I did as a younger man. I've been able to get through it in 40 minutes in recent years, but it now requires more focus than I remember when I was younger. Each time I try to improve upon my own personal "best time," my success depends on a sharp focus on every step. I've found that verbally sounding out the word "focus" while running can help. I've also learned to apply this regime to my job. Participation means you stay in the entire race and try not to miss a step. You may be the coach on the sidelines sometimes as a leader, but the best leaders are also players.

You may be the coach on the sidelines sometimes as a leader, but the best leaders are also players.

Participating, in the grand scheme, means sharing in the struggles and triumphs experienced by your staff. This entails being available as needed to facilitate the work of others and to anticipate problems and provide solutions before your staff is affected. Taking an interest in the personal lives of your staff is also one dimension of participation. You aren't trying to be anyone's best friend, but you do want to demonstrate concern and awareness that your staff has a life outside of the office.

Going back for a moment to my personal illustration of running, I remember my high school track coach one day saying this to us sweaty young runners: "Boys, some day you'll be telling tall tales to your children about how fast you could run." I found this amusing at the time, and really had no idea about what he was saying. Thirty-eight years later, I know why he said this: The joy of participating in a team gives added meaning to individual efforts. This is what you want to do for your team—get down there with them, don't neglect the coaching aspect, but play in the game too!

Building Upon the Foundation

Once the cornerstones of a building are laid and found to be secure, it's time to build the superstructure. I've listed in the sections that follow important activities that will naturally flow out of your leadership position. If they don't seem to come out naturally for you, you need to reexamine the foundation. The building up of a team has many joys for the leader and you don't want to miss these pleasures of leadership. Heaven knows, we have enough headaches trying to manage the development process, so a little joy can go a long way.

Mentoring

Teaching others to teach multiplies your efforts and effectiveness. This will serve as a working definition of mentoring. Mentoring serves many purposes and the more you give to it, the more you'll receive back for the effort. Did you catch the subtle concept, "teaching others to teach"? Mentoring is more than teaching because it exposes your learning methods to those you mentor. My dad told me the primary reason for going to college was to know where to look up things you needed to know for your job and being able to figure them out when you got there. He was right, and mentoring is like this: You're showing others how to learn while you're imparting knowledge to them.

> *Mentoring is teaching others to teach, and it multiplies your efforts and effectiveness.*

The academic field of pedagogy is properly dominated with heuristic concerns. As a mentor, you want to teach in a manner that stimulates and encourages additional learning and experimentation, and thus improves your staff's problem-solving abilities. Creating software requires good problem-solving skills. You may have hated word problems in mathematics, but all of life, and especially coding, is one big word problem. You are tasked to translate a requirement into a working piece of software, and this means you have to map from the requirement domain to the machine implementation with the result being a rich user experience.

The goal of mentoring is to build future leaders like yourself, or even better than yourself. The more you can make your staff take ownership for the whole development endeavor, the more help you'll have as deadlines draw near. Set aside a day a week if you can for mentoring. This will be a challenge to keep up during certain times in your job, but making a commitment to train your staff will not only be doing them a good deed, but yourself as well. Preparing to mentor always cements ideas in your own mind, reinforces your own understanding of the work, and keeps you in tune with what you ask your staff to accomplish.

A typical example of mentoring could be building in real time a prototype that illustrates a particular method of software construction. Perhaps you work on the staff member's current tough assignment for a few hours together. This isn't micromanaging, but rather a good example of collaboration. Mentoring is putting together the participatory and understanding cornerstones of leadership to build up the quality of your staff.

You don't have to be an old sage to be a mentor. Age doesn't matter, but willingness to impart knowledge does. For a team to become superstars in development, the members are going to need to help each other. You start this process off by being the prime mentor and foster the same attitude of giving among your staff.

There are often two levels of mentoring needed from you: targeted and complete. *Targeted mentoring* is where you help staff in specific ways, such as how to make an API call or write a sorting routine, as often as necessary. You should do this type of mentoring all the time. *Complete mentoring* requires more. This type of mentoring involves a quality of transparency in the relationship that will not be possible between you and all of your staff. Those you're grooming to be your successors—the ones with the greatest promise—are the ones you pour yourself into. You try to form deeper relationships as you attempt to pass on all of your combined knowledge. An artist may teach many classes on art: how to sketch, how to shade, how to determine perspective. Many different students may take these classes and learn some of the artist's skills, but only a few are groomed consistently to take the artist's place. This is the role of the pupil, the apprentice, the replacement. If you're irreplaceable, you'll never be replaced. This has negative implications if you ever intend to be promoted.

Rewarding

Outstanding performance should be rewarded. Your privilege and joy as a leader is to pick the manner and time to dole out the goodies. Maybe it's an increase in pay, a dinner for two at a fine restaurant, or tickets to some awesome sporting event. Make the reward commensurate with the performance and always make it based on merit. If everyone is giving 100 percent, this is what they're paid to do. Rewards are for those who exceed the normal expectations by giving a little bit more.

You'll have corporate guidelines to follow in this area, but be as creative as you can get away with when it comes to rewarding success. Hold a contest with a monetary reward during beta testing to see who fixes the most bugs. You'll have to weigh the performance based on the nature of the bug and who was responsible for creating it in the first place, but this can be done. Here's an example of a weighting scheme:

1. Number of bugs fixed.

2. Complexity of the bug.

3. Time to fix the bug.

4. Success of the solution—did the retest fail or succeed?

5. Effort expended in working with others (when appropriate or needed) to bring about a solution.

6. Your familiarity with the area you're fixing.

7. Your efforts to help other developers when they ask for help on their bugs.

8. Extra effort above and beyond the call of duty.

9. Timely work on other tasks not related to the current release.

10. Your willingness to learn things about the product that may be difficult, tedious, and complex.

11. Your persistence in accomplishing a task even if it seems intractable.

Obviously, monitoring all these items for each bug and staff member will take your time, but it's a constructive method to monitoring, one of the cornerstones of leadership, and associates an element of fun with the process. Notice also how the concept of mentoring has been worked into the preceding list. As a team, you want to be careful to prevent competition between programmers from hindering the overall success of the team. This is why attempting to measure a staff member's effort to help another one is a great way to determine rewards. If I was a sports expert, I'm sure I could come up with a suitable analogy—maybe the number of assists? (Is this baseball, basketball, or both? I don't know.)

In whatever method you choose to reward your staff, be fair and timely. Remember the saying of the rich man when asked how much was enough, to which he replied, "A little bit more." Rewards beyond normal compensation should only be given for performance beyond normal expectations.

Rewards beyond normal compensation should only be given for performance beyond normal expectations.

Correcting

Guidance and reproof are key elements to growth for any programmer. Correcting errors doesn't mean acting like a college professor and putting a big *X* through a calculus problem solution on a test. The leader of a team of programmers guides his or her staff to see their own errors so they learn from the mistake. He or she suggests remedies and works alongside the staff member to achieve a corrected result. This is a very personal activity by the leader and must be exercised with care, but not timidity. You must not allow sloppy code or inadequate efforts to go unchecked.

The chapter on technical leadership (Chapter 6) dealt with code reviews and the consequences of neglecting this important technical role. In a more general way, your correcting activities should focus on the situations where a programmer is giving less than his or her maximum effort. Discover the reasons for this failure. I doubt your department can afford to keep on board a programmer who just squeaks by, doing only the bare minimum to get the job done. As I described in Chapter 3, sometimes dismissal is a necessary step to end a problem person. You don't want to end up at this point if it can be helped. Taking small corrective measures geared toward rehabilitation is a better plan than giving someone the axe.

When you correct a programmer for an error or lack of effort, remember that the process works both ways. If you allow your failures as a leader to remain unchecked, the weight of your reproof will be small. Hypocrisy may be common among humans, but it's also dangerous for a leader of programmers. In Chapter 2, where I discussed watching your weaknesses, I mentioned how your coding style might be emulated by your staff, for better or for worse. As a leader, the amount of effort you put into your job will be noticed by your staff, so keep this in mind when you fault someone else for a lack of effort.

 Hypocrisy may be common among humans, but it's also dangerous for a leader of programmers.

Envisioning

Seeing beyond the next mountain inspires others to follow. Some consider the ability to create a vision for the future that motivates others to be the hallmark of a leader. It's very important, even if your visions are not as grand as those that would create the next killer app. Visions can be small in scale and still inspire workers. A vision for how to create the next version of your company's flagship product in a way that reduces future maintenance is just as significant for your company as having invented the Internet, like Al Gore.

Can a method be formulated for constructing visions? Isn't a visionary someone who listens to the muses and relates what he or she heard? Perhaps in great literature or music the muse plays a role, but in all creative endeavors, the much-used phrase "thinking outside the box" does produce dramatic results. When Alan Turing worked for the British during World War II on decrypting the German Enigma codes, it led to a new vision for computing methods. In a charming brief biography about Turing, the following story is told:

> . . . *Turing from the start visualized the Turing machine undertaking functions performed by the human mind. [Turing] now proposed and analyzed the concept of "intelligent machinery". . . . He used the analogy of a master and pupil. The pupil could outshine his master, developing a qualitatively superior intelligence, using only the information programmed in him by his master. Turing argued further. It was possible (by following the rules that had been fed into it). But "playing against such a machine gives a definite feeling that one is pitting one's wits against something alive." Because the computer could learn, its behavior transcended mechanistic determinism and exhibited an element of freedom which seemed like a living intelligence. . . . Turing was thinking on a level that transcended mathematics, computable numbers, or even computers.*[3]

We all know where Turing's ideas led. The importance of algorithms in the architecture of computer software was the result. Calculators turn into machines that can beat a grand master of chess. Turing thought "outside the box" to give his method a contemporary feel. Being a visionary leader requires this kind of lateral thinking and you're in the perfect position to do this in your organization.

Take your "big picture" understanding of your business, coupled with your technical skills and your administrative insights, and come up with new methods

---

3. Paul Strathern, *Turing and the Computer* (New York: Doubleday, 1997), pp. 75–78.

to improve your staff productivity. This will be visionary in a very practical and welcome sense. You can make your visions a reality by practicing all the skills you've been learning in these pages: Communicate your understanding, delegate actions, monitor progress, and participate in the planting and harvest.

> *You can make your visions a reality by practicing all the skills you've been learning in these pages: Communicate your understanding, delegate actions, monitor progress, and participate in the planting and harvest.*

Adapting

In the first chapter, I outlined the importance of adapting to your leadership role. The need for adaptation will continue as long as you remain a leader of programmers. Adjusting your leadership as the conditions warrant to the needs of the day is a refined attribute of a great leader. None of us can see very far into the future; if we could, we would plan for it better. However, we as a species are very good at adapting to biological forces and changing environments over many generations. You don't have the time to wait for biology, but you do have time to partition your leadership journey into regions of competence and assess your growth. As you meet new challenges in your job, these will test your ability to adapt and help you gain new skills. View tough problems as opportunities for growth rather than the customary "wringing of the hands." I know this sounds a bit like the positive thinking school that I've cast dispersions upon in a previous chapter, but if the shoe fits, wear it.

> *View tough problems as opportunities for growth rather than the customary "wringing of the hands."*

Okay, I may be gathering too many clichés in this discussion. Practical questions to ask yourself about adapting include the following:

- What do I need to change about my management style to face today's issues?

- What new technologies must my staff learn if we're to remain competitive?

- Who do I need to hire in order to gain new competencies for future projects?

- How can I restructure my department so quality is improved while not adversely affecting time to market?

You must ask these questions, and other questions only you can think of, daily to yourself and perhaps to your staff. The answers, of course, must be worked out, but part of adapting is knowing what questions to ask. Become an asker of questions, and encourage dialogue within your staff concerning your common tough issues.

Adaptation proceeds along the lines of science: Experiments are tried and evaluated for success. Failed methods are discarded and new ones are dreamed up. Gradually, the best methods are found and turn into laws. Your job in fostering adaptation, first for yourself and then for your staff, is to be the guinea pig. Don't worry, you won't die from this exercise. Nothing you try will be fatal as long as you measure the results of your new methods periodically and change them as needed.

Will They Follow?

What is your leadership power base? I'm not talking about empire building, but rather how you motivate your staff to follow. I previously said leaders create followers—they do this by their powers of attraction. In this section, I'll present some common reasons why people follow a leader. Some methods are better than others, but all have their place in the scheme of things. You'll find that you must use them all together from time to time, and this is fine. Just be sure to note what works for you and your staff in the corporate setting in which you find yourself and lean into your strengths.

Force

You've hired your staff with the explicit condition that they work in order to receive pay. We often take this simple fact for granted. It's the basis of modern commerce: trading skill for cash. Is this enough to motivate people to do outstanding work? Usually not, but it's a place to start—not a very good place, but a starting point if nothing better is available to motivate your workers.

Resorting to force should be your last option. It may be a choice imposed upon you by the market, however. If you company is behind the curve technically, you'll be forced to gain lost ground. This kind of external force can work if cast into the proper mold by you to your staff. Phrases such as "the market demands" and "our competitors have" are appropriate motivational tools you shouldn't be afraid to use.

> *Phrases such as "the market demands" and "our competitors have" are appropriate motivational tools you shouldn't be afraid to use.*

Don't try the phrase "because I say so" unless you want to come across like an unimaginative parent. True, you are the boss, and when you delegate folks do have their marching orders, but remember, you're trying to herd cats and they usually scatter at the sound of loud noises.

Duty

Some of your staff will follow you because they're of a mindset that emphasizes loyalty to the boss. This is great and you should show appreciation for these motives. You must also earn the right to be the boss, even if you have the title. Again, saying "It's your duty to follow me" will fall flat. This is simply using force. Duty is something created within an individual for personal and internal reasons. You can't teach duty. You may be able to require it in the military, but this isn't what you want for a team of programmers.

A better approach to fostering a sense of duty is to create pride in your department by the merits of your accomplishments as a team. Everyone wants to be associated with a winning team. Just look at the fans of the winning team in the Super Bowl. They didn't even play the game, but they're ecstatic with joy at the outcome. Your job as leader is to make your "locker room" one where duty to the team is a high honor because you're an outstanding group of men and women.

> *Foster a sense of duty by creating pride in your department based on the merits of your accomplishments as a team. Everyone wants to be associated with a winning team.*

Admiration

I would have followed Albert Einstein into any laboratory on Earth because of my admiration for him. Of course, his lab was mostly in his mind so this doesn't work well as an analogy. But you get my drift. Many times people follow a leader just because they admire his or her personal qualities. Again, this is great when it can happen, but most of us aren't always the most admirable.

Can you work in such a way to elicit admiration from your staff? I think you can. Will this help? Yes, to some degree. Admirers can be fickle, as the fans of any fallen movie star will tell you. Admiration that lasts and motivates requires that you're consistent in your management style, leadership effectiveness, and dealings with your staff. This is a tall order, but it's necessary. Consistency is admirable because it fosters a sense of security among your staff that can be used in the tough times to battle against the long odds of bringing a software project in under the deadline. It takes time to build up this kind of consistency; you can't do it in one month and perhaps not in one year. But your daily efforts to strive for consistency will be noticed and will produce a level of admiration from your staff that can be a good motivator.

Admiration that lasts and motivates requires that you're consistent in your management style, leadership effectiveness, and dealings with your staff.

Reward

You might consider rewards as a type of positive force. I discussed rewarding your staff under the section on building upon the cornerstones of leadership. Rewards are usually only a short-term solution to motivation. Most of us fall into the ungrateful posture of asking, "What have you done for me today?" I dislike having to say this, but rewards of the common kind (money, days off, and so on) are just not long-term ways to create a following.

What you want to work for in your staff is the kind of rewards they derive themselves from working with you and on projects you direct. These types of intangible rewards are the most effective. I know we say often that programming has its own inherent rewards as a human activity, but you must go beyond this. You'll begin to create a department that programmers want to work in when your management and leadership skills foster a work environment where people wake up each morning and say, "Oh boy! I get to go to work today." Is this too much to hope for? Maybe it is for certain individuals, but it's worth the effort to try and create an enlivening atmosphere for your staff.

How do you do this? I'm repeating myself in giving the answer but I will because repetition fosters learning: *focus and lead*. You dealt with the focus aspect in previous chapters—you're facing leadership head on in this one. Practice what you're learning and what you find that works for you. Practice does indeed lead to perfection and this has many rewards for your staff.

Knowledge

In our industry, knowledge is power. Programmers are attracted to knowledgeable leaders because they can get what they need from them to do their job. This is a very good method of creating a following. Be the expert or guru in your field and you'll have programmers eager to follow you. Is this too much to expect from yourself when you have so many administrative tasks to perform each day? It might be, but you know that if you don't continue to grow in your depth of knowledge you can't adequately lead your group.

I mentioned the misapplied genius style of leadership in the last chapter. If you're one of these geniuses (not the misapplied type), congratulations. You may indeed have a following, and if you do, treat your people right: Work to impart your great knowledge to them in a manner that will help them rise to your level. I'm not being facetious. Our industry is filled with brilliant programmers and leaders and we need more. Concentrate on mentoring, and with your technical skills you will truly build a great following within your staff.

Generational Dimensions to Leadership

This book, I hope, is being read by leaders of many ages. I'm late into middle age; you may be in early adulthood. Your position on the biological clock affects how you view leadership and approach the problems you face in software development. It may be rare to find an experienced leader in their early 20s, but it isn't unheard of. Being old is also no guarantee of wisdom. Some of us "old" guys and gals have rigid habits that need changing, and we can often learn from those younger than ourselves.

Consider traits usually attributed to youth:

- They are quick to learn.

- They are comfortable with new technology.

- They are reluctant to admit a job is impossible.

- They have a sense of immortality that makes them great achievers.

Is there any law written down that says that these qualities can't be exhibited by an adult regardless of age? There isn't, and youth can serve as a good model for us as we get older.

Consider traits usually attributed to older people (whatever "older" means):

- They are wise because they have a deep and long experience with lifelong learning.

- They have many years of experience with changing technology and they know how to adapt.

- They are more patient because they have learned from their mistakes.

- They have an ever-increasing sense of their own mortality and make the most of each day.

Again, nothing says a younger person can't demonstrate these qualities, once you account for the chronological aspects. We can all learn from each other. You can learn new things from your staff, even if you're the oldest or youngest one on the team. Learning should not be limited by age. In our industry, failure to learn is the quickest way out of the business.

> *We can all learn from each other. You can learn new things from your staff, even if you're the oldest or youngest one on the team. Learning should not be limited by age. In our industry, failure to learn is the quickest way out of the business.*

Other generational differences can be more striking. Modern psychology, emerging as a true science of behavior, has developed a number of studies of the adult life cycle. These studies prove that age does make a difference in how you approach your work life, especially when it comes to leadership positions. If you view your life as you do the solar year, with its seasons, the following passage illustrates the view that age grants you different perspectives:

> *To speak of seasons is to say that the life course has a certain shape, that it evolves through a series of definable forms. A season is a relatively stable segment of the total cycle. Summer has a character different from that of winter; twilight is different from sunrise. To say that a season is relatively stable, however, does not mean that it is stationary or static. Change goes on within each, and a transition is required for the shift from one season to the next. Every season has its own time; it is important in its own right and needs to be understood in its own terms. No season is better or more important than any*

other. Each has its necessary place and contributes its special character to the whole. It is an organic part of the total cycle, linking past and future and containing both within itself.[4]

The season of your life will affect how you approach being a leader, how important it is for you to succeed, and how much it hurts when you fail. You're the only one who can determine how your age affects your leadership. There are no fixed rules that make one age better than another.

Generational differences have affected the writing of this book. I began in this industry creating Fortran on IBM punch cards, submitting my deck of cards over the counter at the computer center and waiting days to see if the program ran. I used the first Internet, called ARPANET[5] in those days, and it was a slow, character-based experience. These experiences mark me as from the first generation of nerds—slide rules on the belt and pocket protectors were my standard dress in college. Today, as a leader of programmers, you may be indistinguishable from the MBA down the hall. You may even have an MBA, as well as extensive education in computer science. My generation had to make up these things as we went along. These differences shape our perspectives and will continue to influence the decisions we make as leaders. Whatever your generation, we can all learn from each other's differences. This is where the richest insights and ideas originate.

Marrying Style to Substance As a Leader

Style is the manifestation of behavior that flows from your core personality as you execute leadership principles. Style that matters is married to the substance that makes up what you believe to be important principles of leadership. Style without substance is just technique and of no lasting value. Nevertheless, style is often what we observe in others before we can discern the underlying substance. No two leaders have a style that is exactly alike, thank goodness. Variety feeds technical people and as leaders, we're as varied as the programmers we manage.

We all learn about style from leaders we've followed or admired. We even learn, hopefully, from our own successes and failures as leaders. Business management literature is filled with examples of leaders to follow. I mentioned Jack Welch, the former head of General Electric, in Chapter 2 as someone to seek out for advice. Two other leaders, drawn from the very heart of our industry, are Andy Grove and Bill Gates.

---

4. Daniel J. Levinson, *The Seasons of a Man's Life* (New York: Ballantine Books, 1978), p. 7.

5. ARPA stood for the Advanced Research Projects Agency, later known in the 1970s as DARPA, where the D stood for defense, as in missiles, smart bombs, stealth technology, and all the other dreadful wonders of the cold war.

Andy Grove: Aggressive and Paranoid

Under Grove's leadership, Intel has become the world's largest manufacturer of semiconductors and one of the most admired companies in the world. Grove shepherded Intel to this status during decades of turbulent change and competition in our industry. How did he do it? In the opening chapter of his book about leadership, Grove writes:

> *I'm often credited with the motto, "Only the paranoid survive." I have no idea when I first said this, but the fact remains that, when it comes to business, I believe in the value of paranoia. Business success contains the seeds of its own destruction. The more successful you are, the more people want a chunk of your business and then another chunk and then another until there is nothing left. I believe that the prime responsibility of a manager is to guard constantly against other people's attacks and to inculcate this guardian attitude in the people under his or her management.*[6]

As Grove defines paranoia, it works well from a business perspective. You wouldn't take this approach with your significant other, of course, but it worked for Intel under Grove's leadership. As you read about Intel and Grove's way of leading, you come to understand that his style of responding to change was the hallmark of his success. Change is tough to manage and as a leader it will be one of your more difficult areas to face and something you must face each day.

Grove faced change proactively and with prescience. In spite of mistakes (e.g., the Pentium floating-point flaw), he was able to stay in touch with the grassroots needs of his industry and he respond to the unexpected constructively. Learn from this: Don't become isolated as a leader and lose sight of the forces that affect your industry and your people on a daily basis. If it requires a little paranoia, so be it. Better to expect the unexpected than be surprised when it arrives at your front door.

> *Don't become isolated as a leader and lose sight of the forces that affect your industry and your people on a daily basis. If it requires a little paranoia, so be it. Better to expect the unexpected than be surprised when it arrives at your front door.*

---

6. Andrew S. Grove, *Only the Paranoid Survive* (New York: Random House, 1996), p. 3.

Bill Gates: Driven and Calculating

It's hard not to admire Bill Gates. You may disagree, but when you see the geeky, fresh-faced college dropout in the 1978 company photo[7] and consider what he has created today, you can't avoid being impressed. The Microsoft Empire originated in the driven, visionary, entrepreneurial, and calculating personality of its cofounder. Stories about him are legend. One of Gates' college roommates, relating a story about his poker playing abilities, reported this:

> *Bill had a monomaniacal quality . . . He would focus on something and really stick with it. He had a determination to master whatever it was he was doing. Perhaps it's silly to compare poker and Microsoft, but in each case, Bill was sort of deciding where he was going to put his energy and to hell with what anyone else thought.[8]*

Perhaps the rest is history, but if you fail to see the value in how being driven to success can create success, you're missing a very important point about leadership. I've extolled the value of focus in this book as a key leadership principle. This is a direct result of someone driven to succeed. You may question a leader's motivations, but it's hard to argue with success when many benefit from the result.

I also apply the term "calculating" to Gate's style of leadership. He, like Grove, has been able to see ahead and face change with a plan. For example, have you noticed that the copyright date on most versions of Windows starts at 1981?[9] I see this as evidence of planning refined over many years by a very calculating individual. Sure, Gates hasn't always been first in our industry, but he's made the biggest impact upon what we all do every day as programmers and leaders of programmers. This is where the calculating part of style meets substance and the result is power to lead. Even if you use all non-Microsoft tools and infrastructure, you do this in light (or in spite) of what Microsoft has done and will do.

You: _____ (Fill In the Blank)

In light of the two leadership examples I've related, how would you describe yourself as a leader? Alternately, consider this: As a leader, you have the prerogative to choose your staff based on your knowledge and intuitive evaluation of candidates for employment. What if the tables were turned and your staff could pick the type

---

7. See James Wallace and Jim Erickson, *Hard Drive: Bill Gates and the Making of the Microsoft Empire* (New York: John Wiley & Sons, 1992).

8. Ibid., p. 61.

9. I just looked at an old Windows 98 Second Edition update CD and the copyright date is 1981–1999.

of leader they wanted? Suppose a pool of development managers were available and your staff could interview and hire their leader. Would they choose you? I know this is a tough and a strange question to ask, but it shouldn't be a surprising one when you consider the need for introspection as a manager (Chapter 2) and the negative effects of dark leadership styles presented in the previous chapter (Chapter 7).

I can't fill in the blank in the section title for you. You'll determine what goes after the colon based on your view of your style of leadership. I also can't speak for your team and say they would choose you out of several candidates to lead them. These are private questions only you can ask and answer. However, here is a word of advice I find noteworthy:

> *Leadership doesn't come from a seminar or the shelf at your favorite chain bookstore, nor is it measured in dollars and cents; it comes from working on behalf of your team and acting with a clear head in regard to the larger business goals. Learn to realize that people really are the means of production and that your success depends on your team respecting you for your defense of them from the machinations of outside forces.*[10]

I see the irony in the preceding quote since you probably did buy this book from your local bookstore. However, if this purchase on your part leads you to see the wisdom of marrying your style to real substance, it has served its purpose. The "machinations" you and your team face may not be Machiavellian, but in the spirit of a little healthy paranoia, consider that you're the one who must plan ahead for change and not be overwhelmed by whatever comes.

Summing Up

You may wonder why, at the end of this eighth chapter, in a book of only ten chapters, I've just now gotten to the core of leadership. The reason is that selling you on my concept of leadership is somewhat of a package deal. You have to unwrap the outer layers before you reach the prize. In another sense of a package, like any book, I've tried to make things nice and tidy. We all find books appealing for this very reason, among others. A discerning and discriminating eye, however, will always note the package and understand that the presentation is somewhat different from the reality. This is why "reality TV" has succeeded in many people's view as superior to a more traditional drama. In my opinion, reality TV is a very self-conscious attempt to show real life and fails by virtue of its self-awareness. It's like saying that the undocumented life isn't worth living. (This is supposed to be a joke.)

---

10. Don S. Olson and Carol L. Stimmel, *The Manager Pool: Patterns for Radical Leadership* (New York: Addison-Wesley, 2002), p. 9.

Practice Makes Leadership Real

My main point in this chapter is that you'll find leadership to be an adventure unique to your person, your company, your staff, and the times in which you live. Theory is necessary but practice makes it real. After a few years, you should write your own book or essay on leadership, just to sort it all out in your mind. Here is a case where documenting can be useful. Keep a journal of your experiences if you're inclined to document. Perhaps, if you like this book, tell your fiends about it. It will become a best-seller, and I will thus have opportunities to publish more.[11] We can then collect the journals you keep into a collection of leadership essays. I don't mean to sound too self-serving, but I'm practicing my concept of mentoring in this book. In my season of life, this has become a significant part of my leadership journey.

Build on the Cornerstones

As you move into the light of reality, take these principles I've shared with you. They were shared with me by many colleagues, experiences, and teachers. Spread what you find true and teach others. It is in the telling of truth, or the relating of stories, that you nail down the reality of what you've learned and make it a part of your character.

Do all that you do by staying centered on the cornerstones of leadership:

- **Understanding.** Know where you are going.

- **Communicating.** Impart your understanding clearly.

- **Delegating.** Allow others to help you achieve shared goals.

- **Monitoring.** Track your progress and your team's efforts to achieve your goals.

- **Participating.** Get into the fray and lead by example.

---

11. I'm serious. Send your essays about your leadership experiences to HerdingCats@mindspring.com.

Create a superstructure with your team. Build on the cornerstones by expending effort in

- **Mentoring.** Teach others to teach.

- **Rewarding.** Make success self-reinforcing by rewarding good work.

- **Correcting.** Grow your staff by helping them learn from mistakes.

- **Envisioning.** Motivate by seeing ahead to the next challenge before it becomes a problem.

- **Adapting.** Grow yourself by learning from your own mistakes.

A Look Ahead

In the next chapter, you'll examine your relationship to your boss. This will offer you an opportunity to examine the depth of your leadership abilities. Leading your staff is different from being led by your boss. You need experience in following a leader if you want to learn and practice the full range of being a leader. Take with you into the next chapter the lessons you've read about here and consider how they might apply to your boss. Keep an open mind—your boss has probably experienced all the trials, tribulations, and joys you read about in this chapter and has had numerous occasions to review and improve upon his or her leadership.

CHAPTER 9

Working with
Your Boss

AUTHOR'S NOTE: In this chapter, feminine pronouns are used, for the sake of a clear narrative line, to refer to the boss. I also have another motive: While our industry is traditionally heavy on the male side, women have brought and will continue to bring their special perspectives to software development. Perhaps if we had more women in the beginnings of our industry, we wouldn't be in some of the messes we find ourselves in from time to time.

Don't be intimidated by the title of this chapter, even if you are intimidated by your boss. Once you begin to understand the pressures your boss feels, you can turn your relationship with her into one of your most valuable tools for managing your people and growing as a leader. Remember, she probably has a boss too and has been in your shoes many times before.

If you already have a great relationship with your boss, the ideas I relate in this chapter should have great emotional resonance with you. You and your boss should be a team of two. The strength and agility of your working relationship with your boss will greatly benefit your growth as a leader. Learning to follow is also part of leading and will inform your actions toward your own staff as you work to herd them toward the goals you and your boss establish as priorities.

Understanding the World of Your Boss

The best way to manage your relationship with your boss is to imagine yourself promoted further up the ladder. This may not be your desire, and if you're like most programmers promoted into management, you've gone up as far as you want to go. But if you were in your boss's position, what would you expect of those that report to you? Consider this question and others like it when you work with your boss.

You're perhaps treading on shaky ground because you should not think of managing your boss; instead, think of managing the relationship you have with her using the same level of care as you do toward those who report to you. It's obvious that you want to please your boss. Pleasing sounds nice and warm, but if you aren't careful, you may step out of the bounds of honesty in trying to do this if you don't give careful attention to your motives. Bosses are pleased when the work they delegate is done on time without complaint or whining. Results are what count, not just smooth words aimed to placate and delay correction for a project going badly.

Depending on the structure of your organization, you might have to adjust some of the concepts mentioned here. The general idea I want to convey is that every step up the management ladder brings more responsibility for a wider scope of activity. With this increased responsibility comes increased pressure to perform work via delegation that must travel down several layers of bureaucracy. This chain of delegation, in which you are one link, can be very difficult to manage and inspect.

> *Every step up the management ladder brings more responsibility for a wider scope of activity.*

The authors of the book *The Centerless Corporation*[1] make the following observation: "While the size of today's corporation is approaching staggering proportions, the ability of management to achieve their desired results is weakening." Your boss is fighting this trend. "Desired results" should be everyone's goal. How can you help her achieve this?

In spite of talk of the "centerless" corporation or reengineering the enterprise, most of us still work within some hierarchical structure where one person reports to another and so on. Subordination isn't a bad 13-letter word. How many direct reports does your boss have as compared to you? Do the math. This is one factor to determine as you gain an understanding of your boss's role in your work life. The more people she has to manage should inform you about her administrative challenges, knowing what it takes for you to manage your people. The math might also be misleading. Those above you are ultimately responsible for *all* below. Consider this as you work with her. Her level of responsibility is greater than yours.

---

1. Bruce A. Pasternack and Albert J. Viscio, *The Centerless Corporation* (New York: Simon & Shuster, 1998), p. 15.

Honesty and Deadlines or Slips, Lies, and Videotape?

I mentioned honesty briefly in the preceding section and I wish I could leave it at that, but more needs to be said. When it comes to setting deadlines that can truly be met, honesty becomes a necessary challenge to face with courage. In the sales-driven atmosphere of most companies, time to market is everything. Keeping market share means enhancing software as needed and dictated by market pressures. This can put an enormous strain on your team, which ultimately puts the strain on you. Your boss has an even greater strain because, more than likely, she is accountable to someone too.

Not only is the chain of accountability one factor, but also all the talk of market pressure is very much a reality. Look at the powerful Microsoft marketing machine: You may not like the way they go about it, but you can't argue with their success.[2] Ask any CEO or group of shareholders if they want to have success like Microsoft. Do you think they will say no?

In light of these market pressures, many organizations set dates for software releases without always consulting you. Many times a release plan must be developed far in advance of the actual fully formed business requirements being settled. I discussed this in Chapter 3, where the difference between a wishful and realistic project plan was illustrated. It's worth repeating the principles again. *Ideally* you would like to plan as follows:

1. Establish the business requirements.

2. Create the software design that will successfully implement the requirements.

3. Prototype the design to uncover any flaws and adjust the design or requirements as needed.

4. Develop a project plan that adequately accounts for all the work and testing the development effort will demand.

Once the plan is created, a release window time frame can be established and any promises to the sales department are based on this date. As with any development project, the release window should be contingent upon successful beta testing.

---

2. Maybe you could, but what's the point? I've made a good living using their products for many years and you probably have too.

Of course, we don't live in an ideal world, hence the tales of programmers with sleeping bags near their desks for those all-nighters. Your only recourse is to learn to survive reality.[3] What does this have to do with honesty? Well, it's your job to know that what you're being asked to do is unrealistic because of the following real-world conditions:

- Business requirements are not fully completed, but you must begin the design now to try to meet the release date established by others.

- Your design is always changing because the requirements are in flux.

- You don't have time to prototype or, worse, the prototype becomes the code.

- The only plan you have is to work backward from the sales-driven release date to determine how long you have to do actual development.

In spite of this reality, you must still try your best to meet the deadline. Our industry is immature and the pressures from the marketplace demand that we attempt to be heroes. So, again, honesty means admitting the challenge openly is a lot to bear, but you will attempt it anyway. Does this make sense? If it does, send me your resume in an e-mail—I want you on my team.

A word about being a hero.[4] This might seem like a wonderful idea at the outset of your career, but many never achieve this status consistently. What you should strive for is to maintain a balance between expectations and effort with honesty as your foundation. In other words, you might miss a deadline once or twice, and no one will be surprised. You can get over this. What you can't get over is not being honest about your promises. If you must promise, be sure the caveats are fully stated to your boss. Make promises by qualifying them with the level of confidence you feel appropriate for the conditions of the particular development effort you're about to undertake. Repairing your reputation is a lot harder than fixing bugs in a released product.

> *You should strive to maintain a balance between expectations and effort with honesty as your foundation. Repairing your reputation is a lot harder than fixing bugs in a released product.*

---

3. See Yourdon's great contribution to techniques for surviving "death march" projects in his book of the same title. (It's in the Bibliography.)

4. Only those who live in a society such as ours can afford the luxury of even considering hero status. Count yourself lucky to have a good job and do your best. The real heroes died on September 11, 2001 trying to save the innocent.

More on heroes. The flip side of a hero is a fatalist—someone who tries to be a hero, fails, and then blames fate for his self-created dilemma. If you're engaged in a "death march" project, realize that you and your team may suffer the casualties of war. Fatigue sets in after too many all-nighters, and the code begins to suffer. Adding more programmers to an already late project will only prove Brooks' Law.[5] This is why honesty is so important early on in the project-planning process (assuming you have a plan).

Vanity and pride also have a bearing on honesty. I'm at the age where hair spray, mirrors, and time are required to satisfy my vanity each morning. The truth is I'm going bald. I may try to cover it up for my own reasons, but everyone knows and can see the reality.[6] In the same way, the bald truth of your opinion about deadlines is better than a cosmetic tale. I submit the following poem as another[7] illustration about honesty:

Unfinished Business

In the air an odor lingers:

It is the smell of broken promises,

The scent is distinctive, singular

No one would mistake it.

I cannot. My nostrils are full of it.

Helping Your Boss Plan for Success

Her job is to know what is needed when; yours is to know how. That was a fairly awkward sentence, so let's try again. Planning usually is initiated for the enterprise by your boss, and you're brought in to fill out the details. No, this isn't getting any clearer, is it? That is my point. Planning is like this: Take two steps forward and one step back. It's like a recursive procedure: You have to continually drill down on a big plan to flush out the details that will eventually be your job to manage. This is where you help your boss by imagining the implications of her grand plan. Planning involves more perspiration than inspiration.

---

5. "Adding manpower to a late software project makes it later." See Brooks, op. cit., p. 25.

6. If you were a woman, would you date a guy who tried to use one hair to wrap around his head like a turban to conceal the truth? Probably not. If you know of such women, send me their phone numbers.

7. We must drill down a bit more on honesty, even if you feel like you're at the dentist without novocaine.

Some companies view your department as a factory, where they feed in the specifications and out comes the product. Were this true, I think I would change professions or at least become the owner of a factory instead of the labor foreman. There is real talk of software factories in many consulting firms—usually they're overseas and reflect on the high cost and low return on investment that many software development departments in America exhibit. Edward Yourdon's two books on this subject, *Decline & Fall of the American Programmer* (Yourdon Press, 1993) and *Rise & Resurrection of the American Programmer* (Yourdon Press, 1996), address the reasons why planning is often neglected or badly done in software development circles. Perhaps our insistence on programming as an art form is to blame.[8] If we were building a rocket to the moon, we'd have a plan.

Speaking of the American space program, how is it that in the 1960s we were able to land a man on the moon with less software power than exists in your typical PDA? It was because men and women planned for success with the tools on hand. In Gene Kranz's memoir[9] about mission control, he describes the following principles that led to the professional excellence of his department:

Discipline. Being able to follow as well as lead, knowing that we must master ourselves before we can master our task.

Competence. There being no substitute for total preparation and complete dedication, for space will not tolerate the careless or indifferent.

Confidence. Believing in ourselves as well as others, knowing that we must master fear and hesitation before we can succeed.

Responsibility. Realizing that it cannot be shifted to others, for it belongs to each of us; we must answer for what we do, or fail to do.

Toughness. Taking a stand when we must; to try again, and again, even if it means following a more difficult path.

Teamwork. Respecting and utilizing the ability of others, realizing that we work toward a common goal, for success depends on the efforts of all.

---

8. I know I've freely used the terms "craft" and "art" in this book and I've been somewhat reluctant to embrace software as an engineering discipline. This was a conscious choice: I spent many years as a hardware engineer and I'm very familiar with the disciplines of applied science. I still prefer to consider our work an art, but from time to time the hard sciences can help us out. See the next chapter for further discussion on this subject.

9. Gene Kranz, *Failure is Not an Option* (New York: Simon & Schuster, 2000), p. 393.

Kranz goes on to say that the "greatest error is not to have tried and failed, but that in trying, we did not give it our best effort." He lived by these principles and thus developed good plans, sometimes on the spur of the moment, but he did plan. He had to plan: Lives were at stake. In your case, the software might not kill anyone but a bad plan could damage your career and that of your boss.[10]

Can we take Kranz's principles over into our world? I believe we can and I wouldn't attempt to improve on the wording. They're strong and good words that should be pasted next to our monitors and read aloud every day. As I have mentioned time and again in these pages, leadership fosters much success, and planning is another area where your leadership is needed. Your boss can't do it alone; she may have several other departments to plan for, not just yours. You may consider yourself the engine of your company's business, and perhaps this is a good analogy, but others provide the fuel and maintenance, and govern the throttle. Maybe you're the spark plug. How are you firing? Is your "gap" between management and leadership set right so the power of your passion can create a spark of enthusiasm within your team?

Knowing Your Limits

Your boss is probably better at planning than you are. She got to be where she is because she earned a reputation for getting things done, and this requires good planning skills as well as an ability to execute a plan. In addition, she may be better at most other things than you. What she doesn't always know, however, are your limits as well as you do. If you've been following the narrative up to this point, and I assume if you've read this far you have been, recall the issue of working on your weaknesses discussed in Chapter 2.

Here is an analogy drawn from a software program.

Most of us like to think of ourselves as good technologists, engineers, scientists, programmers, or whatever. Typically these kinds of folks like to play games that challenge their intellectual skills. I've always liked to play chess, even thought I don't think I'm very good at it. In a chess program I use to get better, the software allows you to set the skill level of the chess engine so you can have an enjoyable

---

10. Of course, if you're developing mission-critical software this could be a serious issue. I still don't trust many financial transactions over the Internet because I know the kind of guys who write the software!

game. Now, assuming you want to win, you might need to adjust this skill level from the maximum setting down to one a bit lower. To use the terms from this software,[11] there are eight skill levels:

1. Newcomer

2. Novice

3. Easy

4. Light

5. Moderate

6. Difficult

7. Expert

8. Championship

Your skills at work may fall somewhere on this spectrum; those of your boss probably are higher. The game, however, is always a championship match in the marketplace. Acknowledge your limits as you work with your boss. She will respect your saying "I don't know" more than an opinion that you make sound convincing simply because you haven't got a clue as to the real answer.

> *Acknowledge your limits as you work with your boss. She will respect your saying "I don't know" more than an opinion that you make sound convincing simply because you haven't got a clue as to the real answer.*

Having mentioned chess, this brings to mind the difference between strategic and tactical thinking, two other dimensions to measure your limits by. Chess requires very good strategic skills; tactics will not win the game in most cases unless both players are both in a hurry to determine the winner. Consider these two ways of getting work done, strategy and tactics, as you relate to your boss. Your boss is probably better at strategy than you. If she isn't, help her out; if she is, learn from her. Her job may be best served by you being the tactician while she plays the strategist. Become a team player with your boss and you both will benefit.

---

11. Chess Master 5000. I don't think they'll mind me borrowing their menu structure since this program is an older version. I can't manage a newer and stronger version!

Expecting the Unexpected

You may be in a position within your organization where strategic decisions are made by others and you are charged with carrying them out. Often this can produce a feeling of dread or powerlessness. No one likes being surprised by new work assignments that were not anticipated. Louis Pasteur, the inventor of modern vaccines, said that "chance favors the prepared mind." Write this on the back of your hand or the front edge of your monitor. Our constantly evolving industry will throw you some curve balls from time to time. So will your boss, and when she does this, you need to be prepared.

How do you "prepare" yourself for the unexpected? Good question, and the answers are legion. One key area of preparation is the scope of your knowledge about what is technically possible given the tools on hand or soon to be available. This requires you to be a perpetual student of technology in many fields. While becoming a polymath is beyond most of us today, you can keep up with the industry if you read widely, surf the Internet wisely, and pay attention to business trends. Devote a part of your workweek to investigating and gathering information that may be helpful in the future. Stay away from the "toy" aspect of technology; concentrate on emerging trends demonstrated by those who successfully live on the bleeding edge if you aren't able to do this yourself. Always keep up with the latest beta versions of the tools that you employ in your work. If you can afford a research and development person or department, your ability to prepare for the future will be greatly enhanced. Ask your boss for some help in this area because she may already be better prepared than you. (See the section in Chapter 2 on "Watching Your Weaknesses" for a refresher on agendas for reading.)

Overcoming Organizational Inertia

You are more than likely in middle management and your boss a bit above your level in the pecking order. You have an advantage you might not expect in that you may be more in tune with what is happening in the development world outside the confines of your organization. Your boss may be more isolated due to her position in the company. This condition is common in many companies and, while regrettable, it's often inevitable. It arises due to the increasing concern higher level managers have with the details of the hierarchy below them. They keep their eyes focused on those below and often don't look outward to see what's happening in the industry at large.

Note what Andy Grove has to say about the condition of those high up the food chain:

Senior managers got to where they are by having been good at what they do. And over time they have learned to lead with their strengths. So it's not surprising that they will keep implementing the same strategic and tactical moves that worked for them during the course of their careers—especially during their "championship season."[12]

Grove refers to this condition as the "inertia of success" and it's very dangerous. You can also suffer from this malady, so what I relate here about your boss can also apply to you.

Point Out Industry Trends

Keep your ears tuned and eyes peeled to the condition of your company relative to the competition. Notice how they get things done and measure how you compare. Your boss may be so set in her ways that she doesn't think anyone can derail your company's corporate success. As a technical leader, part of your job is to know what's new in the industry and how it might apply to your development efforts. Your boss may be satisfied with how things are going, even when you're not. Point out how your company's processes can be improved if you believe there is room for improvement. Use examples from your study of new development techniques or coming revolutions in technology to illustrate your insights.

One area to keep in focus, especially when your company is entering a crisis period, is to watch for signs of denial in your boss' attitude toward the problems you face. A crisis often sneaks up on high-tech companies that fail to keep up with the times and then all of a sudden, they must engage in a massive modernization effort. These are turning points for your company and they will directly affect you. You may be in a unique position to be more teachable than your boss and thus can help her see things her past success has blinded her to. Of course, use care and politeness but don't shrink from being bold. You're often the one closest to the front lines and your future success may depend upon sounding the alarm bell when you see your company slipping.

 You're often the one closest to the front lines and your future success may depend upon sounding the alarm bell when you see your company slipping.

---

12. Grove, op. cit., p. 127.

Experiment with New Methods and Techniques

Part of your role as the technical leader is to try out new ways of accomplishing your business goals. You do this not just to have variety, but because you're searching for ways to lower the cost of doing development or to add value to the products and services you offer. Your boss may just ask you to get a job done and leave it up to you in terms of the details. If you sense inertia setting in, try something new to shake things up. Again, use care but be the leader in those things you know will improve your efforts.

Your boss may only be concerned with the final result of your development efforts. You should be too, but if you can beat your deadlines by 10 percent at 20 percent less cost by using new methods or tools, you should take the risk. Show your boss how you did it. She will learn from you by these examples and your value will increase in her eyes, which could mean good things for you as well as your company at large. This is the best way to be a hero, rather than the other, riskier ways I described earlier in this chapter.

Be Sensitive to Timing

The problem with corporate inertia is that it keeps you from acting when economic or technological conditions are demanding your company make a change. If your boss has been highly successful, she may feel invulnerable to change or simply believe it's no problem to conquer. Maybe she's right but it doesn't cost you anything to watch the radar screen for blips that begin to loom on the horizon. Shakespeare had something important to say about timing:

> *The enemy increaseth every day;*
>
> *We at the height are ready to decline.*
>
> *There is a tide in the affairs of men*
>
> *Which, take at the flood, leads on to fortune;*
>
> *Omitted, all the voyage of their life*
>
> *Is bound in shallows and in miseries.*[13]

---

13. See Julius Caesar, Act 4, Scene 2, where Brutus speaks after having murdered Caesar. Don't get any ideas here. I'm aware of the irony of this quotation in the context of working with your boss, but the point about timing in the political drama Shakespeare writes about is equally true in business.

There's usually only one optimal time to act to lead on to fortune. This has certainly proven true in the stock market and it can also be critical in software development. If your company is at a turning point and no one else but you sees it, speak up. Failure to act leads to many miseries, and you can help yourself and your boss avoid these calamities by being sensitive to impending industry conditions that call for a change.

Recognize the Customer Is First

In a technology-driven organization, another type of inertia arises from an exclusive focus on the methods of implementation rather than the results. You are, after all, in business to produce products and services that meet your customers' needs. Notice what one industry leader says about customer service:

> *The best customer service is no customer service. That's right, good service is the kind that doesn't get used because it isn't needed. The goal is to refine products and services so that they're easier to use and understand with every iteration. Successful customer-centered businesses must implement technologies that let them gain deep and meaningful understanding of their customers. The result is an organization equipped to develop the products and services its customers truly want and need. For all of you worried about ROI, here's where an initial investment in customer service will result in lower customer support costs down the line (via gathered and mined customer data).*[14]

If you don't watch for signs of technologically-induced inertia, you may be surprised by the increase in support calls when your latest whiz-bang product hits the market without attention to what the users really wanted or needed. Don't get so carried away with your tools that you lose sight of the end user. Modern technology has many complexities, but it's designed to hide your users from the means of implementation, not put the complexity in their collective face.

Ask your boss to help you gain greater access to marketing information as you plan your next product. If she isn't in tune with this, make a point of reminding her of the importance of listening to the market through the eyes of the sales staff. I've warned you about sales-driven deadlines, but the flip side of these considerations is positive. Without market intelligence, your product or service will only

---

14. See the article by Challis Hodge entitled "Smoothing the Path" at `http://www.webtechniques.com/archives/2001/11/hodge/`. He was the founder and CEO of HannaHodge, a Chicago-based user experience firm. He created the University of Wisconsin's interface design curriculum and guided the user interface development of enterprise Web-based solutions at IBM.

have the narrow perspective you can bring to the business solution. Last year's ideas of what the market demands aren't helpful. You need to be as current with the customer needs of today and tomorrow as you are with the technology you envision will meet those needs.

Summary of Guidelines

I've exposed areas in your relationship with your boss that you need to observe with care. The intention of my dialogue with you here is to help you make the teamwork between you and your boss bring the greatest benefit to both of you. Here's a brief reminder of things to watch out for:

- Understand the unique pressures your boss experiences in her job. Your first response to her should be "Yes, ma'am" followed by a "but" only when you're sure of your facts.

- Value honesty over unrealistic promises regardless of the consequences.

- Help your boss plan, insisting on realistic steps in the plan and a promise to expend the maximum effort in executing the plan.

- Admit when you don't have an answer for your boss. Don't make up stuff just to cover your mistakes.

- Prepare for the unexpected by becoming an expert at what you do. Sometimes the unexpected will come from your boss; at other times, it will come from external conditions. You make your own luck by being prepared.[15]

- Be sensitive to inertia in yourself and your boss that resists needed change, and do something about it before it's too late.

Let me take one last parting shot at your relationship with your boss. Here it is: Treat your boss like you would like to be treated. The Golden Rule isn't just for Sunday school—it works in all areas of life on any day of the week.

---

15. This is my rephrasing of Pasteur's famous saying, "Chance favors the prepared mind." I can't take credit for the paraphrase—I first heard it from my father as a child.

The End Is Near

No, not your career, just this book. The next chapter is the last and it deals with a range of topics that were only partially covered in previous chapters or not discussed at all. I've written this book in a thematic mode, grouping topics under general areas of your work life that you face every day. The next chapter is a shotgun approach that I believe will expose you to the shock of dealing with a variety of topics sometimes outside of the normal flow of your daily job. After all, if software development is an exercise in hitting a moving target, a shotgun is the best way to hit the bull's-eye.

CHAPTER 10

Words without a Song

Software development is usually a linear activity, even when you use an iterative process, and the steps from one phase to the next take place in a logical and linear fashion. The management of the development process, however, is rarely linear. You will find yourself jumping from one problem domain to the next, where the methods to reach one solution don't often help you in another. The best you can do is bring all your intelligence to bear on the challenge of the moment, knowing your goal is to lead others out of chaos and into clarity. You might call this "living on the edge of chaos," and perhaps this describes some of your days at the helm.

The title of this chapter, "Words without a Song," is intended to convey a sense of this "on the edge" condition you often experience. It's loosely based upon a tradition among the Romantic composers, Schubert for example, who were fond of composing songs without words. These are typically some of the most beautiful compositions in the classical repertoire. This chapter is a bit like this in the opposite sense: It has no general melody and you might feel the topics describe here are not particularly beautiful. It may seem that what's related here is a catchall for topics not touched upon in previous chapters—you are correct to assume this. However, there's a deeper method to my madness: Sometimes your job will feel like sets of unrelated and miscellaneous activities. At other times, you'll find yourself considering subjects that are completely outside the scope of your previous experience. This chapter is an exercise in this format[1] and I hope the topics presented can bring some clarity to your job.

---

1.   I also thought that if I entitled this chapter "Miscellaneous Topics" it would generate little reader interest.

The Distributed Workforce

In today's business culture, geographic centralization of development teams is often not possible. Financial forces, key individuals with unique talents, and corporate history may result in you managing a team that doesn't work in the same location. Your efforts to organize collaboration and solitude,[2] two essential needs for your team, will present a major challenge when your workforce is distributed among different time zones or facilities. If you have staff members that telecommute once or twice a week, you'll also need to create methods uniquely tailored for managing their productivity.

> *Your efforts to organize collaboration and solitude, two essential needs for your team, will present a major challenge when your workforce is distributed among different time zones or facilities.*

The Challenge

Consider how development is facilitated when you can successfully manage and provide the following:

- **Solitude.** The ability to work without interruptions or distractions in an environment conducive to abstract thinking.

- **Collaboration.** Sharing ideas in a face-to-face mode until technical consensus is reached within the team or between a pair of programmers working on a common problem.

A team where these two crucial needs are met can be very productive. Writing solid code requires both in an appropriate mixture.

For the distributed workforce, where some staff works alone at home, others share an office with unrelated groups, and still others exist as subteams in yet another location, managing the crucial factors of solitude and collaboration is difficult. You'll have some team members with too much solitude and no means of effective collaboration. Other parts of your team may have very little solitude and even collaborate with all the wrong people. The challenge these conditions bring can be summarized as follows:

- Decisions that would take minutes to resolve if everyone was located in the same place take hours or even days to make.

---

2.   See Chapter 4 where this was discussed.

- Monitoring staff performance and progress is limited to e-mail and telephone conversation rather than direct inspection. This flies in the face of the classic management principle "Don't expect without inspecting."

- Technical design is done primarily through documents rather than an interactive mode. Documents should be the result of collaboration, not the means. The design phase is often lengthened or, in some cases, formally ignored due to time constraints.

- Your team doesn't share the same atmosphere. There is no watercooler banter or friendship building outside the context of work.

- E-mail and instant messaging become the virtual workplace and, while helpful, they're poor substitutes for face time.

- The telephone dominates your working hours as a manager.

Some of these challenges are, of course, present with a centralized team, but the manager of a geographically dispersed team experiences the downside of all these factors each day.

A Solution

If you can't centralize, you must adapt your management style to the circumstances in which your team operates. As you learned in Chapter 1, adaptation is a key skill for leading a team of programmers. Let's apply that skill here to several areas that need special attention when you manage a distributed team.

Planning

First and foremost, the management of task assignments must be carefully thought out and coordinated. This demands that you have planned your project well enough to be able to break them up into assignments that you can give to team members who work alone and can be productive without much collaboration. Of course, you ideally would like all your projects to be this thoroughly planned, but for the dispersed team, it's critical.

You must plan your projects well enough to be able to break them up into assignments that you can give to team members who work alone and can be productive without much collaboration.

If you fail to create adequately defined tasks, the distance between you and the assigned programmer will make refinement of the task more time consuming. In addition, you must design the work so that one person's output can mesh well with another's. A component-driven architecture is ideal for these conditions if it fits in with your overall enterprise strategy. You want the overall construction of the software to be like a factory assembly line where one part snaps into another. A nice idea if you can achieve it. It's possible, but it makes severe demands on your project planning process and design skills.

Planning in general should occur face to face in the initial stages of any new project. This means you'll have to gather everyone in one place at least once to initiate a project design. This costs money, but the time spent in trying to design by e-mail or telephone will cost even more. Make the planning session an opportunity to do team building in addition to design. A yearly retreat to an exotic location can also serve these planning purposes and be a fringe benefit for your team. After you pay for all the round-trip air tickets for a few years, you may want to evaluate spending the same money on permanent videoconferencing links. After a few trips, you could probably pay for a fairly elaborate system that could show a whiteboard on one monitor and various groups on another. You'll have to evaluate the economics of the situation based on your budget. My main concern is that you facilitate your team's ability to communicate by whatever means works for your organization.

Communicating

Thank goodness for Alexander Graham Bell. With the telephone, real-time duplex communication is greatly facilitated. When Bell said, "Come here, Watson," I wonder, however, if he was just tired of talking on the instrument and wanted some face time with his assistant? You would be able to plan your day around more effective and efficient means of communicating if they were all in one place. Nevertheless, unless you rely exclusively on e-mail, the phone might as well be grafted into your right ear when your team is dispersed. If you can afford videoconferencing, this can help aid communication but it isn't always practical or possible for most companies. You may even try the inexpensive PC video camera and appropriate collaboration software if your bandwidth is adequate. I haven't had much success in using these tools.

E-mail, of course, is the primary medium of communication for most teams that are spread out among different locations. For the manager, this means that your inbox usually occupies a large portion of your time each day. Learning to deal quickly with your responses is crucial if you're going to have time to do the other administrative tasks your job requires. Try to limit e-mail to subjects where written words or diagrams are needed to communicate clearly. Use the phone for discussions and e-mail for documentation of decisions.

In spite of the weaknesses of a document-driven design process, you'll come to rely on this method. You'll want to design by contract—that is, establish the public interfaces of objects that must be assembled together at the very beginning of the design. This makes sense even if your team isn't dispersed, but when one developer is in California and another in New England, an agreement on component interaction and interoperability is essential. Invest in good collaboration software for your team and use it as a library for your documents. A number of vendors are competing for market share in the teamware category that can aid your collaboration efforts—you should check them out if you haven't already.[3]

Monitoring

Your job as a manager is greatly complicated when it comes to inspecting what you expect from a geographically scattered team. Your workday will often have to be extended to account for time zone differences. This puts extra demands on you but is the only way to coordinate effectively. Be sure you take care of your own needs as a human with a life if you have to put in 12-hour days on a regular basis. Take breaks in the middle of your day for personal chores when you can or you won't last long under these conditions.

Things can get dicey for you monitoring staff remotely. Have you ever walked up behind one of your staff, observed them surfing the Web, and asked, "Why aren't you working?" They might answer, "I would have been if I knew you were coming!" This might sound funny but it can often describe your reality as a virtual boss. How do you counter the tendency of human nature to play when the boss isn't looking? Only by formally having a plan for individual deliverables and tracking it very closely will you achieve some measure of effective monitoring. The work-breakdown structure for projects might have to be more fine-grained to help you keep from encountering project schedule slips. Again, the telephone and e-mail will be required to facilitate this monitoring need. You'll need to gather weekly and sometimes daily status reports.

A more Orwellian approach might be to have your developers' workstations equipped with remote monitoring software that allows you to see what's on their screen at any time. They, of course, should be aware that their computers are "bugged," but if you really want to check up on an individual, this could be a solution. This approach doesn't do much to build trust, and it might even foster resentment, so you should think long and hard before you employ such measures.

---

3. See http://www.eroom.com, http://www.fox.se/english/starteam/starteam_version_control.htm, and other offerings by IBM and Symantec.

> *Only by formally having a plan for individual deliverables and tracking it very closely will you achieve some measure of effective monitoring.*

The Personal Touch

You'll find your team building efforts more effective if you visit your dispersed staff in their normal work environment as often as you can. When you show up at their workplace, it validates their membership in the team and adds weight to your leadership when you're not present. Doing this will cost time and money, but you'll reap rewards for the investment and mitigate some of the downsides associated with a scattered herd of cats.

Multicultural Factors in Management

America: the true melting pot of the world, or more accurately today, the cultural salad bowl of the planet. Americans aren't the only ones with programming smarts. Learning to manage staff from different national and cultural backgrounds can pose a significant challenge to you as a leader. Methods of communicating and motivating are two areas you must adjust and customize as you spend time learning about your culturally diverse staff. Get to know them socially and learn about their family background and cultural practices. You'll be richer for the effort and your programmer from, say, Russia, will feel that he or she is more valued because you take time to understand his or her unique worldview.

Language and Culture

You must learn to standardize your vocabulary with a multicultural team. You can't deal with everyone like they're all good ol' boys from your neck of the woods. It won't work. Figures of speech, common mannerisms, and even body language differ from culture to culture. Learn to speak more slowly and realize that speaking English as a second language doesn't mean individuals are familiar with American slang or sloppy sentence construction and casual ways of talking. Even the British have significant differences in the use of the English language that might surprise you.[4]

---

4.   They would never use the term "rich user interface." They think this simply means expensive.

> *You can't deal with everyone like they're all good ol' boys from your neck of the woods.*

Other cultural practices will surprise you or be worth incorporating into what you consider normal for an employee. Did you know that men in the Philippines commonly hold hands in public as a sign of friendship? When someone from India visits your home for the first time, he or she usually brings a gift. An Australian might seem closely aligned with American culture, but do you know what they do with Vegemite?[5] What about the observance of typical American holidays? Will staff in Bangalore be observing Thanksgiving or working? You must understand these differences and learn to become a citizen of the world, allowing the best of each culture to become part of your leadership skill set.

Motivating and Controlling the Team

Motivating programmers with money might be the lowest common denominator in your American bag of management tricks, but it's also the least effective way of building teamwork in a multicultural environment. What do you do? You consider all the factors that can motivate the team you have or others you might want to hire. A recent survey of 100 non-U.S. employees conducted by Dene Bettmeng revealed the following:

> *Most employees viewed the corporate culture, policies and use of technology as the main advantages of working for a U.S.-based corporation. Specifically, they like their career growth prospects, compensation and benefits, and the ability to use and learn new technologies. These people felt that working for any U.S.-based firm was generally superior to companies headquartered in other countries. Along with the benefits cited above, they appreciated the political stability, fast pace and strong team environment.*[6]

As with any team, knowing your people makes the difference between success and failure as a leader. With a multicultural team, you have more to learn and this can be a personally rewarding experience for you. It can also be a personally devastating experience. With good American talent often hard to come by, you might

---

5.   Vegemite is a vegetable paste commonly put on toast. It's somewhat equivalent to peanut butter but not nearly as tasty.

6.   Dene Bettmeng, reporting in Network World Fusion (http://www.nwfusion.com/careers/2001/0402man.html) on international relations.

be tempted to try overseas consultants. I have seen it work, and I have seen it fail miserably. Some cultures do not encourage employees to challenge or even ask the boss to clarify their assignments. This can lead you to believe that your foreign consultants understand what you've asked for until you see the end product. Tread very carefully in this area.

Cat Fight! The Foreign Legion

The decision was made to get three projects completed quickly by bringing in 12 foreign consultants. We asked that they be at the expert level or higher—at least, that's what we asked for. All of them ended up being from India, a nation with a growing reputation for producing good programming talent. I was supposed to get them arranged into teams by specialty and begin the projects. I'd been a part of all the interviews and had chosen each according to his specialties, but we where only able to have phone interviews. This is where my first learning experience occurred. Of course, it was only apparent after the interviews were completed and the teams were on board that I learned what kind of trouble I was getting into.

- **Lesson 1.** I learned, after the fact, that during the phone interviews the consultants were provided with lengthy cheat sheets that have the answers to every question you could possibly think of. I would ask, "What data modeler do you prefer?" There would be a pause and they would say, "Could you repeat the question, I didn't quite understand." All the while they were searching their cheat sheets for the topic in question. Then they would reply, "ERStudio is my favorite, but here are its weaknesses. I also like ERWin, and here are its strengths." You get the point—word for word from the sheet the answers I heard made perfect sense. I thought I had found a group of geniuses. This impression was corrected rapidly after the projects began.

  After the projects commenced, I learned several more painful lessons. All of these new learning experiences flowed from cultural issues that I had no idea would be a factor in managing foreign teams.

- **Lesson 2.** When a person from India nods that means no, not yes. Do you realize how confusing this can be when you take for grated that a nod signals agreement?

- **Lesson 3.** Typically, a worker from India will never challenge, correct, or question a superior in front of someone else. This means they will agree to everything you say even if you're completely wrong. Some of them will then simply do the work their way after any meeting, no matter what was said. I thought I must really be a great team leader since reaching consensus was never so easy with American programming teams.

- **Lesson 4.** Often, the consultants never admitted that they didn't understand me. They said multiple times that everything makes sense and then they went off and coded something completely different.

- **Lesson 5.** Indian census records indicate that over 200 distinct dialects exist in India—all of these people where from different parts of the country (some didn't like each other) and their only common language was broken English. Lots of smiles and nods didn't help make up for the communication gaps.

- **Lesson 6.** Even though I had hired all the consultants from one firm, they all actually worked for different consulting companies. They were subcontracted, sometimes five levels deep. I was paying $125.00 an hour for their services, and some of them were making $15.00 while others made $55.00.

My lessons were learned too late. Only one of the projects was a success, the rest were miserable, costly failures. I will never ever try this again.

Evaluating Software Development Methodologies

In the beginning, programming was conducted by a priesthood of engineers and scientists far removed from the hustle and bustle of the business center. Today the computer is ubiquitous and the business use of the technology has demanded quality software delivered on time and within the allocated budget. Let me take a deep breath and you go ahead and have a good laugh for both of us at this last sentence. No, seriously, we can't laugh: The era of the hacker producing products on his or her terms is fading. Business expects our profession to be conducted with all the care and attention to the bottom line that any group in the company would give. This is where the fun begins. Almost everybody with public recognition in our industry claims to be an expert and wants to sell you on their unique methodology for development.

I'm different—I only want to sell you on the idea of becoming eclectic in your use of development methods. Use and enhance what has proven to work for you, your team, and your company. Create and tailor methods to fit your enterprise and ensure they all have one goal in common: Deliver quality software promptly. In the sections to follow, I'll survey significant schools of thought with a focus on the philosophy behind the methods. I'm not discussing design schools here. Structured programming, object-oriented design, and the design pattern movement are more concerned with construction details than an overall development methodology. Architectural concerns (discussed in Chapter 6) are also not the primary focus. I'm taking a step back from the details and giving you a 30,000-foot view of the whole shebang.

Create and tailor methods to fit your enterprise and ensure they all have one goal in common: Deliver quality software promptly.

Software Engineering

During the late 1960s, when the engineering geniuses of the day put a man on the moon with less computing power than a modern calculator,[7] the term "software engineering" began to have currency. It's derived from the belief that software can be manufactured based on the proven disciplines of traditional engineering. For extremely large software projects, especially those initiated by the government or large defense contractors, this approach has had some successes and many spectacular failures.[8] This method was often employed when the hardware was evolving at the same time the software was being created. Few commercial applications were built using these methods. The IEEE defines the method as follows:

> *Software engineering is the application of a systematic, disciplined, quantifiable approach to development, operation, and maintenance of software; that is, the application of engineering to software.[9]*

You may be nonplussed by this definition, as I am. Budgetary concerns are secondary using these methods, but minimizing the number of defects in the code is primary.

The operative words from the IEEE definition can be expanded, in my opinion, as follows:

- **Systematic:** A process can be established to control all aspects of development.

- **Disciplined:** Execute the proper methods consistently and quality software can be delivered.

- **Quantifiable:** All requirements can be known and mapped to methods of implementation.

---

7.   The first practical microprocessor was developed in 1971.

8.   See Glass, *Software Runaways*, op. cit.

9.   See *IEEE Standard Computer Dictionary* (Institute of Electrical and Electronics Engineers, 1990).

Before you gasp at my expansion of these core terms, wouldn't you agree that we all would like to achieve the level of certainty, accuracy, and completeness this method promises? We would, of course. One of the long-time proponents of software engineering writes the following about the myth of the super programmer:

> *There is a common view that a few first-class artists can do far better work than the typical software team. The implication is that they will know intuitively how to do first-class work, so no orderly process framework will be needed. If this were true, one would expect that those organizations who have the best people would not suffer from the common problems of software quality and productivity. Experience, however, shows that this is not the case.*[10]

Do you see the tension building? It's "man" against "machine," where in the case of software engineering, the "machine" is a disciplined team working under a common methodology. The "man" in this case is the guru who produces software like magic from his cauldron of skills. This is all an unnecessary and somewhat artificial debate. You need good people and you need a good process: It takes both to build great software. The question then becomes, Is software engineering a good process?

The reviews are mixed. If you were building a new air traffic control system, you might think this approach would be appropriate. Think again. The software engineering approach had a lot to do with the massive failure of the FAA's Advanced Automation System that promised in the 1980s to modernize air traffic control. The promises were never fulfilled but millions of dollars were spent.[11]

Some still swear by software engineering as *the* correct methodology, while others find it impractical or not applicable to everyday development projects in the Internet era. I suggest you explore the literature on your own, try some of the ideas, and reach your own conclusions. This school does have many good ideas and if you can adapt them to work for you, go for it. In my opinion, software engineering is more of a wish than a reality and I've learned to look elsewhere for methods that work for me and my team.

Microsoft Solutions Framework (MSF)

You may question me bringing in a method proposed by a vendor of tools. Go ahead, but Microsoft has created a very well-thought-out and, of course, well-marketed approach. A number of companies[12] have required all development

---

10. Humphrey, op. cit., p. ix.
11. See Glass, Software Runaways, op. cit., p .56 (Section 2.1.4).
12. Mine, of course, is one of them.

personnel to attend weeklong courses sponsored by Microsoft to teach their methods. Certainly, a company of the stature of Microsoft, whose primary business is commercial software, has something worthy to say on the subject of development.

The key idea behind MSF is coordination of teams with specific areas of responsibility for the development process. Rather than repeating the marketing hype, I will share a few details here because they're more indicative of Microsoft's thinking than the public relations gloss or any clever restatement of their philosophy. Taking a page from their manual,[13] you find their disciplined approach centered around three ideas:

1. A services-based application model that encourages developers to view an application as a network of services in which features and functionality can be packaged for reuse across functional boundaries.

2. An iterative development life cycle process model that is delivery-focused, risk-driven, and has four primary milestones.

3. A scalable development team model consisting of six equally important team roles.

Are you waiting expectantly to find out what these "four milestones" and "six roles" are? Take their course—I don't want to do anymore marketing for them than I have to. They have some excellent ideas and I've adapted a number of them in my own development methodology. Well, okay, I guess you don't have the time to do the research and you did buy my book, so here are the details.

MSF milestones focus on the team approval of the following:

1. **Vision/Scope:** An emphasis on the scope of the effort rather than the requirements.

2. **Project Plan:** Customers and team agree on the deliverables, priorities, and expectations.

3. **Scope Complete/First Use:** The first beta release of the complete product.

4. **Release:** The product or service is released to operations and support groups.

---

13. *Solutions Development Discipline Workbook* (Redmond, WA: Microsoft Corporation, 1996), pp. 1–17.

MSF teams have roles centered upon the following:

1. **Product Management:** Articulates the vision of the product from a business perspective.

2. **Program Management:** Develops functional specifications and maintains the schedule.

3. **Development:** Builds the product or service that meets the specification and customer expectations.

4. **Testing:** Ensures all issues are known before the software is released.

5. **User Education:** Ensures every user is capable of getting the most out of the product.

6. **Logistics:** Ensures a smooth rollout, installation, and migration.

So, what's not to like? Actually, there is much to admire in the MSF approach if you have enough people to staff the recommended teams and execute the defined processes. They claim, in the course presentation, to use MSF at Microsoft. From reading the literature out of Microsoft Press in the past 10 years, I believe they do.[14]

Your homework assignment for today is to find out on your own if MSF will work for your team and company. It encompasses more than just development; it attempts to structure your whole enterprise toward the goal of shipping good enough software. I have found MSF to be helpful, but also in need of adaptation to the realities of corporate culture and some degree of recalibration for many of the prescribed teams.

Extreme Programming (XP)

XP is the new kid on the block from one perspective and as old as bugs caught in relays[15] from another. Let me explain. The key feature of XP is team programming with a focus on the code itself as the medium of communication for requirements,

---

14. A prime example, and probably the origin of many of their ideas, is Jim McCarthy's *Dynamics of Software Development* (Microsoft Press, 1995).

15. The purported origin of the term "bug" was an insect preventing a relay from working in an ancient (pre-1950) computer.

change, and understanding of the software's purpose. One of the leading proponents of XP, Kent Beck, writes that XP makes two sets of promises:

> *To programmers, XP promises that they will be able to work on things that
> really matter, every day. They won't have to face scary situations alone. They
> will be able to do everything in their power to make their system successful.
> They will make decisions that they can make best, and they won't make
> decisions they aren't best qualified to make.*

> *To customers and managers, XP promises that they will get the most possible
> value out of every programming week. Every few weeks they will be able to
> see concrete progress on goals they care about. They will be able to change
> the direction of the project in the middle of development without
> incurring exorbitant costs.*[16]

How does XP help you deliver on these promises? By adopting a discipline
that forces the best practices of programming to be rigidly followed by the programming team, that's how. Instead of entrusting certain aspects of development
to a management team, XP centers the entire effort on the team doing the actual
building of the software.

Daily testing by a two-person team drives the development process—no one
goes off alone into his or her cube to write code only exercised by the testing
group a month from the origin of the code. Integration of code modules follows
immediately after development and that is tested by the programming team right
after the integration is done. All other previous test scripts are rerun at each point
of new code integration to ensure that changing one thing didn't break another.
Short release cycles and even shorter design iterations are the hallmark of XP.

XP is designed to work on projects that can be built with small teams
(between two and ten people) who have direct access to customer inputs and
management buy-in of team decisions. XP is a process controlled by the development team where the programmer is the heart of the methodology. For the
businessperson, there's also a role to play, more one of encouragement than management. The primary management role of the team is carried by the coach, the
programmer who is responsible for the entire development process.

The *X* in XP stands for "extreme," and many in our industry consider it an
appropriate moniker. Some despise the name even when they admire the
method.[17] I believe there's much good to be gleaned from the publications

---

16. Kent Beck, *Extreme Programming Explained* (Reading, MA: Addison-Wesley, 2000), p. xvi.
17. See the Feedback section of the magazine *Software Development*, November 2001.

and practices of this "new" methodology. You should invest time at
`http://www.extremeprogramming.org` and see for yourself what you can adopt or embrace from this very active and vocal group in our industry. Actually, in the spirit of XP, you can't take away part of the methodology and mix it with other styles: You are either "extreme" or not at all. I don't buy into this exclusive way of thinking, but I do understand the motive behind the hype. The proponents are really saying be disciplined about your work or get out of the profession. I *can* buy into this philosophy and so should you.

Agile Development

You'll see more and more of the term "agile" in your days ahead, searching for methods that work for you and your team. The nature of any effective software development method should, of course, be agile; that is, able to adapt to changing requirements and evolving technology even during the building phase of a project. Most software professionals have come to acknowledge that agility is the Holy Grail of development methodologies. A key group of software professionals has even formed an alliance to promote the concept of agility.[18] They have published a manifesto outlining four choices that should be made to ensure your methods are agile:[19]

1. Individuals and interactions over process and tools.

2. Working software over comprehensive documentation.

3. Customer collaboration over contract negotiation.

4. Responding to change over following a plan.

The authors acknowledge while there is value in the items on the right of their list of choices they put more weight and value in the items on the left.

There are many similarities between the so-called agile school and XP. Indeed, the founders of XP, among others, took part in the meeting that created the manifesto. In truth, the agile methodology is more of an idea that should circumscribe any process or planning you institute to build software. In Chapter 6, where technical design methods were discussed, I promoted the term[20] "adaptive software development" as central to your success as a technical leader. This is cut from the same cloth of agility.

---

18. Visit `http://www.AgileAlliance.org`.

19. See Alistair Cockburn, *Agile Software Development* (New York: Addison-Wesley, 2002), Appendix A.

20. This term is from Jim Highsmith's book of the same name. See the Bibliography.

Most software professionals have come to acknowledge that agility is the Holy Grail of development methodologies.

What distinguishes agile methods from all others is the emphasis on responding to change constructively and adaptively, rather than seeing change as something to eliminate as a factor or resist as a force in the development process. With this understanding, you can see that XP is a college in the agile university of learning. Any method that tries to control change by freezing requirements and focusing on a predefined process will result is some pretty cold software. To quote Cockburn:

> *A person might believe that following a defined process is crucial to project success. This person would consequently spend a great deal of effort measuring and controlling adherence to the process. A person really convinced that process is key would not notice for a long time the absence of correlation between following a process and the project outcome.*[21]

In other words, an agile methodology takes the blinders off and helps you see things you might ignore if you're a slave to any process.

To list the steps to follow in any agile development method would be contrary to the spirit of the concept of agility. Any agile methodology is focused on creating a way of seeing the development process as an interactive and collaborative effort between programmer and consumer. While some see this as a methodological trend, in my opinion it's the only way of coming to grips with the messy business of creating quality software.

I encourage you to explore the literature available on agile methods. There are many resources to examine.[22] Even more important, measure your current methods by the standard of agility. If a poorly defined business requirement is clarified close to the code-complete date, can your team respond without an unacceptable delay? Most of us only moan when the requirements change during the development cycle, but our moaning belies the reality that the deeper you work to implement a requirement, the more you'll uncover ambiguities and need to reiterate back through the product definition phase. Agile methods are designed to eliminate the moaning and help you embrace the certainty of uncertainty.

---

21. Cockburn, op. cit., p. 5.

22. See Cockburn, op. cit., for many examples, and http://www.adaptivesd.com for a related online exploration.

Craftsmanship: The Heart of Any Successful Method

I've guided you down a path in this brief discussion of development methodologies that leads, in my opinion, to only one conclusion: Software must be created by craftsmen, not engineers. This may be a hard concept for some of you to swallow. Having come from a hard science and engineering background in earlier careers, I've resisted believing that artistry is superior to science when it comes to software. I've now concluded that resistance if futile.[23] Take a quick look back in time at a 1990[24] headline from one of the leading technical magazines:

> *Software Companies Bugged by Lack of Quality Control – As commercial software becomes more complex, the hunt is on for a way to ride herd on the millions of lines of code needed for complex packages.*[25]

The article following this headline speaks about the software maturity framework (see Chapter 6 where I reference the Software Engineering Institute's Capability Maturity Model) and number of errors per line of code. More effort is expended in this article discussing ways to measure failure than addressing the real issues: People create software, not processes executed by automatons.

People create software, not processes executed by automatons.

What kinds of people create software? Craftsmen. Once you see that a craftsman doesn't ignore science and engineering, you'll no longer resist placing artistry ahead of science. Indeed, you'll consider ways to marry the artist and scientist/engineer in each of us to create the approach best suited for growing code into useful and quality software products. I agree with Pete McBreen in the preface to his book on software craftsmanship where he writes the following:

> *Craftsmanship is a return to the roots of software development: Good software developers have always understood that programming is a craft skill. Regardless of the amount of arcane and detailed technical knowledge that a person has, in the end, application development comes down to feel and*

---

23. You didn't think I would leave out a reference to *Star Trek: The Next Generation*, did you?
24. Remember that in 1990, there was no Windows, and the graphical Internet wasn't a reality.
25. *Electronic Business*, October 15, 1990, p. 147.

experience. Someone can know all of the esoteric technical details of the Java programming language, but that person will never be able to master applica-tion development unless he or she develops a feel for the aesthetics of software. Conversely, once a person gets the feel for software development, the specific technical details become almost irrelevant. Great developers are always picking up and using new technology and techniques; learning a new technology is just a normal part of the life of a software developer.[26]

In the spirit of craftsmanship, create your own development methodology. Learn from others who have documented their processes, but test all truth by experience.[27] After all, the very heart of science is to allow experiments to reveal truth. You are thus embracing a strong scientific and engineering principle when you follow the artisan into the workshop and come out with quality software.

In the spirit of craftsmanship, create your own development methodol-ogy. Learn from others who have documented their processes, but test all truth by experience.

Revolutions in Technology

Sometimes vaporware creates quite a stir. Call it an intellectual fire drill if you want. Do you remember the hype about things that never really materialized in our industry? Here's a brief list:[28]

- The $500 network computer would free the world from Windows.

- MSN was going to destroy AOL. (Not yet—now AOL owns Time-Warner.)

- Intuit, having resisted Microsoft, still had a better product in Quicken.

- OS/2 was a better DOS than DOS and a better Windows than Windows.

- Java would take over desktop application development. (We'll see. . . .)

You can add your own nostalgic items to the preceding list if you want, but I only report these to remind you of how we must use caution in our ways of

---

26. McBreen, op. cit., p .xv.

27. This was the approach recommended by Leonardo that I discussed in Chapter 6.

28. I'm borrowing heavily here from David Coursey, the AnchorDesk editor at
     http://www.zdnet.com, from an article he wrote on October 12, 2001.

dealing with the Next Big Thing. As some marketing campaigns are found of say-ing, the next-generation technology usually means it won't be ready until the next generation.

Revolutions do occur in our industry, but we usually see signs of the coming change long before new ideas take hold and influence our development efforts. The ability to see the proverbial handwriting on the wall is my concern for you. According to Sun Tzu in *The Art of War*:

> *When in difficult country, do not encamp. In country where high roads intersect, join hands with your allies. Do not linger in dangerously isolated positions. In hemmed-in situations, you must resort to stratagem. In a desperate position, you must fight.*[29]

To heed this wise advice and avoid the "desperate position," your technical strategy must be developed long before the revolution arrives. As Sun Tzu says, when in "difficult country . . ."—I believe we can apply this to software develop-ment. Expanding on our Chinese philosopher's wisdom, I recommend the following strategic concerns be part of your long-term planning goals.

Don't encamp: Don't put your programmers in a position where they know only one language and one vendor's infrastructural implementation of architectural solutions to business problems.

Join hands: See the previous point. Work with as many solution providers as possible that have proven records of accomplishment. Hire consult-ants as needed from time to time to graft new knowledge into your team. Engage in team learning by building small prototypes with new tech-niques to prove their suitability for more extensive projects.

Don't linger: Success can produce inertia in an organization and cause you to lose sight of new competitors or opportunities for growth. Stay flexible in your methods and tools. Learn to be uncomfortable when you're comfortable.

Become a student of trends by reading widely and surfing the Internet wisely. Get to know a few good sources of information and stick with them as means of extracting what you need to know.[30] Most important, work with your boss and your team to develop a comprehensive strategy that can serve as a game plan for you in the ever-changing world we live in as developers.

---

29. I'm quoting from the version of this classic edited by James Clavell. Sun Tzu, *The Art of War* (New York: Dell Publishing, 1983), p. 37.

30. I recommend TechRepublic (http://www.techrepublic.com) as a starting point for good summaries of relevant topics.

Economic Woes

These two words often go together. You rarely hear someone speak of economic joys, do you? In recent memory, the dot-com bombs surface as we think of economic woes. Yet risk taking is very much a part of what we do every day in software development, so we often learn a lot from the failures as much as we do from the successes. We could blame the dot-com failures on investment bankers, but this would not inform us as software professionals. Surely, greed, avarice, and all the other attendant vices of capitalism contributed to the failures. At the heart of the woes, however, are people like you and me who lost their jobs and suffered emotional and intellectual pain from the experience. My focus in this section is on what you can do to prevent hard times while you have an opportunity to do something constructive.

Probably the single most important thing you can learn from economic hard times is that unless your company makes a profit, the end may be near.[31] So, obviously, the best way you can prevent economic hard times from affecting your company is to watch the cost of development and strive to be cost efficient. Of course, this is a little bit like the advice to buy low and sell high if you want to make money on Wall Street. Sound advice if you can get the timing right, but then, timing is everything, isn't it?

And this brings me to my major point about economic concerns. If timing is critical, certainly consistency is the mainspring that keeps your company's economic clock in sync with reality. What I mean by this is that you should observe the following rules as the leader of your team.

- You are a businessperson as well as the head techie. Think about cost as much as you do about code.

- Know what it really costs to run your department. Get monthly data on the cost of your facilities, people, equipment, services, and tools.

- Track the final dollar cost of a project against the projected cost. See how far off you were in the estimate and learn from the experience how to be more realistic in your estimates. Remember the cliché "an ounce of prevention is worth a pound of cure."

- Control the salaries of your staff. Keep them in line with what they're worth and what the market will bear for your location.[32]

---

31. The dot-coms were/are famous for this lack of profit. This might not apply to Amazon.com for now, as it hasn't for several years, but time will tell. I'll be sorry to see them go if they fail, and I'll be surprised that all the hundreds of dollars I've sent them over the years didn't make a difference!

32. I talked about this in Chapter 1 (in the "Motivating with Money" section) and Chapter 3 (in the "Promotions and Raises" section) but it's worth repeating here.

If you have to lay off individuals, do your best to help them find other work by writing letters of recommendation[33] and making phone calls. If you're in danger of being laid off yourself, start looking around for new work before the axe falls (if possible). It's much easier to move from one job to the next rather than from the unemployment line to a new opportunity.

Alone at the Top

A leader will often feel alone when he or she is out in front of the team charting new territory. This is the price of leadership, and when coupled with the shift in your responsibilities from full-time programmer to manager of programmers, a sense of loss can often plague you. As previously mentioned, there's often no one to pat you on the back and say you've done a good job. If you're still in the process of learning to adapt to administrative work, you might find yourself in a rather uncomfortable place emotionally.

What I'm writing here might seem like a bit of psychological projection, but since I've experienced the range of emotions I describe, just call it a memoir. You'll get over feeling like a fish out of water and there are actions you can take to help.

Devoting Time to Research

To help your code-withdrawal symptoms, devote more time to researching new technologies and write some code with new tools or techniques. You shouldn't commit to coding on active projects unless you just don't have the staff to carry the load. When you're in charge of the development process, it's hard enough to manage all the intermediate milestones of others. Don't increase your project management duties by being the only one of your staff who hasn't finished his or her coding assignment because you were too consumed managing the work of others. I know you want to get in there and write some code, and participating in the actual work is part of leadership, but do so judiciously.

As a leader, determining the suitability of new software tools, techniques, and architectures should be one of your primary technical jobs. As a leader who mentors his or her staff, you can't teach until you know the lay of the land in the new world into which you want to lead your team. This kind of research takes time and great technical skill, so devote your past experience as a top-notch programmer to this pursuit.

---

33. Sometimes legal concerns will prevent you from doing this. Check with your boss about company policies in this area.

Turning Administration into an Engineering Discipline

While I didn't speak very highly of software engineering as a helpful development methodology, I do believe you can apply engineering to administration. Automate your project planning and weekly work assignments if you haven't already done so. I discussed this in Chapter 4 but it's worth reviewing again. Administration can suck up your time and leave little for other critical activities, so use your programming skills to bring some order to the flow of information that crosses your desk.

Study the works and lives of business leaders who've managed to conquer their administrative burdens and go on to achieve great ambitions. They had to write memos, make phone calls, and all the rest that goes along with daily administrative activities, but they still found time to achieve greatness for their company, their staff, and themselves. You can do the same if you stop thinking of administration as something to avoid rather than control.

Making Strategic Planning a Science

In the previous chapter (Chapter 9) I discussed helping your boss plan for success. It might, however, become your primary job to plan the strategy for your company in the years ahead from a technical perspective. You should thus begin to focus on the skills you need to create strategic plans that can create the future rather than just predict the possibilities. This kind of planning isn't easy. Many so-called white papers written by corporations for planning are more an exercise in assuaging fears that the future has been thought about rather than accounted for. There's a difference between just thinking about the future and really planning for it.

As you develop a strategy for the future, examine the past very carefully for clues about where you've been and how past plans have either been successful triumphs or miserable failures. Become a historian of your company's technology and a futurist for the years ahead. It may be a cliché to say those who fail to learn from history are doomed to repeat it, but it's worth recognizing the truth in this timeworn proverb.

You'll begin to make your strategy scientific when you establish your plans on proven prototypes rather than speculations about vaporware. Who says that strategic documents can't have a little code under the covers? As part of your plans, demonstrate the viability of new ideas and techniques by employing proof-of-concept sections in your monographs. Block diagrams showing future architectural implementations are helpful, but when they're backed up by the substance of "a work in progress," they take on more weight.

Learning to Increase the Value of Your Relationships

I'm sure you already value many relationships in your life and work. But, hey, I'm talking to a very techie crowd and sometimes we tend to be a little socially withdrawn. Maybe this doesn't describe you, so pardon the intrusion. Nevertheless, is there a limit to the value we should put upon our relationships at work? From a paranoid perspective, maybe the answer to this question is yes, but this isn't "good paranoia."[34] I'm not talking about all the touchy-feely stuff you might suspect. I'm referring to the value each individual has on your team as a person into whom you invest time and energy, helping him or her to grow as a programmer and potential leader. It's a shame the Army has stopped using the slogan "Be all that you can be," because as a leader you're sometimes like a drill sergeant trying to get the most out of his or her troops.

> *It's a shame the Army has stopped using the slogan "Be all that you can be," because as a leader you're sometimes like a drill sergeant trying to get the most out of his or her troops.*

Never forget that a true leader is always trying to get the most productivity out of his or her staff. You'll get more out if you put more in. This means that all formal and casual interactions with your staff, at the end of the day, are all work related. You're the boss and you'll always be perceived in this light by your staff. You can't really be one of the "guys" anymore in the way you may have been as a programmer on the team. Thus, how you manage your relationships with your team should always be conducted in the light of who you are in the company.

---

34. See Chapter 8 where I discussed Andy Grove's constructive use of the word "paranoia."

Finale

If this has been a chapter of words without a song, it's only fitting that it has a summary in keeping with the beginning metaphor. I've introduced you to a whole lot of miscellaneous topics with only one theme: Herding cats requires you to consider a wide range of problems as opportunities to create order out of chaos. You've considered the following range of topics:

- Distributed workforces place stringent demands on your project planning and monitoring activity.

- Managing multicultural teams requires you to become a citizen of the world and shed as many of the national traits that would lead to miscommunication and lack of motivation for your diverse staff.

- You will constantly need to refine your development methodologies. Striving to make agility an overriding characteristic of any process you institute is paramount to your success.

- Revolutions in technology can be foreseen and prepared for. Strategic planning based on understanding the nature of coming change is central to not being caught in a desperate battle to catch up when the revolution comes.

- Economic hard times may come, but you can mitigate their impact by always working to make your company profitable. This starts with you managing your department as a businessperson as well as a technical person.

- Leadership can be lonely but there are actions you can take to compensate for this reality. Don't become isolated. Be proactive and creative in your research, administration, planning, and dealings with people.

Being a leader is a great adventure. I believe our industry offers many exciting opportunities to explore, create, and in general have all the variety each of us craves as technical people expanding ourselves to become true pioneers in peopleware and software. Relish each moment of your day, seize it, and make it count for you and your staff.

Into the Fray

It's time to move on and get back to the daily battles you face in your job. I close this book with an extended metaphor, asking you to envision yourself as a ship on a stormy sea. This sea is software development in the twenty-first century, and it's likely to be as turbulent and as wonderful as that of the twentieth century. To navigate this sea successfully, you'll need a deep and strong rudder to stay your course, a large and sturdy sail to catch the wind, and an anchor to keep you steady. I hope this book will help you keep your boat afloat.

The Rudder

Rudders guide ships—what's guiding yours? It should be a combination of the two most important themes this book discussed. These themes can be summed up in two words: *focus* and *lead*. As you mature as a leader of men and women with your eyes fixed on the goal of delivering great software, constantly look for ways to sharpen your focus. Look for opportunities to practice leadership—they'll be all around you if you keep your eyes open. All the ideas and techniques discussed in the preceding pages were aimed at helping you become a better leader. You have to become a good manager in order to create time to lead, so manage well by keeping your focus on the priorities you've established as urgent and important. This is what "focus" means—deflecting distractions so you can keep working on tasks that count.

In our business there are many interesting things you could be doing. The technology you employ to solve business problems can also create great distractions. You must learn to discriminate between necessary solutions and the ones that, while good, aren't germane to your company's success. Planning is one part of this discrimination task and executing the plan another. Organizing your administrative life can also help you focus by eliminating distractions. Ostensibly, a clean desk *is* a sign of a healthy mind while clutter can indicate uncertainty about priorities. Notice I used the word "ostensibly" because this refers to outward appearances: What's critical is the inner state of your organization about all things work related.

Review your priorities as you go into the development fray. Are people first? They must be because without them code doesn't get written. The more you pour yourself into those who work for you, the more they'll truly embrace and act upon your shared goals. Many people simply say, "I work for Company X"; what you want to achieve is programmers who say, "I work for _____ (fill in your name here)." This type of loyalty doesn't happen overnight and requires patient investment on your part in each team member's work life.

The Sail

Sails catch wind to provide movement. The atmosphere within which we all work in software development is filled with turbulence, and thus "wind" is abundant. Learning to tack both with and against the wind is vital if you're to keep moving in the right direction for your company. No matter which "camp" you've made your home as a developer, the winds of change have been blowing strong this past decade.

If you've been Microsoft-centric, there have been strong winds blowing from the northwest. You can discern the source of these winds over the past few years, a result of thoughtful planning and some not so thoughtful. What do you think Windows 98 Second Edition was all about? What about all the service packs to Visual Studio? Can you recall the various released version numbers for ADO? Have you run Microsoft's product that attempts to identify which version your machine is closest to relative to ADO?[1] You just get used to Windows 2000 and then along comes XP (extra pricey?). All this and the next version of Visual Studio creates a paradigm shift for VB programmers that promises to change the way you write code in a dramatic way.

The Java and C++ worlds have had their changes, too, and more will likely follow. Sun kept Java a secret for a number of years—even the name was a break with the tradition of naming languages. It was to be called "Oak," but this name was already taken. The word "Java" was apparently created to give a "jolt" to the burgeoning Internet development market. It worked, we've all been jolted. Then there are the worlds of CORBA and COM, or is it CORBA and COM+? No, maybe it's CORBA and SOAP. Maybe XML will bridge the gulf! You get the picture.

Changes are inevitable in our kind of world with evolving business requirements and technologies. Mix this with users who can barely keep up with it all, not to mention programmers (yours, mine, Microsoft's, and so on) who often repeat their own mistakes. These conditions make for stormy weather.

---

1.   I'm speaking about the program called ComCheck that Microsoft gives out for free on their download site for figuring out the DLL Hell ADO can create.

Coping with these storms demands that you work toward creating good enough software while constantly raising the bar of what "good enough" means. You have to negotiate deadlines with your boss, argue with the business analyst concerning what's possible to accomplish with software, cope with glitches in the network infrastructure—the list could go on and on. No wonder your work product often feels incomplete. It doesn't just feel that way, it is! Perhaps only an ideal world can yield an environment in which a completely bug-free program can be produced, but if you aren't aiming for the ideal, then you're aiming too low. Set your sights on quality and you'll achieve a measure of respect from your coworkers and favor in the marketplace.

To raise the bar of "good enough" requires passion, an essential fuel for powering your leadership journey. It is passion that will help you sail through the storms. Balance your life between work and whatever else gives you joy and you'll create passion. Lose your passion through excess in any area of life and you'll become fatigued and fail. Strive to maintain passion for your work and your life by making all your endeavors an adventure.

Another thought about "balance." In today's workplace, the nature of balance is more accurately described as "blending." This can be especially true if you work from home either full-time or nights. With PDAs, laptops, always-on Internet connections using Virtual Private Networking, and other tools of the trade, you never really get away from work. Thus, trying to balance whatever you call your life with work may mean that you spend 15 contiguous hours where any given hour you might be doing something personal or something work related. How do you break away, a necessary activity for recharging your batteries? I can't supply the answer, but you can and must or else your passion will fade and burnout will result. It's hard to rekindle a fire once the fuel has been all used up.

The Anchor

Anchors keep us steady and must be deployed from time to time in our work and our life. Just knowing the anchor is on board can be comforting during stormy weather. Your leadership skills can be an anchor. Herding cats, an activity in which this book attempts to guide you, requires leadership skills often beyond the average programmer. A programmer by his or her very nature is concerned with objects that can be told what to do. When you create an object with certain public interfaces, you expect it to exhibit these alone when you access it from another object. People are different. They can show many faces at one time or an unexpected face under certain conditions of stress. Your job is to learn to understand and work with the unexpected facets of your people in an attempt to get them all moving in the same direction. You must be very clear about this direction and you must use *attractors*. No, I'm not talking about the esoteric constructs of chaos theory, but rather the need to draw your people unto yourself by being a strong leader. A great manager can't do it. A creative and productive programmer can't do it. But *you* can, if you focus on building your character as a leader. I'm not talking about techniques here. You can polish your positive thinking techniques as much as you want—they won't attract your folks. The reflected brilliance of your consistent and thoughtful leadership ways will work.

You must consistently reevaluate the effectiveness of your leadership. Consider the following analogy: Software problems are often caused by conflicting DLL versions. We call this "DLL Hell" and it often plagues our programming work. Isn't it amazing how fast these problems can be solved after you run the "restore" CD for the operating system? This may be analogous to what you have to do from time to time to improve your leadership. You can't continue piling on management techniques and hope this will solve your problems. Sometimes you have to take the *zero-based* approach: Think fresh each day and think outside the box. Specifically, the "box" is your present method of conducting your affairs within your department. Refresh your understanding and commitment to the fundamentals of leadership as often as necessary. What should you be doing that you're not doing? What should you stop doing? Leading programmers isn't going to just happen because you have the position of manager, team leader, director of development, or even CIO. You must earn the right to lead and this will only occur if you recognize your weaknesses and strive to correct them. Your strengths may go unpraised, but the effects will be felt among your people and in your organization. Your weaknesses will be noticed, talked about, and brought up to you; this is the way the world works. Lean into your strength.

I know I've been preaching to you a bit in this book. Well, a lot actually. Maybe that's why you read to the end: You needed a good sermon. I hope it has been an edifying one and will help you in all the days ahead.

J. Hank Rainwater

January 2002

Caring for Your Pet: The Administrative Director Software

Open source software has many benefits and some drawbacks. Standards are the greatest concern, but if you have the source at least you can institute your own standards. I'm making my source code for the Administrative Director, my pet, available to you so you can organize for success with a little head start. This software is intended for personal use and cannot be sold or refactored and sold in any form. You can download it by navigating to `http://www.apress.com` and following the links under Downloads.

The software (described in Chapter 4) was constructed with Visual Basic 6.0, service patch 5. The database is Access 2000 and the project references the standard VB items as well as the following:

- Microsoft Data Source Interfaces

- Microsoft ActiveX Data Objects 2.6 Library

- Crystal Reports version 8.5 (various components)[1]

- Microsoft Direct Speech Synthesis

- Microsoft Agent Control 2.0

- Microsoft Scripting Runtime

- Microsoft Direct Speech Recognition

---

1. Crystal Reports 8.5 has more DLL files that you can shake a stick at. I have the full developer edition installed and there are many files needed for the reports to work. The Package and Deployment Wizard in VB 6.0 doesn't correctly identify the files needed.

In terms of components out of the ordinary, the project references an older calendar control created by MSCAL.OCX[2] that shipped with Access 97 and a custom date control called MyData.OCX that's available as part of the downloaded code.

You can take out or substitute references and components as you desire. You'll have to modify the code accordingly, of course.

An INI file governs program configuration and requires a directory structure dictated by this file. For each "resource" defined in the database table of the same name, a folder must exist so reports can be exported to the proper place. A template folder contains the Crystal Reports files the program uses. The self-extracting file containing the code will create an appropriate folder structure. The database comes populated with sample data.

The database has lookup-type tables that you can populate as you see fit. I haven't taken the time to make a number of the tables, such as the projects table, to be used via a join from the task table. This choice also simplified reporting using Crystal Reports and so any change would affect these report templates. Feel free to add to the code and send me your solution. You can send me questions at herdingcats@mindspring.com and I hope I can provide some answers for you.

And now, here are some additional views of software screens in the application that might be helpful to you in organizing your personal information flow. Figure A-1 displays the parent container window.

While the Today screen described in Figure 4-3 (Chapter 4) is essential for tracking your administrative life, you need more. According to my theory of organizing administration, you need to view tasks based on the three primary dimensions associated with tasks: Project, Source, and Assigned. You use the Project view (see Figure A-2) when you want to focus on all the tasks required to monitor a project's progress. The Assigned view (see Figure A-3) is for tracking who is doing what, and the Source view (see Figure A-4) reminds you who (or what process or committee) is expecting you to get things done. Figures A-2 through A-4 show views of these three user interfaces. They're sizable MDI-child windows, so you can have as many open as you can stand.

---

2.   I'm suspicious about this OCX. It doesn't show any dependencies on other files (other than the standard Windows API files), but I couldn't get it to work on a machine that never had Access 97. I've made a version of the software using the calendar control that is part of VB 6.0 so you can substitute this control if you get a bad reference error when trying to load the code.

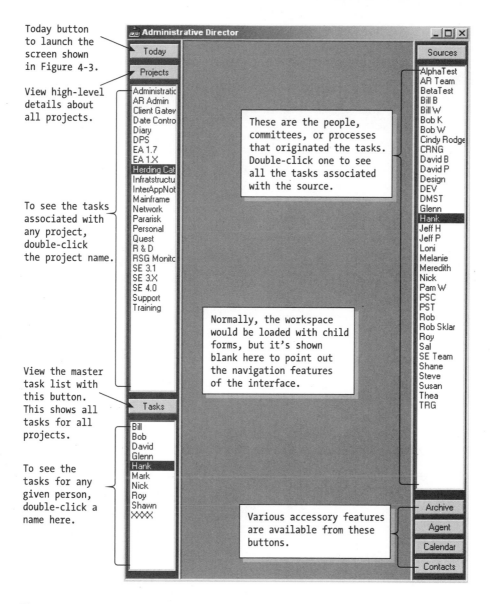

Today button to launch the screen shown in Figure 4-3.

View high-level details about all projects.

These are the people, committees, or processes that originated the tasks. Double-click one to see all the tasks associated with the source.

To see the tasks associated with any project, double-click the project name.

Normally, the workspace would be loaded with child forms, but it's shown blank here to point out the navigation features of the interface.

View the master task list with this button. This shows all tasks for all projects.

To see the tasks for any given person, double-click a name here.

Various accessory features are available from these buttons.

Figure A-1. Parent (MDI) container window (no child windows loaded)

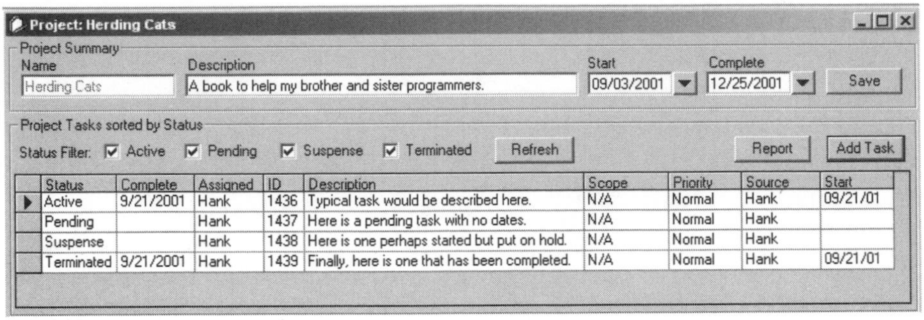

Figure A-2. Project view

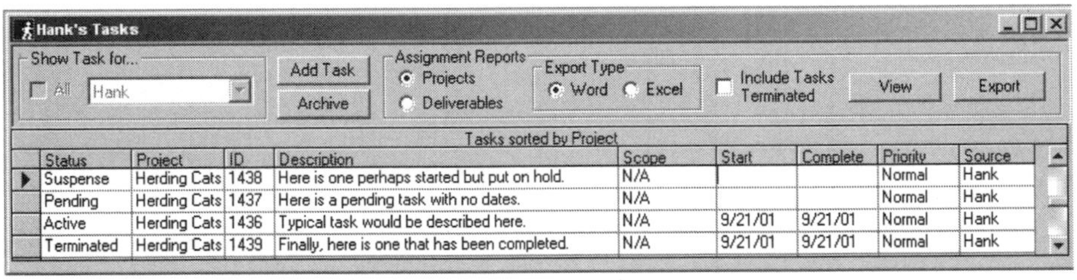

Figure A-3. Assigned view

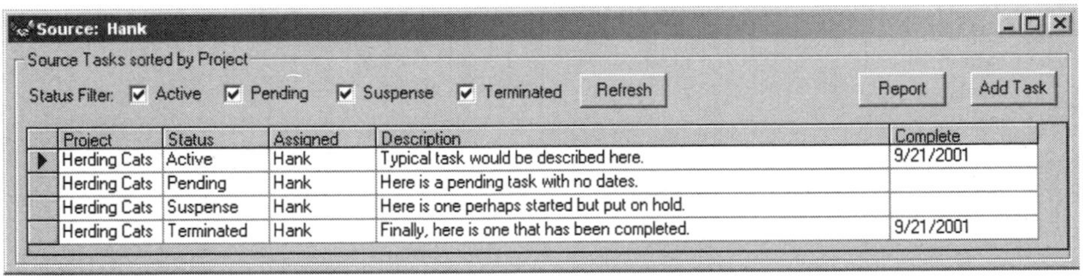

Figure A-4. Source view

From each of these screens you can produce a report useful for e-mailing to your staff, carrying into meetings, sending to your boss, or just poring over when you have to correlate your activities with those of another department. Until groupware reaches some level of maturity, there will often be a disconnected relationship between various departments for tracking differing kinds of work, each of which dictate a unique style of administration. Thus, cut-and-paste methods are often required to manage your task lists and hence the concept of "death by a thousand cuts" is often used to describe this administrative reality and nightmare.

For quick access to these primary views, the three list boxes on the perimeter of the parent MDI window described in Figure A-1 allow quick launching. These list boxes contain data-driven lists of the names of projects, resources to which tasks can be assigned (usually these are people), and sources, the origin of the tasks you're working on or tracking. Double-clicking any list item launches a view of tasks arranged in a manner consistent with the purpose of the view.

I find it helpful to create a separate Source item for my boss so that I can keep track of those tasks that originate with her. Nothing is more embarrassing (not to mention career threatening) than forgetting something specifically assigned by your boss.

Several of the grids support functions presented with pop-up menus fired from a right-click of the mouse. You can try these or look in the code for the event code.

That's about it. You can play with the source code to learn more. Have fun with your pet and treat him nicely.

Poking Your Pet in the Eye: Code Review of the Administrative Director

In Chapter 6 I spoke about being a code cop in the section entitled "The Code Police." While it's difficult to remain objective while policing your own code, I'm going to attempt to do so here. Since I called my code a "pet project," I thought the title of this appendix would give you a hint of what I'm up to in this analysis. The purpose of this appendix is to guide you through a code review process and note things you should observe when examining the code your team writes.

Having the source code loaded will make reading this appendix easier. As noted in Appendix A, you can download the code from the Downloads area of http://www.apress.com.

Context and Origin of the Software

I wrote the Administrative Director code after becoming disenfranchised with a previous Web-based product I had created for managing the administrative details associated with software development. I was in a bit of a hurry in writing the code critiqued here and used the project to prove a number of architectural ideas. It was a fun experiment and successful from my perspective.

I would not consider this code to have the quality of an off-the-shelf product you could buy, but it ain't bad either, and it's served my administrative needs well.

The Rules of the Game

I'll examine the code from the perspective of Chapter 6's "Guidelines for Design" that I repeat here for convenience. Good code should

- **Follow programming standards appropriate for your language.** This will ensure that the construction techniques of objects dictated by your architecture won't vary widely from programmer to programmer.

- **Encourage strong cohesion within your objects.** Objects aren't just containers for a bunch of procedures, they're organs that perform a specific function. The heart doesn't try to breathe and the lungs don't try to pump blood.

- **Discourage coupling between your objects.** Unless you have a significant other, coupling isn't a good thing because it makes maintenance a nightmare. When objects are coupled, divorcing them later costs time and money.

I'll also throw in a few other observations that I know to be weaknesses in the code. Most of all the shortcomings of the code are due to time pressure and the fact that this was a tool that only I would use. I haven't claimed to be infallible in this book, so you shouldn't be surprised at my confessions.

Did I Follow Appropriate Standards?

I think I did for the most part. I've been using VB since version 1.0 and I've written good and bad code over the years, just like you. My working definition of appropriate VB standards is to attempt to map OO concepts into a language that doesn't fully support object orientation.

In Chapter 4 I identified the Task concept as a central organizing principle of the software, and if you examine the code you'll see an object called clsTasks and a helper object called clsTask. These two class modules encapsulate all the user interactions and data handled by the software relative to tasks. The two forms (frmTask and frmTasks) that deal with the GUI side of handling tasks are children of the clsTasks object. Other objects, such as clsToday, when dealing with tasks, use local instances of clsTasks to do work. This is good and illustrates object reuse.

Here are the module level declarations of clsTasks:

```
'---private objects and events
Private mo_DataService As clsDataService '---data for the object
Private mo_PickList As clsPickList '---pick list needed for forms
Private WithEvents mf_Tasks As frmTasks '---all the tasks on frmTasks
Private WithEvents mf_Task As frmTask '---an individual task on frmTask
Private mo_DataGrid As DataGrid
Private WithEvents mo_DataProvider As clsDataProvider '---host data
Private ml_CurTaskID As Long '---currently selected task ID
Private ms_Project As String '---used when working from frmProject
Private mo_ProgConfig As clsProgConfig
Private ms_TaskFilter As String
Private mo_Task As clsTask
Private mb_NeedRefresh As Boolean
Private ms_Resource As String
Private ms_Source As String
'---public objects and events
Public Event TaskUpdated()
```

What do we have here? Well, we have some comments, but none that describe the purpose of this central object. *Bad cat!* How is anyone else supposed to figure out the purpose of this object if nothing here describes it? They won't without tracing through the code. I know the code since I wrote it, but a newcomer will have a mystery on his or her hands.

If you were to respond to this code as a manager, you would insist that comments be added to the header of the module showing who created it and when. You would also want an overview of the module, showing the public procedure names and what they do to make the object work.

There are some good things in the preceding code snippet. Note that the variables have appropriate names where m identifies the scope (module) and the next letter indicates the type of variable (1 indicates long, s indicates string, b indicates Boolean, and so on).

Let's look at a specific procedure. Here's one that starts up the whole process of showing a task form:

```
Public Sub Show(Optional sResource As String = "")
    If (mf_Tasks Is Nothing) Then
        SetHourglass
        Set mf_Tasks = New frmTasks
        Load mf_Tasks
        Set mo_DataGrid = mf_Tasks.grdTasks
        '---load tasks
```

```
            LoadTaskGrid
            '---Load resource combo
            mo_PickList.LoadPickList mf_Tasks.cboResource, PIC_RESOURCE
            '---configure task list
            ms_Resource = sResource
            mf_Tasks.Configure ms_Resource
            If sResource <> "" Then '---set data provider for individual task display
                ms_TaskFilter = "Assigned =" & Chr$(39) & sResource & Chr$(39)
                mo_DataProvider.Filter ms_TaskFilter
                mo_DataProvider.Sort "Status"
            End If
            SetReady
        End If
        With mf_Tasks
            .WindowState = 0
            .Show
            .ZOrder 0
        End With
End Sub
```

Again, comments are sparse but the names of the procedures called do indicate their purpose, so to some extent the code is self-documenting. However, what's lacking again are any module-level comments to show this is a key routine, since it's public in scope.

What About Cohesion and Coupling?

For the answer to the question in this section's heading, you'll have to take my word for it, since as you've seen in the previous section, comments in the code aren't written to explain where to go to understand the general flow or structure of the code. Nevertheless, I submit the following data for your observation and have inserted comments about cohesion and coupling.

The program is controlled by clsApplication, an object that exists with global scope in the program. From this object, all other objects are created and managed at a high level. For example, in the appropriately named procedure clsApplication.StartApplication, you'll see the main MDI parent form created and other auxiliary objects brought to life. This is good, from the standpoint of program flow.

Note the module level declarations in clsApplication:

```
Private WithEvents mf_Parent As mdiManager
Private WithEvents mo_Projects As clsProjects
Private WithEvents mo_Tasks As clsTasks
Private WithEvents mo_Today As clsToday
Private WithEvents mo_Archive As clsArchive
Private mo_Contacts As clsContacts
Private mo_DataService As clsDataService
Private mo_Reports As clsReports
Private mo_ProgConfig As clsProgConfig
Private mo_PickList As clsPickList
Private mc_Tasks As New Collection '---collection of clsTasks objects
Private mc_Projects As New Collection '---collection of clsProjects objects
Private mc_Sources As New Collection '---collection of clsSource objects
Private mo_User As clsUser
Private mo_Source As clsSource
Private ms_DSN As String 'used for where connected
```

Here, except for the lack of module comments, you see all of the child objects of clsApplication. If you knew to look here, you could eventually navigate your way down the object hierarchy of the program.

A heavy use of events is implemented in the program to keep the code in the forms fairly light. In most cases, the class modules are parents of forms named in such a way to indicate their relationship. For example, clsProjects fires up frmProjects, and whenever an event happens on a form, it raises an event in its parent that controls the action. This keeps all the code in one place, for the most part, and thus enforces encapsulation.

Each main object in the program (clsTasks, clsProjects, and clsToday) uses a local copy of a data provider object called clsDataProvider. This is a VB class module whose data source behavior is set to the value of vbDataSource. clsDataProvider is brokered via clsDataService by means of the function named GetDataProviderRS, which is named to show that the data provider record set is being retrieved. Most of the SQL statements that control the program are located here. At the very least, the use of the prefix "Get" indicates action and serves as a clue about the purpose of the procedure. I've already poked my pet enough about the lack of comments so I won't say any more about this weakness.

In terms of data access, the object clsDataService is the public interface for the logical data tier. clsDataProvider, described in the previous paragraph, is the means of communication between the GUI-side layer and the data. In clsDataService you'll find a child object called clsDataAccess, which actually makes the connection to the database and executes SQL statements passed in from its parent object. This partitioning of services is key to minimizing coupling, and I believe it makes the Administrative Director fairly easy to maintain and enhance.

Other Strengths and Weaknesses

I've only touched lightly upon areas you might review in this example. Here are other confessions that might be things to watch for in your own code review.

How Is the Database Connection Maintained?

It's created at start-up, kept open, and passed around as needed to objects that need data. For a two-tier program for one user, this might be fine. To scale this program to more than one user would reveal this wasn't a good design choice. It was expedient and saved time. Does this make up for the choice? For me, it's fine since I don't intend for this software to be extended, but in general you see how time pressures force shortcuts that you could later regret.

What Is the Role of Recordsets in the Program?

The ones that are dynamic are opened in each object and kept alive, just like the database connection. Again, this makes the program more responsive for one user on one physical machine, but it limits the program's capability to scale. Disconnected recordsets would have allowed the program to be more scalable.

Lack of joins between tables is another area relative to recordsets that is a clear weakness in the code. In other words, I actually store the project name in the task table data store rather than a foreign key reference to the project table. This results in never being able to rename a project. *Bad cat!* I allowed the need for speed to override my better judgment. Also, in defense of this choice, generating reports with Crystal Reports was simplified by having a non-normalized recordset to pass into the template file. Creating the template was also easier since I could use the Crystal Designer program to open the database table directly and drop the fields on the template. I could have implemented other solutions, but the one I did was fast and enabled me to generate weekly reports for my team quickly.

Are Any Magic[1] Numbers Used?

No. For the most part, private and public enumerated types are used in the program to make it more readable. (See basMain for the enums with global scope.) In a few cases, control arrays are referenced numerically rather than by enums, but for the most part you can know what a parameter value does by looking at its definition.

Summary

In this brief exercise, the need for speed was most often given as an excuse for code weaknesses. I think this is telling, and it will probably be your greatest challenge to address in code reviews. As the leader, you're supposed to set a pace that will allow quality development to occur. In the case of this particular project, I was both the leader and the coder, so I blew in on both counts. If you want to take me to task on any issues relative to my code, you can send your questions or rants to herdingcats@mindspring.com.

I encourage you to reread Chapter 6 from time to time just to remind yourself of the principles of good technical leadership. As I wrote this chapter, it forced me to own up to some of my personal failings as a leader and I was reminded again of the danger of knowing what to do but failing to act on the knowledge.

---

1. This refers to numbers that just magically appear to have an important role because you can't find any definition of their value.

Resources for Cat Herders

This bibliography contains works referenced in the footnotes as well as others related to the subject matter of this book. An attempt has been made to include works published recently in order to help you build a good library of counselors.

I've annotated the books in the category of "Software Development" to help you determine if you should look deeper into the author's thinking. In my opinion, you can't have too many books, as long as you read them. Of course, you should be choosy, and I hope my notes will help you pick out the resources that will speak to you and become nourishment for your mind and heart.

Software Development

I've broken down the references in this area according to my subjective view of each book's importance in our field. I consider all worthy of your inspection.

The Classics

Brooks, Frederick P. *The Mythical Man-Month: Essays on Software Engineering, Anniversary Edition.* New York: Addison-Wesley, 1995.
Drawn from his experience as a project manager on the IBM 360, Brooks exposes principles of development that were original at the time of the writing and proven over and over again in the years since as axioms in our industry. His classic rule, "Adding manpower to a late software project makes it later," has been validated time and again. This book should be required reading for all managers. The technology of Brooks' day may be out-of-date, but his insights into the human tasks of programming are not.

Weinberg, Gerald M. *The Psychology of Computer Programming, Silver Anniversary Edition.* New York: Dorset House Publishing, 1998.
The other classic in our field. Weinberg, who continues to make significant contributions to our field today, created a landmark work in this book, which

was originally published in 1971. He was one of the first to focus in depth on the human dimensions of programming and leadership, marrying psychology with technical understanding of the process of development. You'll find many ideas in this book as relevant today as they were revolutionary when first proposed.

Cream of the Crop

Beck, Kent. *Extreme Programming Explained: Embrace Change*. Reading, MA: Addison-Wesley, 2000.
Beck catches a lot of flack from the software engineering school, but the methods he proposes and practices makes perfect sense if you've been down in the trenches writing code. As a manager, you may find his approach to be, well, extreme, but also necessary to making small teams work well together. This book isn't for those who think writing code is a solitary adventure.

Cockburn, Alistair. *Agile Software Development*. New York: Addison-Wesley, 2002.
The term "agile" may be relatively new, but the methods described in this excellent work account for the real conditions we experience daily trying to map business requirements into software that can actually be implemented. If your scope creeps during development (when does it not?), this book will help you identify ways to react positively to change.

DeMarco, Tom, and Timothy Lister. *Peopleware: Productive Projects and Teams, Second Edition*. New York: Dorset House Publishing, 1999.
Whenever a computer-oriented book goes into its second edition, you know it must be good. Such is the case with this work by two leaders at managing the people side of software development. This edition covers areas of space planning, team building, people management, and many other topics central to getting a handle on leading programmers from chaos to order.

Highsmith, James A., III. *Adaptive Software Development*. New York: Dorset House Publishing, 2000.
This book will become a classic, I predict. You may find it a bit heavy-going from time to time, but this is only because Highsmith makes you think deeply about the nature of the software development processes. The subtitle of the book is "A Collaborative Approach to Managing Complex Systems," and he does a great job of explaining the complexity of what you and I do each day as leaders and programmers. His explanations of collaboration alone are worth the price of this book. Highsmith's book is a good companion to Cockburn's book on the same subject.

Hunt, Andrew, and David Thomas. *The Pragmatic Programmer.* **New York: Addison-Wesley, 2000.**

A wonderful book! Every programmer on your team should read this book. The authors' advice is culled from years of experience and you'll be constantly nodding in agreement as you read through this book. Their admonitions about preventing software entropy from overtaking your development efforts are a key feature of their practical approach to managing code.

McBreen, Pete. *Software Craftsmanship.* **New York: Addison-Wesley, 2002.**

McBreen has produced a brave and worthy polemic backed up with facts that should be promoted in the rank and file of our industry. He subtitles his book "The New Imperative" even as he describes how craftsmanship is a return to the roots of software development. If you believe in coding as an art, this one is for you. If you don't believe coding is an art, read this book anyway—it might change your mind.

McCarthy, Jim. *Dynamics of Software Development.* **Redmond, WA: Microsoft Press, 1995.**

A well-written and insightful book on what goes on behind the scenes as teams attempt to deliver software on time. Many of the lessons Microsoft learned about development are encapsulated in this book and it's filled with passion, intelligence, and practical advice. McCarthy speaks the language of "agility" in this book before the term gained as much currency as it has today. This work is a good candidate for a book review during your weekly staff meetings.

Noteworthy

Brown, William H., et al. *AntiPatterns: Refactoring Software, Architectures, and Projects in Crisis.* **New York: John Wiley & Sons, 1998.**

This work and the next one are wonderful examples of how the wrong practices lead to instant learning opportunities. You'll find your own experiences validated in this book and many helpful techniques for getting out of trouble with code.

Brown, William H., et al. *AntiPatterns in Project Management.* **New York: John Wiley & Sons, 2000.**

Geared toward the leadership side of the antipattern movement, this book nicely supplements a number of ideas presented in Chapter 7 on the dark side of leadership. This book can offer a mirror to you for evaluating your leadership style.

Constantine, Larry L. *Beyond Chaos: The Expert Edge in Managing Software Development*. New York: Addison-Wesley, 2001.

This is a collection of essays by various writers pulled together under one cover by Constantine in this book. The topics range from people to process to deadline pressures, and a whole section is devoted to leadership and teamwork.

Constantine, Larry L. *The Peopleware Papers*. Upper Saddle River, NJ: Yourdon Press, 2001.

Constantine is in the same league with DeMarco and Lister (see the "Cream of the Crop" section) and he offers a collection of his articles published in several leading development magazines over the years. You can open this book at any point and begin reading. The author's insights into managing people are especially helpful.

Glass, Robert L. *ComputingFailure.com*. Upper Saddle River, NJ: Prentice Hall, 2001.

A collection of failure stories by Glass, this one covering some of the more recent notable failures during the dot-com boom. Great storytelling and perspectives on the relationship of money to software failures.

Glass, Robert L. *Software Runaways*. Upper Saddle River, NJ: Prentice Hall, 1998.

Glass has done an excellent job over the years writing on project failures, and he's enlightened us with his observations. He writes from the software engineering perspective and his retelling of recent history is both engrossing and insightful.

Maguire, Steve. *Writing Solid Code*. Redmond, WA: Microsoft Press, 1993.

The emphasis is on bug-free C code in this book and the principles can be applied to any language. Compare this work with the book by McConnell mentioned in this section. They're both from the same era and are good supplements to each other.

Malveau, Raphael, and Thomas J. Mowbray. *Software Architect Bootcamp*. Upper Saddle River, NJ: Prentice Hall, 2001.

This book is one of a series from the Worldwide Institute of Software Architects (WWISA). It serves as a great introduction to software architecture, especially for those who think architecture is just design on steroids.

McConnell, Steve. *Code Complete.* **Redmond, WA: Microsoft Press, 1993.**

A classic for C programmers. This book contains practical insights that remain relevant for today's coding challenges. The section on naming conventions is very helpful to mention just one, and everything McConnell writes about will help you create self-documenting code.

Olson, Don S., and Carol L. Stimmel. *The Manager Pool: Patterns for Radical Leadership.* **New York: Addison-Wesley, 2002.**

If you want to compare yourself as a leader of programmers to others, this book is for you. A lot of psychology is wrapped around leadership patterns in this work, and the authors have done a good job of exposing behaviors that are common among software managers.

Sewell, Marc T., and Laura M. Sewell. *The Software Architect's Profession: An Introduction.* **Upper Saddle River, NJ: Prentice Hall, 2002.**

Another in the WWISA series. This one is by the president of the institute with his wife, a clinical psychologist. Good reading here. If you want to see the role of a software architect in relationship to the classic profession of architecture in general, pick up this quick-to-read volume.

Yourdon, Edward. *Death March.* **Upper Saddle River, NJ: Yourdon Press, 1999.**

Another instant classic. We've all been on death march projects and wondered why. Yourdon not only shows why but also how to get out of it, if you're willing to pay the price. The subtitle, "The Complete Software Developer's Guide to Surviving 'Mission Impossible' Projects," pretty well describes the contents.

Yourdon, Edward. *Decline & Fall of the American Programmer.* **Englewood Cliffs, NJ: Yourdon Press, 1993.**

This book, written by a leader in our industry, was a real eye-opener for many when it was first published. Many of the topics contained in Yourdon's book have been expanded by many other writers since. The title might seem depressing, but the contents are still relevant today. It has served as a textbook in many college courses.

Yourdon, Edward. *Rise & Resurrection of the American Programmer.* **Upper Saddle River, NJ: Yourdon Press, 1996.**

This is a sequel to Yourdon's other work described previously and it's equally compelling. Yourdon's long experience in the field makes him an expert at relating trends, and this work is an excellent companion to the more gloomy title he published a few years before.

Helpful

Bullock, James, Gerald M. Weinberg, and Marie Benesh, eds. *Roundtable on Project Management.* New York: Dorset House Publishing, 2001.
This book is a collection of conversations that occurred on the Web related to project management. The insights about knowing when a project is in trouble from the people and process side is very entertaining as well as helpful in avoiding your own disasters.

DeMarco, Tom. *The Deadline.* New York: Dorset House Publishing, 1997.
DeMarco is a leader in writing about the people side of software and this book is in the form of a novel. It has many insights on project management told in a style that makes you want to keep turning pages.

Freedman, Daniel P., and Gerald M. Weinberg. *Handbook of Walkthroughs, Inspections, and Technical Reviews.* New York: Dorset House Publishing, 1990.
Though somewhat dated, there aren't many books on this topic and this one gives a thorough plan for conducting technical reviews.

Humphrey, Watts S. *Managing the Software Process.* New York: Addison-Wesley, 1989.
Written from the perspective of the school of software engineering, this classic by Humphrey should be read even it you don't agree with his approach. It might seem dated, but many general principles are still valid and worth contrasting with competing schools of development methodologies.

Jones, Capers. *Applied Software Measurement.* New York: McGraw-Hill, 1991.
This work is one in a series by the Software Engineering Institute. (The preceding book by Watts Humphrey is another.) The subject of measuring software quality is a tough one and while you might just think "if it works release it," the principles described in this book will force you to do a bit more testing before you compile.

Kerth, Norman L. *Project Retrospectives.* New York: Dorset House Publishing, 2001.
If you need an up-to-date perspective on how to review projects, this is it. The author is a leader in the field, one who doesn't have much press. I have found many of his suggestions practical and insightful.

Whitehead, Richard. *Leading a Software Development Team: A Developer's Guide to Successfully Leading People & Projects.* New York: Addison-Wesley, 2001.

> Whitehead has put together a very comprehensive book for the new leader of programmers in this book. It has a question and answer format that gets right to the heart of many of the questions we all have about herding cats.

General Management and Leadership

Carlson, Richard. *Don't Sweat the Small Stuff at Work.* New York: Hyperion, 1998.

Champy, James, and Nitin Nohria. *The Arc of Ambition.* New York: Perseus Books, 2000.

Covey, Stephen R. *Principle-Centered Leadership.* New York: Simon & Schuster, 1992.

Covey, Stephen R. *The 7 Habits of Highly Effective People.* New York: Simon & Schuster, 1989.

Grove, Andrew S. *Only the Paranoid Survive.* New York: Random House, 1996.

Katzenbach, Jon R., and Douglas K. Smith. *The Wisdom of Teams.* New York: HarperCollins, 1999.

Pasternack, Bruce A., and Albert J. Viscio. *The Centerless Corporation.* New York: Simon & Shuster, 1998.

Welch, Jack. *Straight from the Gut.* New York: Warner Business Books, 2001.

Software Language-Specific Works

Appleman, Dan. *Moving to VB .NET: Strategies, Concepts, and Code.* Berkeley, CA: Apress, 2001.

Foxall, James D. *Practical Standards for Microsoft Visual Basic.* Redmond, WA: Microsoft Press, 2000.

Hollis, Billy S. *Visual Basic 6 Design, Specification, and Objects.* Upper Saddle River, NJ: Prentice Hall, 1999.

Miscellaneous Works

Blake, William. *The Complete Poetry and Prose of William Blake.* Edited by David V. Erdman. Berkeley, CA: University of California Press, 1982.

Elliot, T. S. *Collected Poems 1909-1962.* New York: Harcourt Brace Jovanovich, 1971.

Kauffman, Stuart. *At Home in the Universe.* New York: Oxford University Press, 1995.

Kranz, Gene. *Failure Is Not an Option.* New York: Simon & Schuster, 2000.

Levinson, Daniel J. *The Seasons of a Man's Life.* New York: Ballantine Books, 1978.

Merton, Thomas. *No Man Is an Island.* New York: Harcourt Brace Jovanovich, 1955.

Raymond, Eric S., ed. *The New Hacker's Dictionary, Third Edition.* Cambridge, MA: The MIT Press, 1998.

Rich, Adrienne. *The Dream of a Common Language.* New York: W.W. Norton & Company, 1978.

Shenk, David. *The End of Patience: Cautionary Notes on the Information Revolution.* Bloomington, IN: Indiana University Press, 1999.

Strathern, Paul. *Turing and the Computer.* New York: Doubleday, 1997.

Tzu, Sun. *The Art of War.* New York: Dell Publishing, 1983.

Wallace, James, and Jim Erickson. *Hard Drive: Bill Gates and the Making of the Microsoft Empire.* New York: John Wiley & Sons, 1992.

Ullman, Ellen. *Close to the Machine.* San Francisco: City Lights Books, 1997.

Yeats, William Butler. *Selected Poems and Three Plays of William Butler Yeats.* Edited by M.L. Rosenthal. New York: Collier Books, 1986.

Index

Numbers and Symbols

4GLs. *See* fourth generation languages (4GLs)

A

adaptation, importance of in leadership role, 166–167

adapting, practical questions to ask yourself about, 166–167

Adaptive Development Life Cycle, benefits of following, 114

Adaptive Software Development (James A. Highsmith, III), 114, 236

administration
customizing yours, 70–71
managing, 41–44

administrative activities, creating software to direct, 65–70

Administrative Director software
appropriate standards for, 228–230
caring for, 221–225
code review of, 227–233
cohesion and coupling in, 230–232
context and origin of, 227
creating, 65–70
guidelines to follow, 228
how the database connection is maintained, 232
importance of comments in, 229–230
parent (MDI) container window, 223
the role of recordsets in, 232
Today screen, 69
Web site address for downloading, 221

administrative distractions, typical, 43

administrative filter, for navigating to your goals, 42

age group, effect of on your leadership, 172

Agile Alliance, Web site address, 207

agile development, vs. extreme programming (XP), 207–208

Agile Software Development (Alistair Cockburn), 207, 236

amateur programmer, 11

ambition, making it work for you, 24–25

analogist programmer, 9–10

analogy, programmers that are good at, 9–10

analysis viewpoints, managing design forces with, 109–110

AntiPatterns in Project Management (William H. Brown et al), 78, 139, 237

AntiPatterns: Refactoring Software, Architectures, and Projects in Crisis (William H. Brown et al), 7, 237
for examples of mortal programming sins, 51

Appleman, Dan, *Moving to VB.NET: Strategies, Concepts, and Code* by, 241

Applied Software Measurement (Capers Jones), 119, 240

architect programmer, 6–7

architecture, planning before choosing your technology, 28

ARPANET, 172

artist programmer, 7–8

Assess Your Level of Cool test, 2–3

Assigned view, Administrative Director software, 224

assignments, distribution of to your programmers, 73

At Home in the Universe (Stuart Kauffman), 114, 242

attitudes, managing yours and your staffs, 76–77

B

Bacon, Francis, essay *Of Innovations*, 26

Beck, Kent, *Extreme Programming Explained: Embrace Change* by, 157, 206, 236

Beyond Chaos: The Expert Edge in Managing Software Development (Larry L. Constantine), 76, 238

bibliography
general management and leadership books, 241
miscellaneous works, 242
software development books, 235–241
software language-specific works, 241

Blake, William, *The Complete Poetry and Prose of William Blake*, ed. David V. Erdman, 23, 242

bonuses, for programmers, 16–17

book review, adding to your weekly staff meetings, 89

books, reading to stay current in your primary programming language, 32

bosses

helping them plan for success, 183–185

summary of guidelines for working with, 191

understanding the world of, 179–180

working with, 179–192

breeds of programmers, characteristics of, 6–12

Brooks, Frederick P., *The Mythical Man-Month: Essays on Software Engineering, Anniversary Edition* by, 13, 235

Brooks' Law, 183

Brown, William H. et al,

AntiPatterns in Project Management by, 78, 139, 237

AntiPatterns: Refactoring Software, Architectures, and Projects in Crisis by, 7, 51, 237

C

Carlson, Richard, *Don't Sweat the Small Stuff at Work* by, 75, 241

cat fight

asleep at the wheel, 117–118

disagreements between programmers, 14

The Foreign Legion, 200–201

green card blues, 55

the outsider, 94–95

the owner who couldn't let go, 135

Champy, James, *The Arc of Ambition* by, 241

change, basic flavors of, 80–81

change management, 80–81

checklists, daily inspection for managers, 38–39

Chess Master 5000, skill levels in, 186

Churchill, Winston, quote by, 54

Close to the Machine (Ellen Ullman), 5, 242

clsApplication, module level declarations, 231–232

clsTasks, module level declarations, 229

Cockburn, Alistair, *Agile Software Development* by, 207, 236

code comments, importance of good in software design, 120–121

Code Complete (Steve McConnell), 239

code modules, importance of testing when complete, 158

code police, importance of code review by, 118–119

code reuse vs. design reuse, 103–105

code standard violations, importance of correcting immediately, 122

cohesion and coupling, weak as coding standards violations, 122

collaboration and solitude, needed for software development, 194–195

Collected Poems 1909–1962 (T. S. Elliot), 118, 242

comments, importance of in good code, 120–121

communicating

as a cornerstone of leadership, 154–156

the goal of, 154–155

importance of for managing a distributed workforce, 196–197

communication, elements of effective, 155

complete mentoring, 162

computers, types needed by programmers, 83–84

ComputingFailure.com (Robert L. Glass), 50, 238

conference calls, using as meetings, 99–100

consistency, striving for in leadership role, 169

Constantine, Larry L.

Beyond Chaos: The Expert Edge in Managing Software Development by, 76, 238

The Peopleware Papers by, 94, 238

constructionist programmer, 7

consultants, guidelines for hiring, 53–54

control issues, list of things you can and can't control, 71–72

cookie, 3

correcting errors, as part of your leadership role, 164

Covey, Stephen R.

The 7 Habits of Highly Effective People by, 18, 241

Principle-Centered Leadership by, 241

cowboy programmers, managing, 13

cracker, 3

craftsmanship, of software development, 209–210

criticism, dealing with in leadership role, 145–146

customer service, importance of, 190–191

D

da Vinci, Leonardo, a case study of philosophy in action, 124–126
daily inspection checklist, for managers, 38–39
danger signs, of overload in leadership role, 144–146
dark empire builders
    characteristics of leaders, 143
    flirting with darkness, 144–146
    in a leadership role, 142–144
deadlines, setting and following up on, 27
deadlines and honesty, importance of in leadership role, 181–183
Death March (Edward Yourdon), 239
Decline and Fall of the American Programmer (Edward Yourdon), 184
delegating, as a cornerstone of leadership, 156–157
delegation
    importance of for success, 29
    importance of in leadership, 5
DeMarco, Tom
    The Deadline by, 240
    Peopleware: Productive Projects and Teams, Second Edition by, 25, 236
design documents, importance of, 29
design forces, managing with analysis viewpoints, 109–110
design meetings
    dynamics and issues of a typical, 90
    guidelines for, 91
    importance of note taking in, 91–92
    leading, 90–94
design reuse vs. code reuse, 103–105
developers, pitfalls of adding to a late project, 157
development team, importance of interpersonal relationships in, 14
diplomacy skills, importance of, 93–94
distractions
    deflecting, 44–46
    some typical administrative, 43
distributed workforce
    challenge of working with, 194–195
    lessons learned about multicultural, 200–201
    motivating and controlling the team, 199–200
    solution for working with, 195–198
    value of visiting periodically, 198
documentation, importance of for project success, 29

Don't Sweat the Small Stuff at Work (Richard Carlson), 75, 241
dot-com companies, economic woes of, 212–213
duty, fostering a sense of in your department, 168
Dynamics of Software Development (Jim McCarthy), 17, 205, 237

E

Eisenberg, Ronni, *Organize Your Office* by, 64
Elliot, T. S., *Collected Poems 1909–1962*, 118, 242
Emerson, Ralph Waldo, *Self-Reliance* by, 89
employee performance reviews, gathering information for, 96
engineer programmer, 8
envisioning, as part of your leadership role, 165–166
equipment, needed by programmers, 83–84
Erickson, Jim, *Hard Drive: Bill Gates and the Making of the Microsoft Empire* by, 174, 242
expectations, controlling those of others, 75–76
extreme programming (XP), 205–207
    vs. agile development, 207–208
    how it works, 206–207
Extreme Programming Explained: Embrace Change (Kent Beck), 157, 206, 236

F

facility management, importance of, 82–84
Failure is Not an Option (Gene Kranz), 184, 242
fan-in and fan-out, 122
filing system, creating to organize your projects, 64
firing practices, importance of documenting problems, 56
focus, importance of in leadership role, 43–44
fourth generation languages (4GLs), creating bad architecture with, 110
Foxall, James D., *Practical Standards for Microsoft Visual Basic* by, 241

Freedman, Daniel P., *Handbook of Walkthroughs, Inspections, and Technical Reviews* by, 240

G

gardening metaphor, for software development, 105–106
Gates, Bill, example of leadership role of, 174
Gelb, Michael J., *How to Think Like Leonardo da Vinci* by, 124–125
genius vs. leader, 141–142
Glass, Robert L.
    ComputingFailure.com by, 50, 238
    Software Runaways by, 50, 238
goals, importance of providing written for your programmers, 88
green card blues, 55
Grove, Andy, *Only the Paranoid Survive* by, 173, 241
guidelines, for design meetings, 91

H

hacker, 3
Handbook of Walkthroughs, Inspections, and Technical Reviews (Freedman and Weinberg), 240
Hard Drive: Bill Gates and the Making of the Microsoft Empire (Wallace and Erickson), 174, 242
herding cats, leading the herd, 41–59
Highsmith, James A., III, *Adaptive Software Development* by, 114, 236
hiring practices, guidelines, 53–54
Hodge, Challis, *Smoothing the Path* article by, 190
Hollis, Billy S., *Visual Basic 6 Design, Specification, and Objects* by, 111, 241
honesty and deadlines, importance of in leadership role, 181–183
How to Think Like Leonardo da Vinci (Michael J. Gelb), 124–125
Humphrey, Watts S.
    Managing the Software Process by, 47, 240
Hunt, Andrew, *The Pragmatic Programmer* by, 105, 237

I

IEEE Standard Computer Dictionary, definition of software engineering, 202
ignoramus programmer, 11–12
"inertia of success" defined by Andy Grove, 188
information, organizing into knowledge and action, 62–70
information flow, understanding and organizing incoming, 72–77
inspection checklist, for managers, 38–39
instant messaging, using to convey information, 45
intimidated programmer, 11

J

job description, importance of having written for job applicants, 53
Jones, Capers, *Applied Software Measurement* by, 119, 240
journals, reading to stay current in your field, 32
Julius Caesar, quotation about timing from, 189

K

Katzenbach, Jon R., *The Wisdom of Teams* by, 241
Kauffman, Stuart, *At Home in the Universe* by, 114, 242
Kerth, Norman L., *Project Retrospectives* by, 98, 240
Kranz, Gene
    Failure is Not an Option by, 184, 242
    leadership principles described by him, 184–185

L

language and culture, multicultural factors to deal with in, 198–199
leaders
    common reasons why people follow, 167–170
    vs. geniuses, 141–142
    importance of being knowledgeable in your field, 170
    working to elicit admiration from staff, 168–169

leadership
    building on the cornerstones,
        176–177
    building upon the foundation,
        161–167
    communicating as a cornerstone of,
        154–156
    cornerstones of, 152
    delegating as a cornerstone of,
        156–157
    effect of age on, 171–172
    expecting the unexpected, 187
    foundations of, 151–160
    generational dimensions to, 170–172
    importance of acknowledging your
        limits, 186
    importance of knowing your people,
        199–200
    importance of monitoring software
        design, 158–159
    pitfalls of participating in the coding,
        159–160
    practice makes it real, 176
    the role of mentoring in, 161–162
    understanding as a cornerstone of,
        152–154
leadership role
    adapting to new, 1–20
    of Andy Grove of Intel, 173
    answers to skills questions, 34–36
    antipatterns in management, 130–132
    avoiding eclipses, 147–148
    being sensitive to timing, 189–190
    of Bill Gates, 174
    the blinding light of misapplied
        genius, 140–142
    building and managing your staff,
        53–58
    building trust between you and your
        staff, 136–137
    consequences of the unfocused style,
        138–140
    creating a vision for the future,
        165–166
    daily inspection checklist, 38–39
    danger signs to look for, 144–146
    dark empire builders, 142–144
    the dark side of, 129–149
    dealing with project scope creep,
        46–50
    dealing with unfocused managers,
        137–140
    describing yourself as a leader,
        174–175
    devoting time to research, 213
    examining your skills objectively,
        21–22
    firing practices, 56
    getting help with unfamiliar language
        areas, 52
    grooming your replacement, 58
    hiring practices, 53–54
    how your work has changed, 24
    importance of adapting to, 166–167
    importance of character in, 2
    importance of delegation to, 29
    knowing your limits, 185–186
    leading the herd, 41–59
    learning to increase the value of your
        relationships, 215
    living on the edge of chaos, 193–216
    making strategic planning a science,
        214
    managing meetings, 87–102
    managing promotions and raises,
        56–58
    marrying style to substance in,
        172–175
    methods of correcting your
        programmers, 164
    vs. micromanagement, 134
    multicultural factors in, 198–200
    organizing for success, 61–85
    preparing yourself for the
        unexpected, 187
    re-evaluating success, passion, and
        ambition in, 24–25
    reading to improve knowledge and
        experience, 32–33
    review of, 151–177
    striving for consistency in, 169
    surviving and emerging from an
        eclipse, 146
    turning administration into an
        engineering discipline, 214
    value of visiting your distributed
        workforce, 198
    watching for your weaknesses, 31–33
    working to improve your skills, 23–25
leading vs. managing, 61
*Leading a Software Development Team: A
    Developer's Guide to Successfully
    Leading People & Projects* (Richard
    Whitehead), 241
Levinson, Daniel J., *The Seasons of a
    Man's Life* by, 171–172, 242
Lister, Timothy, *Peopleware: Productive
    Projects and Teams, Second Edition*
    by, 25, 236

M

magician programmer, 9
Maguire, Steve, *Writing Solid Code* by, 238
Malveau, Raphael C., *Software Architecture Bootcamp* by, 108, 238
management
    antipatterns in, 130–132
    multicultural factors in, 198–200
management role. *See* leadership role
managers, types of unfocused, 138
managing vs. leading, 61
managing meetings, practicing the principles of effective leadership in, 100–101
managing the leader, 21–39
Managing the Software Process (Watts S. Humphrey), 47, 240
McBreen, Pete, *Software Craftsmanship* by, 57, 237
McCarthy, Jim, *Dynamics of Software Development* by, 17, 205, 237
McConnell, Steve, *Code Complete* by, 239
meetings
    avoiding unnecessary and ineffective, 26
    for consensus and action, 101
    criteria for one-on-one, 95–96
    managing, 87–102
    with other groups, 97–98
    project retrospective, 98–99
    simple agenda for weekly, 87
    using conference calls for, 99–100
mentoring
    as part of your leadership role, 161–162
    typical example of, 162
Merton, Thomas, *No Man Is an Island* by, 81, 242
micromanagement, the shadow of, 132–137
micromanagers
    advice for, 136–137
    vs. good leaders, 134
    variations of, 133–134
Microsoft Solutions Framework (MSF), 203–205
minimalist programmer, 9
money, using as a motivating force, 16–17
monitoring
    importance of for managing a distributed workforce, 197
    techniques for in code design, 158

motivational tools, external forces as, 167–168
Moving to VB.NET: Strategies, Concepts, and Code (Dan Appleman), 241
Mowbray, Thomas, *Software Architecture Bootcamp* by, 108, 238
MSF milestones, focus of, 204
MSF teams, the processes roles are centered upon, 205

N

naming conventions, importance of following in software design, 120–121
natural selection and time, 25–29
Ninjitsu, 2
No Man Is an Island (Thomas Merton), 81, 242
Nohria, Nitin, *The Arc of Ambition* by, 241
note taking template, example of, 93

O

object-oriented design concept. *See* OO design concept
Olson, Don S., *The Manager Pool: Patterns for Radical Leadership* by, 175, 239
one-on-one meetings, criteria for, 95–96
Only the Paranoid Survive (Andy Grove), 173, 241
OO design concept, for designing and constructing software, 41–42
organization
    helping your company be successful, 77–84
    importance of for success, 27
    to insure control, 71–77
    some elementary principles of, 64–65
    for success, 61–85
    turning information into knowledge and action, 62–70
organizational inertia, overcoming, 187–191
organizational software, creating to direct administrative activities, 66–70
Organize Your Office (Ronni Eisenberg), 64
overload, danger signs of in leadership role, 144–146
overtime, controlling for yourself and your staff, 74–75

P

paper chase, pros and cons of, 63–65
paranoia, defined by Andy Grove, 173
participatory leadership, pitfalls of, 159–160
passion, preserving yours for success, 24–25
Pasternack, Bruce A., *The Centerless Corporation* by, 180, 241
pedagogy, the academic field of, 161
people problems, working to solve, 76–77
Peopleware: Productive Projects and Teams, Second Edition (Tom DeMarco and Timothy Lister), 25, 236
performance reviews, gathering information for, 96
personal information manager (PIM) software, managing the paperless chase with, 65–70
philosophy in action, a case study of, 124–125
phreaking, 3
PIM software. *See* personal information manager (PIM) software
ping, 3
planning, importance of for managing a distributed workforce, 195–196
Practical Standards for Microsoft Visual Basic (James D. Foxall), 241
praise, importance of, 15–16
Principle-Centered Leadership (Stephen R. Covey), 241
process management, 80–81
product development, importance of project definition for, 79–80
product management, importance of appropriate, 78–79
product management group, working with for better program development, 79
product modification, questions to ask before making, 81
product testing, importance of, 82
productivity, measuring yours, 30–31
program anomaly, 12
programmer
    amateur, 11
    analogist, 9–10
    architect, 6–7
    constructionist, 7
    cowboy, 13
    ignoramus, 11–12
    intimidated, 11
    magician, 9
    minimalist, 9
    salad chef, 12
    scientist, 8
    slob, 10–11
    speed demon, 8–9
    toy maker, 10
programmer-manager, your role as, 24–25
programmers
    adapting to leading, 1–20
    building a good team from scratch, 13–14
    determining what they are worth, 16–17
    encouraging the intimidated, 11
    gathering strays, 51
    importance of organizing collaboration and solitude, 82–83
    importance of praise and recognition to, 15–16
    leading into great work, 5–6
    major breeds and their characteristics, 6–9
    minor breeds and their characteristics, 9–10
    the mongrels and their characteristics, 10–12
    recognizing breeds of, 6–12
    some pitfalls of managing, 4–5
    tools needed by, 83–84
    working with the breeds, 12–14
programming
    balancing purity with practicality, 28
    importance of continuing after promotion, 21
    joys provided by, 13–14
project definition, importance of for good product development, 79–80
project management software, using to convey information, 45
project plans
    example of realistic, 49–50
    example of unrealistic, 48
    principles of realistic, 181
    real-world conditions that affect, 182
project post-mortems. *See* project retrospective meetings
project retrospective meetings, importance of, 98–99
Project Retrospectives (Norman L. Kerth), 98, 240
project scope creep
    dealing with, 46–50
    example of, 48

Project view, Administrative Director
    software, 224
promotions and raises, managing, 56–58
"proof of concept" exercise, 111–113
psychology assessment test, Web site
    address for, 53

R

raises and promotions, managing, 56–58
rapid application development (RAD),
    110
Raymond, Eric S. ed., *The New Hacker's
    Dictionary, Third Edition*, 4, 242
recruiting guidelines, 53–54
remote monitoring software, for viewing
    your developers' workstations, 197
retrospective meetings, typical questions
    to research in, 99
rewards
    example performance weighting
        scheme, 163
    granting for outstanding
        performance, 162–164
    as a motivating force for your staff,
        169
Rich, Adrienne, *The Dream of a Common
    Language* by, 121, 242
*Rise & Resurrection of the American
    Programmer* (Edward Yourdon), 184,
    239
Roundtable on Project Management
    (Bullock, Weinberg, and Benesh,
    eds.), 240

S

salad chef programmer, 12
salaries and promotions, managing,
    56–58
salary rates, for programmers, 16–17
scientist programmer, 8
scope bloat. *See* project scope creep
scope creep. *See* project scope creep
*Selected Poems and Three Plays of
    William Butler Yeats*, ed. M.L.
    Rosenthal, 242
Self-Reliance (Ralph Waldo Emerson), 89
Sewell, Marc T. and Laura M., *The
    Software Architect's Profession: An
    Introduction* by, 107, 239
shadows, avoiding in leadership role,
    147–148
Shenk, David, *The End of Patience:
    Cautionary Notes on the Information
    Revolution* by, 31, 242
slob programmer, 10–11

Smith, Douglas K., *The Wisdom of Teams*
    by, 241
software, typical process of delivering, 47
software architects, role of, 107
software architecture
    design forces in planning, 108–109
    enforcing the laws of, 118–119
    goal of, 103–105
    philosophy in action, 123–126
    the primacy of, 106–110
    results of bad, 123
    tools for creating reusable system
        designs, 108
    violation of standards, 120–121
Software Architecture Bootcamp
    (Malveau and Mowbray), 108, 238
Software Craftsmanship (Pete McBreen),
    57, 237
software design
    design step 0, 111–113
    design steps 1, 2, 3, 2, 1, 4 ..., 113–117
    a fresh look at, 110–117
    guidelines for, 115
    importance of code review, 118–122
    importance of documenting new
        code modules, 158
    results of poor, 123–124
software design principles, common
    violations of, 119–122
software development
    bibliography of reference books,
        235–242
    characteristics of companies most
        successful at, 119
    craftsmanship of, 209–210
    economic woes in, 212–213
    evaluating the methodologies of,
        201–210
    gardening metaphor for, 105–106
    guiding your ship on a stormy sea,
        217–220
    pitfalls of participatory leadership,
        159–160
    preventing major disasters in, 51
    reasons for disasters, 50
    rules to live by, 212–213
    strategic concerns for long-term
        planning goals, 211
software engineering, 202–203
    balancing purity with practicality, 28
    importance of avoiding complexity
        in, 8
Software Runaways (Robert L. Glass), 50,
    238
    solitude and collaboration, needed
        for software development, 194–195

Solutions Development Discipline Workbook (Microsoft Corporation), about Microsoft approach to software engineering, 204

Source view, Administrative Director software, 224

speed demon programmer, 8–9

staff meetings, weekly, 87–89

staffing, managing, 53–58

Stimmel, Carol L., *The Manager Pool: Patterns for Radical Leadership* by, 175, 239

Straight from the Gut (Jack Welch), 33, 241

Strathern, Paul, *Turing and the Computer* by, 165, 242

system architecture

    importance of controlling, 73–74

    proving it works from top to bottom, 111–113

T

Tablet PC, using as an organizational tool, 63

targeted mentoring, 162

task concept

    displaying and organizing tasks, 68–70

    an implementation of, 67–68

task lists, for weekly staff meetings, 88–89

tasks, displaying and organizing, 68–70

team building, importance of, 41–59

technical leadership

    a bird's-eye view, 126–127

    devoting time to research, 213

    experimenting with new methods and techniques, 189

    a guideline for success, 116–117

    importance of studying industry trends, 188

    learning to increase the value of your relationships, 215

    making strategic planning a science, 214

    philosophy and practice of, 103–127

    recognizing the customer is first, 190–191

    the shadow of micromanagement, 132–137

    turning administration into an engineering discipline, 214

    your role of managing architecture and design, 103–105

technology

    planning your architecture before choosing, 28

    revolutions in, 210–211

telecommuting, allowing to minimize programmer distractions, 46

teleconferencing, for meetings, 99–100

template, example for design meeting note taker, 93

testing, products before releasing, 82

testing applicants, guidelines for, 53–54

The 7 Habits of Highly Effective People (Stephen Covey), 18, 43

The Arc of Ambition (Champy and Nohria), 241

The Art of War (Sun Tzu), 211, 242

The Centerless Corporation (Pasternack and Viscio), 180, 241

The Complete Poetry and Prose of William Blake, ed. David V. Erdman, 242

The Deadline (Tom DeMarco), 240

The Dream of a Common Language (Adrienne Rich), 121, 242

The End of Patience: Cautionary Notes on the Information Revolution (David Shenk), 31, 242

The Manager Pool: Patterns for Radical Leadership (Olson and Stimmel), 175, 239

The Marriage of Heaven and Hell (William Blake), 23

The Mythical Man-Month: Essays on Software Engineering, Anniversary Edition (Frederick P. Brooks), 13, 235

The New Hacker's Dictionary, Third Edition (Eric S. Raymond), 4

The Peopleware Papers (Larry L. Constantine), 94, 238

The Pragmatic Programmer (Andrew Hunt and David Thomas), 105, 237

The Psychology of Computer Programming: Silver Anniversary Edition (Gerald M. Weinberg), 52, 235–236

The Seasons of a Man's Life (Daniel J. Levinson), 171–172, 242

The Software Architect's Profession: An Introduction (Marc T. and Laura M. Sewell), 107, 239

The Wisdom of Teams (Katzenbach and Smith), 241

thinking, the role of in your new leadership role, 17–19

Thomas, David, *The Pragmatic Programmer* by, 105, 236–237
time and natural selection, 25–29
timing, importance of being sensitive to, 189–190
Today screen, for administrative director software, 69
tools, needed by programmers, 83–84
toy maker programmer, 10
trade magazines, reading to stay current in your field, 32
Turing, Alan, decryption of the German Enigma codes by, 165–166
Turing and the Computer (Paul Strathern), 165, 242
Tzu, Sun, *The Art of War* by, 211, 242

U

Ullman, Ellen, *Close to the Machine* by, 5, 242
understanding
    as the first cornerstone of leadership, 152–154
    tasks involved in, 154
undocumented feature offering (UFO), 12
unfocused managers, dealing with, 137–140

V

vaporware, the stir it creates, 210–211
vertical thinking, 33
viewpoint, 109
Viscio, Albert J., *The Centerless Corporation* by, 180, 241
Visual Basic 6 Design, Specification, and Objects (Billy S. Hollis), 111, 241

W

Wallace, James, *Hard Drive: Bill Gates and the Making of the Microsoft Empire* by, 174, 242
weak cohesion and strong coupling, as coding standards violations, 121–122
Web site address
    Agile Alliance, 207
    for psychology assessment test, 53

Weinberg, Gerald M.
    Handbook of Walkthroughs, Inspections, and Technical Reviews by, 240
    The Psychology of Computer Programming: Silver Anniversary Edition by, 52, 235
Welch, Jack
    seeking out as advisor, 172
    Straight from the Gut by, 33, 241
Whitehead, Richard, *Leading a Software Development Team: A Developer's Guide to Successfully Leading People & Projects* by, 241
work assignments, distribution of, 73
worker density, impact of on productivity, 46
working hours, controlling for yourself and your staff, 74–75
workweek, managing for yourself and your staff, 74–75
worm, 3
Writing Solid Code (Steve Maguire), 238

Y

Yeats, William Butler, *Selected Poems and Three Plays of William Butler Yeats*, ed. M.L. Rosenthal, 23, 242
Yourdon, Edward
    Death March by, 239
    Decline and Fall of the American Programmer by, 184
    Rise & Resurrection of the American Programmer by, 184, 239

Notes

Notes

Notes

Notes

Notes

Notes

Notes

Apress Titles

ISBN	PRICE	AUTHOR	TITLE
1-893115-73-9	$34.95	Abbott	Voice Enabling Web Applications: VoiceXML and Beyond
1-893115-01-1	$39.95	Appleman	Appleman's Win32 API Puzzle Book and Tutorial for Visual Basic Programmers
1-893115-23-2	$29.95	Appleman	How Computer Programming Works
1-893115-97-6	$39.95	Appleman	Moving to VB. NET: Strategies, Concepts, and Code
1-893115-09-7	$29.95	Baum	Dave Baum's Definitive Guide to LEGO MINDSTORMS
1-893115-84-4	$29.95	Baum, Gasperi, Hempel, and Villa	Extreme MINDSTORMS: An Advanced Guide to LEGO MINDSTORMS
1-893115-82-8	$59.95	Ben-Gan/Moreau	Advanced Transact-SQL for SQL Server 2000
1-893115-48-8	$29.95	Bischof	The .NET Languages: A Quick Translation Guide
1-893115-67-4	$49.95	Borge	Managing Enterprise Systems with the Windows Script Host
1-893115-28-3	$44.95	Challa/Laksberg	Essential Guide to Managed Extensions for C++
1-893115-44-5	$29.95	Cook	Robot Building for Beginners
1-893115-99-2	$39.95	Cornell/Morrison	Programming VB .NET: A Guide for Experienced Programmers
1-893115-72-0	$39.95	Curtin	Developing Trust: Online Privacy and Security
1-59059-008-2	$29.95	Duncan	The Career Programmer: Guerilla Tactics for an Imperfect World
1-893115-71-2	$39.95	Ferguson	Mobile .NET
1-893115-90-9	$49.95	Finsel	The Handbook for Reluctant Database Administrators
1-893115-42-9	$44.95	Foo/Lee	XML Programming Using the Microsoft XML Parser
1-893115-55-0	$34.95	Frenz	Visual Basic and Visual Basic .NET for Scientists and Engineers
1-893115-85-2	$34.95	Gilmore	A Programmer's Introduction to PHP 4.0
1-893115-36-4	$34.95	Goodwill	Apache Jakarta-Tomcat
1-893115-17-8	$59.95	Gross	A Programmer's Introduction to Windows DNA
1-893115-62-3	$39.95	Gunnerson	A Programmer's Introduction to C#, Second Edition
1-893115-30-5	$49.95	Harkins/Reid	SQL: Access to SQL Server
1-893115-10-0	$34.95	Holub	Taming Java Threads
1-893115-04-6	$34.95	Hyman/Vaddadi	Mike and Phani's Essential C++ Techniques
1-893115-96-8	$59.95	Jorelid	J2EE FrontEnd Technologies: A Programmer's Guide to Servlets, JavaServer Pages, and Enterprise JavaBeans
1-893115-49-6	$39.95	Kilburn	Palm Programming in Basic
1-893115-50-X	$34.95	Knudsen	Wireless Java: Developing with Java 2, Micro Edition
1-893115-79-8	$49.95	Kofler	Definitive Guide to Excel VBA
1-893115-57-7	$39.95	Kofler	MySQL

ISBN	PRICE	AUTHOR	TITLE
1-893115-87-9	$39.95	Kurata	Doing Web Development: Client-Side Techniques
1-893115-75-5	$44.95	Kurniawan	Internet Programming with VB
1-893115-46-1	$36.95	Lathrop	Linux in Small Business: A Practical User's Guide
1-893115-19-4	$49.95	Macdonald	Serious ADO: Universal Data Access with Visual Basic
1-893115-06-2	$39.95	Marquis/Smith	A Visual Basic 6.0 Programmer's Toolkit
1-893115-22-4	$27.95	McCarter	David McCarter's VB Tips and Techniques
1-893115-76-3	$49.95	Morrison	C++ For VB Programmers
1-893115-80-1	$39.95	Newmarch	A Programmer's Guide to Jini Technology
1-893115-58-5	$49.95	Oellermann	Architecting Web Services
1-893115-81-X	$39.95	Pike	SQL Server: Common Problems, Tested Solutions
1-59059-017-1	$34.95	Rainwater	Herding Cats: A Primer for Programmers Who Lead Programmers
1-893115-20-8	$34.95	Rischpater	Wireless Web Development
1-893115-93-3	$34.95	Rischpater	Wireless Web Development with PHP and WAP
1-893115-89-5	$59.95	Shemitz	Kylix: The Professional Developer's Guide and Reference
1-893115-40-2	$39.95	Sill	The qmail Handbook
1-893115-24-0	$49.95	Sinclair	From Access to SQL Server
1-893115-94-1	$29.95	Spolsky	User Interface Design for Programmers
1-893115-53-4	$44.95	Sweeney	Visual Basic for Testers
1-59059-002-3	$44.95	Symmonds	Internationalization and Localization Using Microsoft .NET
1-893115-29-1	$44.95	Thomsen	Database Programming with Visual Basic .NET
1-893115-65-8	$39.95	Tiffany	Pocket PC Database Development with eMbedded Visual Basic
1-893115-59-3	$59.95	Troelsen	C# and the .NET Platform
1-893115-26-7	$59.95	Troelsen	Visual Basic .NET and the .NET Platform
1-893115-54-2	$49.95	Trueblood/Lovett	Data Mining and Statistical Analysis Using SQL
1-893115-16-X	$49.95	Vaughn	ADO Examples and Best Practices
1-893115-68-2	$49.95	Vaughn	ADO.NET and ADO Examples and Best Practices for VB Programmers, Second Edition
1-893115-83-6	$44.95	Wells	Code Centric: T-SQL Programming with Stored Procedures and Triggers
1-893115-95-X	$49.95	Welschenbach	Cryptography in C and C++
1-893115-05-4	$39.95	Williamson	Writing Cross-Browser Dynamic HTML
1-893115-78-X	$49.95	Zukowski	Definitive Guide to Swing for Java 2, Second Edition
1-893115-92-5	$49.95	Zukowski	Java Collections

Available at bookstores nationwide or from Springer Verlag New York, Inc. at 1-800-777-4643;
fax 1-212-533-3503. Contact us for more information at sales@apress.com.

Apress Titles Publishing SOON!

ISBN	AUTHOR	TITLE
1-893115-91-7	Birmingham/Perry	Software Development on a Leash
1-893115-39-9	Chand	A Programmer's Guide to ADO.NET in C#
1-59059-000-7	Cornell	Programming C#: A Guide for the Non-C++/Java Programmer
1-59059-009-0	Harris/Macdonald	Moving to ASP.NET
1-59059-016-3	Hubbard	Windows Forms in C#
1-893115-38-0	Lafler	Power AOL: A Survival Guide
1-59059-003-1	Nakhimovsky/Meyers	XML Programming: Web Applications and Web Services with JSP and ASP
1-893115-27-5	Morrill	Tuning and Customizing a Linux System
1-893115-43-7	Stephenson	Standard VB: An Enterprise Developer's Reference for VB 6 and VB .NET
1-59059-007-4	Thomsen	Building Web Services with VB .NET
1-59059-010-4	Thomsen	Database Programming with C#
1-59059-011-2	Troelsen	COM and .NET Interoperability
1-59059-004-X	Valiaveedu	SQL Server 2000 and Business Intelligence in an XML/.NET World
1-59059-012-0	Vaughn/Blackburn	ADO.NET Examples and Best Practices for C# Programmers
1-893115-98-4	Zukowski	Learn Java with JBuilder 6

Available at bookstores nationwide or from Springer Verlag New York, Inc. at 1-800-777-4643; fax 1-212-533-3503. Contact us for more information at sales@apress.com.

books for professionals by professionals™

About Apress

Apress, located in Berkeley, CA, is a fast-growing, innovative publishing company devoted to meeting the needs of existing and potential programming professionals. Simply put, the "A" in Apress stands for *"The Author's Press*™*"* and its books have *"The Expert's Voice*™*."* Apress' unique approach to publishing grew out of conversations between its founders Gary Cornell and Dan Appleman, authors of numerous best-selling, highly regarded books for programming professionals. In 1998 they set out to create a publishing company that emphasized quality above all else. Gary and Dan's vision has resulted in the publication of over 50 titles by leading software professionals, all of which have *The Expert's Voice*™.

Do You Have What It Takes to Write for Apress?

Apress is rapidly expanding its publishing program. If you can write and refuse to compromise on the quality of your work, if you believe in doing more than rehashing existing documentation, and if you're looking for opportunities and rewards that go far beyond those offered by traditional publishing houses, we want to hear from you!

Consider these innovations that we offer all of our authors:

- **Top royalties with *no* hidden switch statements**
  Authors typically only receive half of their normal royalty rate on foreign sales. In contrast, Apress' royalty rate remains the same for both foreign and domestic sales.

- **A mechanism for authors to obtain equity in Apress**
  Unlike the software industry, where stock options are essential to motivate and retain software professionals, the publishing industry has adhered to an outdated compensation model based on royalties alone. In the spirit of most software companies, Apress reserves a significant portion of its equity for authors.

- **Serious treatment of the technical review process**
  Each Apress book has a technical reviewing team whose remuneration depends in part on the success of the book since they too receive royalties.

Moreover, through a partnership with Springer-Verlag, New York, Inc., one of the world's major publishing houses, Apress has significant venture capital behind it. Thus, we have the resources to produce the highest quality books *and* market them aggressively.

If you fit the model of the Apress author who can write a book that gives the "professional what he or she needs to know™," then please contact one of our Editorial Directors, Gary Cornell (gary_cornell@apress.com), Dan Appleman (dan_appleman@apress.com), Peter Blackburn (peter_blackburn@apress.com), Jason Gilmore (jason_gilmore@apress.com), Karen Watterson (karen_watterson@apress.com), or John Zukowski (john_zukowski@apress.com) for more information.